6.9.77

International Trade
Under Communism –
Politics and Economics

INTERNATIONAL TRADE UNDER COMMUNISM – POLITICS AND ECONOMICS

FRANKLYN D. HOLZMAN

BASIC BOOKS, INC., PUBLISHERS

New York

To

Bonnie and Larry

and

Rose and Alfred

Library of Congress Cataloging in Publication Data

Holzman, Franklyn D.
  International trade under communism—politics and
  economics.

  Includes bibliographical references and index.
    1. Communist countries—Commercial policy.
2. Communist countries—Foreign economic relations.
3. East-West trade (1945-   ) I. Title.
HF1531.H65   382'.09171'7   76-7489
ISBN 0-465-03381-4

Contents

Contents

Chapter 5

Chapter 6

List of Tables

CHART

Acknowledgments

My greatest debt in the writing of this book is to my colleague, Benjamin J. (Jerry) Cohen, editor of this series. His criticisms of my first draft, particularly of the third and fourth chapters, led to revisions which substantially improved the manuscript. I also benefited from criticisms of the first draft of the third chapter by Edward Hewett and Robert Legvold, and of the third and fourth chapters by Sara Paulson. In a more general way, the manuscript benefited from my regular contact at the Russian Research Center at Harvard with my many colleagues in political science as well as in economics, from the able bibliographical assistance provided by Susan Gardos, and from typing help by Mary Towle, Rose di Benedetto, Christine Porto, and others. Various drafts of the manuscript were also typed almost errorlessly by Mrs. E. P. Goodwin and Sarah Bollinger.

Despite all this assistance, the ruble stops here.

Preface

The purpose of this book is to explain how the international economic system of the Communist bloc operates and, more particularly, how economic factors constrain, are constrained by, and otherwise interact with political, diplomatic, strategic, and military forces in international relations. For the most part, the book focuses on the U.S.S.R. and the other nations of Eastern Europe with which the U.S.S.R. is most closely associated—Bulgaria, Czechoslovakia, East Germany (the German Democratic Republic, or G.D.R.), Hungary, Poland, and Rumania. These nations, along with the Mongolian People's Republic and Cuba, currently make up the fully participating members of the Council of Mutual Economic Assistance (CMEA, CEMA, or Comecon), the customs union counterpart in Eastern Europe of the European Economic Community in Western Europe. Very little reference is made in this book to Mongolia or Cuba, or to Albania (which left CMEA in the early 1960s), Yugoslavia, China, North Korea, or North Vietnam. The European CMEA nations have much closer relationships with each other than they do with the other Communist nations, and their relationships with the non-Communist world are more alike. In this book, reference is made to Communist nations, socialist nations, centrally planned economies (CPEs), and so forth. Unless otherwise indicated, these terms usually refer to the European CMEA nations and not to the other Communist countries.

The first chapter introduces the reader to some of the fundamental political and economic characteristics of the Communist nations, an essential prerequisite to understanding their foreign trade and investment behavior. The most obvious differences between Communist and Western capitalist nations are the much greater political and economic centralization and control in the former, as exemplified by one-party electoral systems and public ownership of virtually all means of production. Despite these two major differences, there is a remarkable similarity in some of the major goals of the two systems. Both are geared to rapid growth, full employment, and price stability (although under capitalism the immediate needs of the consumer receive more attention, while under Communism there tends to be a more equitable distribution of income and wealth as a result of the elimination of private property).

The big differences, however, are not so much in goals as in means and intensity of implementation. Most important, of course, is the use of central planning by direct controls to operate a national economy in the U.S.S.R. and Eastern Europe, as opposed to the decentralized operation of the market under Western capitalism. Moreover, central planning by direct controls, with its lack of free markets, inevitably involves the development of what are often termed "irrational" price structures which reflect neither supply nor demand forces accurately. Central planning and public ownership of means of production also mean that the goals and incentives of enterprise management differ from those in a capitalist enterprise. All these features of Soviet bloc societies have implications for their international economic relations. To the extent that economic reforms are introduced in the U.S.S.R. and Eastern Europe—and, as we point out in the last section of Chapter 1, reforms have been introduced over the past decade—both domestic and international economic behavior will differ somewhat from that of the earlier postwar period.

Foreign trade behavior is the subject of Chapter 2. The reasons for some of the socialist bloc idiosyncrasies in trade are easy to explain. Under nationalization of industry and central planning, it is logical that foreign trade also be nationalized and be conducted by a state monopoly. With central planning, it is to be expected that foreign trade will be planned and that trade with other nations will be organized in the framework of annual (and longer) bilateral trade agreements. Under central planning, with government decisions determining the distribution of exports and imports, tariffs become unnecessary for the protection of domestic enterprise. The reasons behind these features of Communist foreign trade behavior are obvious. Less obvious is the impact of central planning, irrational prices, etc., in other areas. Among the questions to which answers are provided in Chapter 2 are the following.

Why have the currencies of the Soviet bloc nations always been inconvertible? Why is trade among CMEA members always rigidly bilaterally balanced despite serious efforts toward multilateral agreements, whereas CMEA trade with the West is multilateral? Why do the CMEA nations trade so much smaller a part of their gross national product (GNP) than do capitalist nations? Why were tariffs suddenly introduced by many of the Eastern nations in the 1960s? Why do the socialist nations trade among themselves at world prices, which are unrelated to their own domestic price structures? Why does devaluation of the ruble, zloty, or lev not encourage exports and discourage imports, thereby improving the balance of payments, as is the case in the West? Given the lack of rational price systems, how do the Communist nations decide what to import and export? Why do these nations always have serious balance-of-payments problems in their trade with the West? These are some of the questions to which answers are provided in Chapter 2. In the last section of that chapter the actual and potential impact of the economic reforms on foreign trade behavior is explored.

The next three chapters, utilizing this background material, explore the politics and economics of Communist international relations in different areas of the world.

In Chapter 3, the course of *intrabloc* political and economic relations since World War II is traced and analyzed. Preliminary to this, three simple theoretical models which should illuminate the historical record are presented. The first sets forth the complex interrelationships which exist between political and economic power. A second explores the process of economic integration in order to evaluate, later, Soviet bloc attempts to integrate their economies. Finally, a model of economic warfare is presented as a framework against which to evaluate the U.S.S.R.'s attempts to coerce Yugoslavia, Albania, and China into following its lead. It is also used, in Chapter 4, for evaluating the Cold War arsenal of economic weapons employed by the United States against the U.S.S.R. and Eastern Europe.

The first postwar decade was characterized largely by Soviet application in intrabloc relations of its superior political and military power for its own political and economic aggrandizement. The nations of Eastern Europe were walled behind an "iron curtain," their leaders subservient to Stalin's wishes. Their economies were exploited through reparations, joint stock companies, and the like. The restructuring of Eastern European trade toward the U.S.S.R. and each other constituted a violent economic break with past profitable channels and, according to our economic integration model, caused losses to all concerned. Relations between the U.S.S.R. and Eastern Europe changed sharply during Khrushchev's early years. The political costs of economic exploitation and political subjugation had become too high and bloc cohesion was threatened. The U.S.S.R. was forced to trade economic profits for political favor and to rule with a slightly less arbitrary hand. Even Khrushchev's economic warfare against China and Albania was only a pale image of Stalin's attempt to subdue Yugoslavia. Attempts were made under Khrushchev's regime to integrate the socialist economies not just through ordinary commodity trade, but by coordinating plans, planning a further division of labor, undertaking joint projects, and the like. Despite elaborate attempts, very little progress was made, for reasons discussed in detail in Chapter 3. On matters like these, economic decisions have profound political implications, and vice versa. As a result, sustained and bitter debates took place, with the U.S.S.R. and Rumania the major antagonists, as to whether CMEA should or should not have supranational powers. Lack of progress toward integration is also related to problems connected with central planning as these are expressed in intrabloc foreign trade pricing problems, the flow of capital, the flow of labor, technical cooperation, currency inconvertibility, and so forth. Some of these economic contacts between the socialist nations have political dimensions around which conflicts have been generated; others are purely economic.

The past seven or eight years have been marked by the widespread introduction of economic reforms, a renewed attempt at integration through the famous *Comprehensive Program*, and enunciation of the so-called Brezhnev Doctrine shortly after the invasion of Czechoslovakia in August 1968. It is interesting to consider why the U.S.S.R. intervened to stop Czech economic reform but did not intervene to reverse the liberal Hungarian economic reform. Or why the Soviets kept their hands off the Polish riots in December 1970. Or why Rumania has been able to shift so much more of its trade to the West than other members of CMEA and has also been able to impede CMEA integration unilaterally by using its veto power without feeling the might of the Soviet fist. Another recent issue of interest is the apparent conflict between the goals of greater Eastern bloc integration through the Comprehensive Program and the détente-inspired increase in East-West trade.

East-West relations are the subject of Chapter 4, "West" here referring to the advanced industrial nations. East-West trade is, of course, dominated by politics. In the decade immediately after World War II, East-West trade was negligible, not because of considerations of comparative advantage, but because of the Cold War. The United States and the U.S.S.R. were the major antagonists in the Cold War, of course, and the smaller nations in each camp demonstrated, as soon as it became feasible, that they preferred to reap the gains from East-West trade, leaving the politics to their patrons. The United States was least willing to forgo East-West economic warfare and stubbornly continued its attempts to hurt the Communist nations for many years after other Western nations had abandoned their trade controls. These efforts were a failure, of course, and had it not been for the war in Vietnam, détente might have come almost a decade earlier. By the early 1960s, economic factors were very favorable to renewed East-West trade. The CMEA economies which had done well in the 1950s were running into unanticipated difficulties which generated, among other things, the economic reform movements of the 1960s. For reasons discussed later, the reforms did not work as well as expected and CMEA turned to the West for help. With the Vietnam War over, the East-West scene has since been dominated by détente, "linkage" politics, joint ventures, a rapid expansion of East-West trade, and the like.

In Chapter 5, CMEA's trade with and aid to the non-Communist Third World is studied. In overall quantitative terms, the economic relations of socialist nations with less developed countries (LDCs) have not been very important, amounting to only about 1 percent of world trade. Nevertheless, for a number of reasons, they have taken on much more economic, political, and military importance than their size would seem to warrant. For one thing, the LDCs provide an important competitive arena in which the Eastern and Western nations vie for political and economic influence. For another, Soviet economic influence has often been focused very strategically. Cases in point are the Aswan Dam, the Middle East wars, the Bhilai and Bokharo steel plants in India, and support of Cuba (after Castro's takeover). Motives behind CMEA trade with and aid to the LDCs are quite complex, and an attempt is made in Chapter 5 to analyze them. As it turns out, the interplay of politics and economics differs, depending on whether one is concerned with trade, economic aid, or military assistance. Furthermore, policies regarding each of these areas have changed from time to time. Many interesting questions can be raised. What led to the sudden interest in LDC trade and aid in the mid- and late-1950s? Why did aid to black Africa and Latin America suddenly decline in the mid-1960s? In what respects are CMEA aid and repayment terms different from Western terms? In what respects did Brezhnev and Kosygin modify Khrushchev's approach to the LDCs? What kind of markets (relative to the West) do the socialist nations provide for LDC exports? Do the CMEA nations bear their fair share of the burden of extending aid to the LDCs? How successful was CMEA aid in achieving its goals? These and other questions are confronted in Chapter 5.

Chapter 6 is an attempt to peer ahead. The future of intrabloc relations is discussed primarily in terms of the political and economic advantages of, and obstacles to, radical economic reforms. Another important variable is the rising economic cost to the U.S.S.R. of maintaining high levels of CMEA trade—a cost which has been borne willingly in the past for political reasons but which might become too high, especially given the rising value of Soviet raw materials for the West. East-West trade is, of course, the other side of the intrabloc trade coin. The problems that divide the CMEA nations lead them to greater East-West trade, but there are potential impediments. To mention a few: the present détente is certainly not robust and no one would be surprised if U.S.-Soviet relations cooled again; Eastern hard currency balance-of-payments problems will certainly constrain the future growth of East-West trade; United States and Soviet strategic interests will probably continue to dampen large-scale long-run reliance by either nation on trade with the other.

Finally, in the more distant future, other issues loom large. The gap between the per capita real incomes of East and West on the one hand and the LDCs not in the Organization of Petroleum Exporting Countries (OPEC) on the other is a growing problem, one that will concern both groups of developed nations. Other political-economic problems which will require action are those relating to protecting the environment, arms control, arms trade, and the new and more effective economic warfare such as that implemented by the OPEC nations in the fall of 1973.

International Trade

Under Communism –

Politics and Economics

Chapter 1

The Institutions, Goals, and Internal Economic Mechanisms of the Communist Nations

The differences between the political economy of Communist and capitalist international economic relations stem basically from differences in their respective goals, institutions, and economic mechanisms. Before proceeding to the specific subject of this book, it is necessary, therefore, to set forth some of the organizational characteristics of Communist economies. The sketch that follows is by no means complete and should not be viewed as a substitute for or summary of the many books and articles which have been written on political and economic organizational forms that characterize Communist nations. Our concern here is solely with those aspects of Communist societies that have a specific bearing on international relations. At this stage, moreover, the model which we develop describes a Stalinist-type society of the kind which characterized the Eastern bloc before 1960 and is still a quite accurate description of the U.S.S.R., Rumania, and Bulgaria, but a less accurate one of the other Eastern European nations (particularly Hungary), because of the recent economic reforms. These reforms are discussed in the last section of this chapter.

Political Centralization and Control

The Eastern European nations have one-party governmental systems. In each nation the leaders of that party, the Communist party, wield much more power than the leaders of the dominant party in any Western nation. By hypothesis, the party cannot lose power, although within the party, of course, one faction might oust another. In theory, the leaders of the party (presidium, central committee) are subject to the control of the party members, themselves an elite comprising a minority of the adult population. In practice, however, rank-and-file party members do no more than rubber-stamp decisions handed down from the top; changes in leadership take place via "palace revolts" rather than the ballot box. The formal governmental structure parallels the party structure, and for the most part, important governmental positions are occupied by party officials. The power and control exercised by the Communist party at the highest levels has its counterparts at all lower governmental levels. Furthermore, most economic and other nongovernmental organizations are managed by members of the Communist party who are subject to party discipline.

Clearly, the leadership of Communist nations has more power than Western leadership has to make policy decisions and to implement them without consent of the governed. This does not mean that policy decisions are necessarily different from those which would be made by democratic processes. Nor should it be interpreted to imply that the policies adopted by the governments of Western nations are necessarily always those which benefit or are desired by their populations. The two sets of political systems are obviously both located somewhere on a spectrum which runs from absolute dictatorship to pure democracy (whatever that may mean). Nevertheless, it seems perfectly clear that the Communist nations generally fall in the dictatorship half of the spectrum, whereas the advanced capitalist nations generally occupy the other half.

Nationalization of Industry and Central Planning

PUBLIC OWNERSHIP OF THE MEANS OF PRODUCTION

Most nonagricultural enterprises are nationalized in Communist countries. Nationalization of the means of production is, in fact, one of the very basic distinctions between capitalist and Communist societies. Industrial enterprises, owned by the state, are operated by state-appointed managers, for the most part on an independent financial basis. That is to say, they keep financial accounts and are supposed to finance their expenditures out of revenue from the sale of their products. Presumably, this method of operation imposes a financial discipline on the enterprise which would not exist if all receipts were automatically handed over to the state treasury and all expenditures were financed by the treasury. In practice, financial discipline is less stringent than under private enterprise for a number of reasons, including the almost unlimited ability of a government to subsidize inefficient enterprises and its apparent aversion to closing them down. The major exception to state ownership is agriculture, a large part of which is either privately or cooperatively owned. In either case, government is able to exercise considerable control through its roles as principal supplier of machinery, fertilizers, and the like, major purchaser of agricultural output, and price setter. Outside of agriculture, only very small-scale handicraft-type enterprises remain un-nationalized.

MARKET STRUCTURE: CENTRAL PLANNING WITH DIRECT CONTROLS

Another distinguishing feature of the Communist nations is central economic planning. This is not an unnatural concomitant of state ownership of the means of production, though, as Yugoslavia has shown, it is feasible to have state ownership of most means of production along with little more planning than exists, say, in Sweden or France. A wide range of mechanisms is available to government for setting forth and implementing national plans. On the one extreme, the central planning board and its sub-units can, in theory, issue direct orders to regulate practically every transaction that takes place. At the other extreme, it is possible for the planners to rely for implementation almost completely on price and market mechanisms. Under Stalinist-type central planning, a mixture of techniques has been characteristic. With some exceptions, market mechanisms have predominated in the consumer-good and labor markets. The distribution of consumers' goods in Communist countries is accomplished much as it is everywhere else. The major differences are that the state, rather than private owners, sets prices and makes decisions regarding changes in output.

Needless to say, in the Communist countries, prices are much more rigid and changes in output much less responsive to changing consumers' needs. The distribution of labor is also accomplished largely by market means. Wages are set by the state but wage differentials reflect many of the same considerations as under capitalism: training, skill, pleasantness of job, and scarcity (demand). Workers are relatively free to apply for jobs of their own choosing.

There are no capital markets in the Soviet bloc nations. The rate of investment (and of military spending) is determined by the state, and the funds to finance these expenditures are raised primarily by taxation. The rate of interest has almost no effect on either the supply or demand for capital. The wide range of stocks and bonds and of financial institutions that exist in capitalist nations has no counterpart in the socialist nations of the world today.

Market mechanisms also play a small role and direct controls a large role in the vast number of transactions that take place between enterprises and between enterprises and state organizations. The transactions between enterprises are transactions in intermediate and capital goods products, including commodities like coal, steel plate, machinery, and textiles, which are the outputs of one enterprise and the inputs or investment of another. Procurement of material and other products for the armed forces probably makes up the bulk of the transactions between enterprises and government organizations; purchases by ministries of health and education must also be substantial, however.

Not all these transactions involve direct controls. Enterprises and organizations are allowed to buy and sell freely a large number of products, at fixed prices of course. But these are usually products which are relatively unimportant and widely available. Important products, and these number more than one thousand in the U.S.S.R. at present, are directly controlled by state planning organs. For these commodities, the planners set output and sales targets, determine delivery dates, and tell each enterprise from whom it is to buy its inputs and to whom it is to ship its products. Since there is, in effect, no real market through which supply and demand can seek an adjustment, this particular function, accomplished anonymously by "invisible hands" in the West, must be performed explicitly by the supply planners. This is a laborious process. Under present practice, "material balances" are established for all products so controlled, in which all sources of a commodity are listed on one side and uses or shipments on the other. If the supply and demand for a product do not balance, or if balance is upset by an unpredicted event, serious difficulties are encountered because of the complexity of interindustry relationships. Suppose, for example, that the steel balance shows a one-million-ton deficit, and a decision is made to increase steel output by this amount so that all planned uses of steel can be met. The steel industry will have to be allocated more coal, limestone, machinery, labor, and so forth. A problem arises because the planned balances for each of these commodities is upset, assuming that they were balanced in the first place. In order to produce more coal, limestone, machinery, and so forth, it is necessary to have more steel than the one million tons originally desired; this requires still more coal, limestone, and machinery, and so forth in a many-staged regression. Alternatively, if it had been decided to solve the balance problem by cutting back on shipments of steel (rather than increasing steel output), similar adjustments would have to be made as various enterprises found themselves with less steel than anticipated, were forced to cut back shipments to other enterprises, and so forth.

The complexity of supply planning for thousands of commodities and many tens of thousands of enterprises cannot be overestimated. It is one of the factors that led the nations of Eastern Europe to try to reform their planning systems by relying more heavily on decentralized price and market mechanisms. It was also largely responsible, under the old system, for the widespread illegal use by enterprises of expediters* whose function it was to purchase, outside the plan, commodities which the enterprise should have received under the plan but did not. The need for such "black markets" is underlined by the fact that the authorities make little or no attempt to eliminate them.

Over-Full Employment Planning

In practice, central planning has always been over-full employment planning. Over-full employment planning, also called taut planning, means setting output targets for enterprises and industries which are

*In Russian the word is *tolkach* (pusher).

unrealistic in terms of available resources and possible rates of growth in productivity. This tendency to overcommitment of resources is not unlike that which occurs in capitalist countries during wartime. The result, as under capitalism, is that there is always excess demand by households for consumers' goods and by enterprises for labor and other inputs. This has many undesirable consequences. First of all, it tends to worsen the planning difficulties caused by the inherent complexity of having to balance supply and demand for thousands of commodities and tens of thousands of enterprises. Imbalances are bound to occur, and enterprises are bound to be frustrated even more frequently if the basis upon which the balances are drawn up in the first place is unrealistic. Other consequences are: enterprises resort to hoarding scarce materials whenever possible; the use of expediters is encouraged still further; and managers have an incentive to understate their capacity to produce and overstate their input requirements, thereby passing on inaccurate information to the planners. Finally, taut planning means sellers' markets, that is, enterprises can sell virtually anything they produce. This, in turn, generates a lack of concern among managers for the quality of the products they produce and an insensitivity to the needs of their clientele.

DISEQUILIBRIUM PRICES

Prices in the Communist nations have always been "disequilibrium" and "irrational" prices. They are disequilibrium prices in the sense that if prices were freed, they would not equate supply and demand. This would be the case even if taut planning and excess demand were eliminated. Prices do not, of course, have to equilibrate supply and demand in the market for producers' goods and raw materials since this presumably is accomplished directly by the planners through their method of balances. As a result of planning with direct controls, prices are changed very infrequently and are largely insulated from market forces operating through supply and demand. For example, a reform of wholesale prices, the first wholesale price change in five years, occurred in the U.S.S.R. in 1955. The next change was not to occur until 1967, twelve years later. By that time, it was necessary to alter some twenty million prices, a process which took several years to accomplish. The Czechoslovakian reform of 1968 involved some two million prices. The planners' problems are truly staggering and it is no wonder that prices finally are irrational.

There are other factors behind price irrationality. Until recently enterprise accounts have not included proper charges for rent, interest, and profits; only labor has been adequately accounted for. This practice is based on adherence to the Marxian labor theory of value, and has two implications for costs and prices. First, the costs of production (and possibly the prices) of all commodities are understated to the extent that the costs of land, capital, and "entrepreneurial" activities are not included. Second, and perhaps more important, the relative costs and prices of products are distorted because this failure to account fully for rent, interest, and profits has a different inpact on different products. The costs of petroleum and its products tend to be understated because of the heavy rent element in the industry; similarly, the explicit costs of production of capital-intensive products are on the low side. In the recent reforms, some attempt has been made to include rent and interest charges in enterprise accounts, and price rationality may have improved somewhat for this reason.

Finally, a considerable degree of irrationality has been introduced into prices by the large-scale use of discriminatory excise taxes (called turnover taxes), particularly on consumers' goods, and by the simultaneous extension of discriminatory subsidies to many enterprises, primarily those producing other than consumers' goods. The excise taxes on consumers' goods are often intended to serve social policies, such as high taxes on liquor to discourage drinking, or low taxes on musical instruments to encourage musical activities, and so forth. They are also sometimes differentiated to help equate supply and demand, e.g., goods in very short supply, like automobiles, are heavily taxed; those few goods in excess supply have their taxes reduced.

Most of the Communist nations have recently been trying to reduce or eliminate subsidies to enterprises. Subsidies have often been extended to enterprises producing new products in order to encourage their use, particularly in the first years of production when costs are particularly high. The bulk of the subsidies, however, has originated for negative reasons, that is, either to cover the operating costs of enterprises which are operating at a loss because they are less efficient than others in the industry, or to cover the losses of all enterprises in an industry where wages have risen faster than productivity. Sales taxes plus subsidies result in a price situation in which prices of consumers' goods substantially exceed prices of producers' goods, even for the same or similar products (e.g., passenger automobiles and trucks), and individual prices in both sectors vary widely and unsystematically.

The state of price confusion in the Soviet bloc is quite freely admitted, as the following statement (or understatement) in Communist jargon testifies:

> . . . prices, as is known, do not reflect with adequate completeness and precision the socially necessary labor outlays for the manufacture of goods. Prices of means of production are mainly below value while the prices of many consumers' goods are above value. Moreover, the prices within each of these departments [sectors] also diverge from their value. Thus numerically equal outlays of social labor are expressed in different prices.[1]

Managerial Incentives

The managerial incentive system in Soviet bloc nations is quite complex and no attempt will be made here to describe it in detail. We attempt only to set forth a few salient features relevant to the issues of this book. If there is one major management guidepost under capitalism, it is profits. In order to achieve and maintain a high level of profits, the manager of a capitalist enterprise is motivated on the supply side to keep his costs down and on the demand side to provide a product which is, or appears to be, superior to the products of competitors and to appeal generally to his customers. Under Stalinist-type planning, on the other hand, the manager is faced with many targets, only one of which, and a minor one at that, is profits. Other targets, or success indicators, as they have been called, are: reduce unit costs; reduce expenditures on wages; raise labor productivity; raise capital productivity; maximize quantity of output; and so forth. Many of these targets conflict with each other. For example, enterprises have often increased output at the expense of rising unit costs and declining profits and labor productivity. This is not a trivial example. In fact, until the recent reforms, output targets were the major goals of enterprises and took precedence over dozens of other targets facing managers. Precedence of output targets was assured by attaching the largest managerial bonuses to the achievement of these targets.

The importance of quantitative targets is not really surprising when viewed in the context of central planning with direct controls. For the whole system of "material balances" is one of meshing *quantities* supplied with *quantities* demanded. In theory, at least, profit maximization is bound to be of less interest than output, to authorities intent on equating supply and demand. There are two other major reasons for emphasis on quantity rather than value or profits targets. First, with prices so arbitrary and anarchic, the use of profits as a guide to production decisions loses most of its rationale. Second, as indicated earlier, the Communist nations plan for over-full employment. What this means, in effect, is that they are "pressure" economies, like capitalist nations during wartime. Just as a capitalist nation during wartime has goals of so many tanks, planes, steel plate, mortars, and so forth, the Communist nation presses in peacetime for similar quantitative goals. Thus the Communist system of emphasizing production goals over profits or other goals is simply the counterpart of the capitalist wartime practice of contracting with private enterprise for deliveries on a "cost-plus" basis. In a modified way, this same technique is used even now in the United States in much defense procurement. There is one major difference between the two systems, however, probably related to the fact that in the United States only Defense Department procurement is on a cost-plus basis. I refer to the fact that under central planning the existence of quantitative targets and lack of concern for profits leads to disregard for quality of product, whereas one of the reasons for cost-plus in the United States is the concern to achieve a high level of quality regardless of cost. Very probably, defense procurement in the centrally planned economies is also characterized by high quality standards and is an exception to the general case.

Since the recent reforms in Eastern Europe and the U.S.S.R., production targets, while still maintained, are no longer the basis of managerial bonuses. There are at least two reasons for this. First, as these economies became wealthier and more complex, quality deterioration became a more serious problem. Second, "relative affluence" led to a situation, particularly in the consumer-good market, where the failure of planners and enterprises to cater to the needs and tastes of consumers led to the accumulation of unsalable supplies. This situation is aggravated, of course, by the fact that enterprises cannot exercise the privilege of adjusting prices to clear markets. In some cases—sewing machines in the U.S.S.R. being the most publicized—products continued to be produced even though the warehouses were filling up with unsold goods, because fulfillment of output plans continued to be rewarded with bonuses. In other words, the production sector was almost completely insulated from market feedback. In an attempt to solve these problems, bonuses were tied to sales rather than to output. This is a fitting remedy, of course, for the instances of overproduction. But in those cases where the market is characterized by excess demand—and in the U.S.S.R., at least, they still predominate—enterprises can sell everything they produce and need not worry about quality or the needs of the market.

Economic Goals and Policies

The economic goals of the Communist states are implicit in what has already been stated. Some of these are goals of capitalist nations as well, and differences between the systems, to the extent that they exist, are due to the greater intensity with which goals are pursued in nations run by single parties.

Full employment and stable prices are explicit goals of the Communist nations. The U.S.S.R., at least, does not even admit the existence of unemployment. Absence of mass unemployment was advertised as, and was, one of the obvious advantages of central planning in the prewar period when most capitalist nations were experiencing the Great Depression. Widespread use in the postwar period of Keynesian fiscal and monetary policies substantially reduced these advantages. More recently, however, the development in Western industrial nations of "stagflation," that is, the simultaneous existence of inflation and unemployment and the inability to reduce either without aggravating the other, has increased Communist superiority in these areas. For while the Communist nations do have frictional and structural unemployment related to changing of jobs and to mismatches between job requirements and the distribution of labor skills, the existence of over-full employment planning more or less insures that there will be little, if any, unemployment due to lack of effective demand. Over-full employment planning is not consciously pursued nor is it pursued in order to achieve full employment. Full employment, a by-product of this kind of planning, simply reflects the leadership's impatience to use all resources as fully as possible. As noted, capitalist nations are hindered from pursuing full employment so intensively by the fact that, as full employment is approached, prices begin to rise. The Communist nations are not similarly constrained, since the state controls wages and prices. Control of wages and prices, while making it easier to have full employment, also suffers from drawbacks. It leads to repressed inflation and disequilibrium pricing and the deleterious consequences on resource allocation and incentives for the economy that result.

A related goal of the Communist nations is industrialization and rapid economic growth. This goal stems from several sources: from Marxist ideology, from their status as relatively underdeveloped nations (in comparison with the leading nations of Europe and North America), and from their competition with and desire to outpace the West. In the words of the important *Basic Principles of International Socialist Division of Labor* adopted by CMEA in 1962:

> The economic complex in each country should be developed in a way that will continuously raise the country's economic level. This presupposes, above all, maximum development of each country's socialist industry as the leading branch of the national economy, with priority given to the output of means of production.[2]

In the implementation of economic objectives, the central planners have shown a marked preference for the use of administrative controls over price and market mechanisms. Many economists have argued that this preference was rational at the time that central planning was introduced, because of the monumental changes in institutions and economic structure initially planned. Price and market mechanisms work most efficiently when called upon to effect changes gradually, which is why even capitalist nations fall back on controls in wartime. Another factor behind antagonism toward use of market mechanisms is the Marxist labor theory of value, which, in its crudest form, makes wages the basis of price and denies the importance of interest and rent. In Marxist theory, capital and land simply make labor more productive but are not, in themselves, productive. Since land and capital are not a source of value, there is no need for rent or interest payments or their inclusion in price. Furthermore, since in the Communist nations, land and capital belong to the state, there would, in any case, appear to be no one to whom such payments should be made. Finally, administrative controls usually become associated with the economic and political status of individuals, and for this reason become difficult to eliminate. The force of this consideration is much greater in a one-party system, in which, in contrast to multiple-party systems, there may not be a change in administration for very long periods of time.

Nevertheless, as we shall show below, the recent reforms in Eastern Europe have involved a move toward price and market mechanisms, although these have been substantial only in Hungary and Czechoslovakia (pre-invasion). There are many factors behind the reforms, most of which relate to the economic problems that beset most of these nations under Stalinist-type planning. If there was ever a need for such Draconian measures, it is recognized by many that that need no longer exists. Furthermore, while the ideological bias against private individuals receiving rent and interest income remains, the use of these categories in price formation and resource allocation (the state receiving the income) is now acceptable.

Another policy, corollary to several of the characteristics and policies already discussed, is the priority the state accords to what might be termed the planners' interests over the interests of household and consumer. In fact, it has been this priority principle that has made it feasible, for example, for the authorities to tolerate the uncertainties and disruptions associated with the use of the method of balances and with over-full employment planning. If, for example, without the priority principle, the steel industry did not receive its share of inputs and was unable to produce its planned level of output, the state might find that it was not getting the supplies it needed to produce, say, the missiles and tanks it was counting on. The priority principle insures, on the one hand, that the steel industry receive its full complement of inputs and, on the other hand, that even if steel output is not up to planned levels, producers of missiles and tanks receive their planned allocations. In both contingencies, of course, it is the industries servicing the household which ultimately suffer. This is not to say that the authorities do not wish to improve the lot of their citizens, for they do. At the margins, however, the priority favors those sectors in which the consumer has least direct interest. The priority principle does operate with constraints, of course, as attested to by the uprising in Poland in December 1970.

The Economic Reforms

We have already alluded several times to the economic reforms which have been put into effect in Eastern Europe since the mid-1960s. The reforms and the reasons for their promulgation differ from country to country. Nevertheless, there have been a number of common causes. One dominating feature of the performance of these nations has been a steadily declining rate of economic growth. And the rate of growth has not declined because authorities have lowered the rate of investment, for they have not. In fact, a given rate of investment yields a smaller percentage increase in growth of output today than it did ten and twenty years ago,* and it is necessary to invest more resources in order to get the same rate of growth. Another set of factors behind the reforms is related to the growing complexity of these economies as they become more affluent. The task of the central planning board grows more and more difficult as the numbers of commodities and prices multiply, as consumers become more affluent and are no longer willing to accept low-quality ill-fitting products, and so forth. When the population does not have enough necessities, it is easy to direct the factories to produce so many pairs of shoes, so many sewing machines, etc. Once the basic necessities have been supplied, it becomes necessary to worry about "tastes," i.e., sizes, styles, and colors. For this one needs a market in which consumers can register their preferences. Similarly, in a very complicated economy, it becomes more and more difficult for the planners to give detailed instructions to each and every enterprise and to have a hand in all managerial decisions. To the extent that the central planning board tried to do more than it could handle, it made many wrong decisions. This was as true of agriculture as of industry where, for example, collective farm chairmen in the U.S.S.R.

---

*Technically speaking, the capital-output ratios are rising, i.e., capital productivity is declining.

were often told by the central planners to plant the wrong crops for soil and weather conditions.

The continuing technical backwardness of the socialist nations and the difficulties they have had in introducing new technology into their industries is a problem which undoubtedly contributes to the slowing rates of growth noted above and which, in turn, may be attributed in part to the complexities of central planning and to the difficulties in properly structuring managerial incentives to innovate under these circumstances. Generally speaking, socialist managers have found that as long as they fulfilled their output or sales targets, they received adequate bonuses—so why run the risk associated with innovation? Technical backwardness has also been a major factor behind the strengthening interest in East-West trade over the past decade and particularly in the willingness to engage in cooperative industrial and marketing agreements and joint ventures with Western enterprises (see Chapter 4). Interest in East-West trade, in turn, has been a factor behind the economic reform movement because of the trade difficulties created by non-scarcity prices, non-market mechanisms, and non-functioning exchange rates (see Chapter 2). Foreign trade as a stimulus to economic reform has been much more important to Eastern Europe than to the U.S.S.R. because it plays so much larger a role in their economies than in the U.S.S.R.

This listing by no means exhausts the reasons for the reforms, nor does it apply equally to each Eastern nation. Nevertheless, these are some of the major factors. They are discussed further in Chapter 4.

As noted, the reforms differ substantially from each other. Furthermore, the reform in each nation is a living thing, the subject of continual experimentation, which changes from year to year as the situation changes and which often contains a considerable gap between blueprint and implementation. The spectrum along which the reforms differ is marked mainly by the amount of reliance placed on market mechanisms, as opposed to direct controls.

The Soviet reform has been quite conservative, with little reliance on market mechanisms. The reform which was introduced gradually after 1965 retains most physical production targets, though reduced in number, a rigid system of allocation of materials, and absolute central control over prices (which are changed very infrequently). The changes which have been made were clearly designed not to introduce markets but to improve the functioning of the Stalinist system of planning by direct controls. Thus, for example, managerial bonuses are no longer based on the output target, but rather on sales, to avoid the continued production and embarrassing accumulation of inventories of sewing machines and other products that no one wants. Prices were reformed in 1967 for the first time in twelve years to facilitate decision making, but they have remained relatively fixed since then. Furthermore, since they were never truly market-clearing prices, particularly in the producers' goods area, rationing could not be eliminated. Price formation has also been improved by the inclusion of rent and interest charges. The inclusion of interest charges on capital, a major ideological breakthrough, may help reduce the squandering of capital by management, since capital is no longer free. A substantial percentage of investment decision-making was to be decentralized to the enterprise level. However, this "unplanned" investment has not materialized, partly because it was so difficult to fit into a system in which all major materials and equipment are still rigidly allocated. The manager was also supposed to have much more freedom in determining the kind of work force he needed. Presumably he would no longer be stuck with a particular set of workers as determined by the planning board, each to be paid a given wage. However, managers found that when they tried to change their labor-mix it was almost impossible to fire workers they wanted to dismiss. Finally, the authorities found that many managers, used to the old ways, would not change their working pattern even when they were given new freedoms.

In the early 1970s the U.S.S.R. moved to create large super-firms or "branch associations" which stand between the ministry (industry head office) and the enterprise. Presumably, these associations will attempt to take over some of the burdens of the central planning board, thereby admitting a small amount of decentralization into the system and allowing the board to concentrate on more basic problems. Basically, however, they function as part of a larger direct-control planning system and provide no new freedom for the enterprise—the basic economic unit. The one area in which the associations may improve the functioning of the economy is by permitting a closer relationship between the research and development (R&D) organizations and the industrial enterprises. This was difficult to achieve when the several enterprises producing a similar type of product and interested in the same kind of technological advances had no connection with each other.

The reforms in the Eastern European CMEA nations, except for Hungary, exhibit approximately the same degree of conservatism as the Soviet reform. Poland was the pioneer, having set forth a blueprint for a radical reform in 1956. Primarily for political reasons (discussed in more detail in Chapter 6), this reform failed and so did two later attempts. A fourth reform is currently in the experimental stage. "Industrial conglomerates" have been created which, like the Soviet "branch associations," stand between the ministries and their enterprises. What is not yet clear is how much decision-making power has been delegated by the central planning board to the conglomerates and how much power the conglomerates have taken from the enterprises. From the available literature, it is not apparent that the market has been significantly extended. However, as of fall 1975, there have been reports which suggest that further reforms are being pushed through by the Poles and that their economy may presently become about as liberal as that of East Germany.

Bulgaria, like Poland, had a reform blueprint which involved significant decentralization of economic activity but which also was never implemented. Like the U.S.S.R., Bulgaria introduced, among other things, an interest rate, bank financing of some capital investment, and trusts which took most of the power away from the enterprises. In 1973, the regime introduced still another stage of control with so-called economic complexes, which were, in effect, super-trusts, and which were to coordinate the activities of the trusts. Of critical importance, however, is the fact that no effort was ever made to reduce the scope or compulsory nature of the central plan. If anything, the Bulgarian reform appears to be developing in the direction of greater rather than less centralization.

The Rumanian reform has never been fully implemented and, like the Bulgarian reform and others, appears to have been largely designed to shore up the central planning mechanism. As in the other reforms, intermediate organizations were called "industrial centrals." These were granted even more power than, for example, the Soviet branch associations. From the standpoint of finance and supply, the industrial central, rather than the enterprise, is the basic administrative economic unit in Rumania. Central planning, with its direct control of output and prices, remains unchanged.

The East German reform is probably the most liberal of those already mentioned. The East Germans pioneered the industrial trust in Eastern Europe; their version is generally known by its German acronym, VVB. The VVBs took power from both the central planners and the enterprises subordinated to them. While they were allowed some latitude in setting targets for their enterprises, price-setting remained fully centralized. As in the Soviet and Polish reforms, extensive additional changes of the old Stalinist model took place in the form of price reforms, sales rather than quantity targeting for enterprises, and some decentralization of the investment mechanism. Basically, however, the East German economy remains centrally directed.

The Czechoslovakian (until August 1968) and Hungarian reforms, breaking much more sharply with the Stalinist model, introduced a degree of true decentralization. The Czech economic reform was stopped by Warsaw Pact troops in August 1968, after a substantial degree of liberalization in political and intellectual affairs developed. By 1970, the central plan had been completely reinstituted, enterprises were given targets, prices were frozen, and so forth. The Czech economy has since been as thoroughly controlled as that of the other Eastern European nations.

The Hungarian (like the pre-1968 Czech) reform was conceived as an attempt to establish a socialist market economy in which the major macropolicy issues—such as which industries to develop, rate of investment and military spending, and distribution of income—were to be determined by the planners, with detailed implementation left to market mechanisms. The market was to be guided by the state into the right paths by employment of such instruments as taxes and tax rebates, subsidies, access to short- and long-term credit, and so forth. Plans were established for the various ministries and industries, but these were not binding, simply serving as guidelines, as with the French "indicative planning" system. Enterprises are not given specific targets nor are they required to buy and sell to each other according to government directive; they are free to produce and trade with whom they wish. In theory, prices are supposed to be freed to respond to market conditions, but in practice, most prices have been frozen because of the need to control inflation (a result of over-full employment planning). A large part of investment is now determined by the enterprises themselves, and financed from profits. However, the government power to tax, to control credit, and to license new investment projects insures that its overall development policies are implemented. Profit, rather than output or sales, is the measure of enterprise success as well as the source of bonuses and investment funds.

These are some of the major features of the Hungarian reform model. In practice, it has not been completely successful. As noted, the continued existence of inflationary pressures has necessitated price controls and prevented the kind of price flexibility required for the successful operation of markets. It has been difficult to get the required reallocation of resources which the reform supposedly makes possible, because of social pressures against forcing workers to change their places of work or their skills. As in the Soviet case, the old plant managers cannot be fired and it is difficult to get them to adopt the new ways. Finally, as noted above, the state is still able to exert considerable control over enterprise decisions by the use of indirect regulators such as the various financial instruments noted above. In fact, according to some observers, these regulators are used so extensively as to leave little freedom to the plant manager and market.

Finally, it is worth noting that Yugoslavia, which broke with the Soviet bloc some twenty-five years ago, did at that time establish a true market economy with the added feature of a substantial degree of worker control over enterprises. No other socialist nation, not even Hungary, has come close to the degree of marketization that exists in Yugoslavia. At the other extreme, no "liberalizing" economic reforms have been reported in Cuba, Outer Mongolia, or in the non-CMEA Communist nations.

Chapter 2

Foreign Trade Institutions and Behavior of Centrally Planned Economies: Theory

---

The institutions, techniques, and behavior of the Communist nations in international trade are quite different from those which have evolved under capitalism. Most of these differences are due to the special characteristics of the Stalinist model of central planning as outlined in the previous chapter. Changes in foreign trade behavior can be expected, therefore, as domestic economic reforms are promulgated. These changes are discussed in the last section of this chapter.

State Trading

THE FOREIGN TRADE MONOPOLY AND ITS IMPLICATIONS

In Western nations, most foreign trade transactions are initiated and conducted by private enterprises, that is, exporters and importers. True, most governments engage in some trading operations because of activities relating to international military and aid functions. However, aside from these, the government role is largely regulatory, protective, or macroeconomic and confined to taking measures to prevent smuggling, levy tariffs and quotas, maintain exchange rates at parity, and the like.

In a Communist nation, foreign trade is in the hands of a state monopoly and its operation is fairly centralized. This appears inevitable, given the centralized nature of most other economic activity and the necessity facing the planners of having to dovetail imports and exports into their annual economic plans and, specifically, into their commodity balances. The Soviet monopolistic organization called the Ministry of Foreign Trade is assisted in its efforts by some thirty to forty subministries or foreign trade organizations (FTOs), each of which is operationally responsible for the exports, imports, or both of a particular commodity sector such as ferrous metals, vehicles, or tourism (administered by the Intourist organization). The ministry itself is an administrative, not an operating, organization and stands between the FTOs and the central planning board. In establishing preliminary estimates for the annual national economic plan, the central planning board develops a set of preliminary export and import targets. These targets are not developed out of thin air, of course, but take into account traditional patterns of export and import and also probable forthcoming export and import obligations under the long-term trade agreements that each Eastern nation has with many other nations. The ministry checks these targets in a preliminary and aggregative way (e.g., for balance in payments) and transmits them to the proper FTOs, where they undergo a more detailed plausibility check. The FTOs' views are transmitted back to the central planning board via the ministry. When the final annual national plan is eventually born, the foreign trade targets passed down to the ministry and thence to the FTOs have the force of "law." That is to say, the FTOs are expected to negotiate exports and imports, as planned, with FTOs in other Eastern European countries or with private enterprises in the West. It is very important to note that it is usually the FTOs, not the export-producing or import-using enterprises of a country, which have contact with the FTOs or enterprises of other nations. This artificial separation of consumers from producers cannot help but make foreign trade less satisfactory than it could be, except in the case of completely standardized homogeneous commodities.

A special difficulty that arises in the case of export-producing enterprises is that they have no incentive to produce for export or to meet the special requirements of foreign buyers. Their quantitative targets are not usually differentiated among buyers and their profits are not dependent upon exports. Under the plan, part of their output is shipped to domestic enterprises and part to the FTO. Since, with over-full employment planning, they can usually sell all they produce anyway, it matters little to them whether their products are exported. In fact, if exported goods required special attention, they would prefer not to produce for export, since this would make it more difficult for them to achieve their quantitative targets. Such problems as these have led some of the Eastern European nations, particularly Hungary and East Germany, to allow direct negotiations between some domestic and foreign enterprises without the mediation of the FTO, and also to allow some of the enterprises to keep part of the foreign exchange earned to meet their own needs in foreign markets.

The conduct of trade by a nationalized foreign trade monopoly rather than by private individual exporters and importers has three additional major consequences. First, the Communist nations take an entirely antimercantilist view of foreign trade, that is, trade is conducted primarily to obtain essential imports. Exports are considered not as an end in themselves but purely as a means to finance the necessary imports. If some of the Communist nations have on occasion mounted intensive export programs, this has only been because of balance of payments pressures related to rising import requirements. More basically, exports are viewed as a loss of resources, not a gain. In the West, of course, the level of exports is always just as important a goal as, if not more important than, the level of imports. Some individual traders export, others import, with the gains to the economy presumably reflected in the private profits in each case. One implication of the Communist approach is that the foreign trade monopoly is apt to put less effort and concern into export promotion and marketing than into imports. Thus exports tend to suffer from neglect at the national level as well as at the level of the producing enterprise.

Second, since the foreign trade monopoly is in charge equally of exports and imports, there is some tendency to take a barter approach to foreign trade rather than to approach export and import transactions completely independently, as is the case with private enterprise. Under these circumstances, profitability may often be assessed on the basis of "terms of trade," that is, value of imports received for exports sold, rather than on the basis of profit on each individual transaction. Hence, for example, the Ministry of Foreign Trade might be willing to sanction the sale of a commodity at a loss if by doing so it could earn sufficient foreign exchange to purchase another commodity whose value to the economy was deemed very great. This attitude has implications for the evaluation of dumping by Communist nations.

Third, since foreign trade is completely controlled by a state monopoly, tariffs are unnecessary and, where they exist, redundant.

TRADE THROUGH TRADE AGREEMENTS

Most foreign trade is conducted within the framework of bilateral long-term agreements (usually lasting five years). This is to be expected, given the existence of extensive central planning by direct physical controls. A strong motive of planners, faced with an extremely complicated task, is to reduce uncertainty as much as possible. The trade agreements constitute an attempt to reduce the uncertainties of foreign trade. The five-year agreements usually specify minimum flows of trade and the flows of key products. Annual negotiations fill in the details, such as the amounts of each commodity, prices, delivery dates. All the Communist nations have trade agreements with each other, and it is these which are referred to above; most also have agreements with some Western nations. The agreements they make with each other are much more binding than those with Western nations. That is to say, Western governments can open up their borders to exports and imports of particular products and can encourage contacts between private traders and Communist trade associations, but they cannot guarantee the consummation of a transaction in the same way a Communist government can. In this regard, East-West trade agreements, while better than nothing, are much less satisfactory to the Eastern nations. Where trade agreements do not exist, as for example in U.S. trade with the Soviet bloc (as of 1972), trade nevertheless takes place on an ad hoc basis, often on a basis of long-term contracts with individual capitalist enterprises.

TRADE AVERSION

Until about ten years ago, it was commonplace for specialists to say that Communist countries were autarkic, that is, they tried to eliminate trade to the fullest extent possible. This was an overstatement based on several observations. First, the U.S.S.R. in the 1930s almost closed its economy to world trade. By 1937, exports and imports each amounted to only one-half of one percent of GNP compared with from 10 to 12 percent before the Revolution and 3 to 4 percent in the early 1930s. Second, Soviet economists in that period actually said that their country traded only to free itself of the future necessity to trade. Third, in the early postwar period, most of the nations of Eastern Europe and China tended to trade on a much smaller scale than comparable Western nations or than they had traded as capitalist countries before World War II.

In recent years, the trade-GNP ratios of the U.S.S.R. and the nations of Eastern Europe have risen, and economists of these nations have explicitly denied that autarky is a goal. Nevertheless, the trade of many of these nations, particularly that of the Soviet Union, is clearly below the level which would obtain if capitalism prevailed (see Table 2.1).* The lower level of trade is partly due to the effect of the cold war. But

TABLE 2.1
Participation in World Trade, 1967

	PERCENTAGE SHARE IN WORLDS				
	AREA	POPU-LATION	NATIONAL INCOME	INDUS-TRIAL OUTPUT	FOREIGN TRADE
The West[a]	26.4	21.5	63	55	69.3
Socialist nations[b]	25.6	35.5	23	38	11.3
Third World[c]	48.0	43.0	14	7	19.1

[a]Canada, United States, all of Europe (except the eight socialist countries), Japan, South Africa, Australia, and New Zealand.

[b]Albania, Bulgaria, Czechoslovakia, East Germany, Hungary, Poland, Rumania, the U.S.S.R., Mainland China, Mongolia, North Korea, and North Vietnam.

[c]Countries other than Western or socialist nations.

SOURCE: Josef Wilczynski, *The Economics and Politics of East-West Trade*, London: Macmillan, New York: Praeger, 1969, p. 24.

*The figures in Table 2.1 tend to overstate the relatively low trade levels of the Communist countries because of the importance of the U.S.S.R. and Communist China in their totals. These two nations are very large, with widely varied resources, and have low trade-to-GNP ratios on this account, as well as for reasons relating to central planning.

it is also due to specific features of central planning with direct controls. The result is more properly called trade aversion than autarky.

Probably the major factor behind trade aversion is the desire on the part of the central planners to minimize disturbances to their commodity "balances." They view foreign trade as inherently risky and are unwilling to depend on foreign sources of supply which are outside their direct control, if they can be avoided without too great a cost. In actual fact, however, foreign sources of supply, particularly Western sources, are probably as dependable as domestic enterprises whose reliability, especially in an overfull employment milieu, is not particularly good. Their attitude on this matter must be viewed therefore as determined more by psychological and ideological than pragmatic considerations. Second, all nations endeavor to achieve a degree of self-sufficiency for military reasons. Such desires are likely to reduce trade to a greater extent where industry is nationalized than where economic activity is largely in private hands. In fact, it is worth observing that although under private enterprise international trade takes place wherever profitable opportunities are available unless governments intervene, under central planning in a Communist nation foreign trade does not take place except by a specific act of government. Third, the prevalent irrationality of internal prices in Communist countries must certainly enhance trade aversion by making it difficult for the planners, since they recognize that their prices are irrational, to determine what should and should not be traded. All sorts of ad hoc devices have been developed in an attempt to get around this problem. Fourth, the rigid bilateralism of intrabloc trade undoubtedly lowers the level of trade, since in most instances bilateral balance is achieved by having the stronger (in a foreign trade sense) of the two trade partners reduce its exports rather than increase its imports (of unwanted goods). On the other hand, the latter possibility undoubtedly also sometimes occurs and some uneconomic trade is thereby generated.

Pricing, Exchange Rates, and Trade Choices

FOREIGN TRADE PRICING AND EXCHANGE RATES

An exchange rate is the price of one currency in terms of another. Where trade is allowed to flow freely and prices and exchange rates are allowed to seek their equilibrium levels, the relative prices of currencies reflect, roughly, the purchasing power of each currency in its own country of internationally tradable goods. There is, in other words, an organic connection between the prices of tradable goods in each country and world prices; in a world without friction the prices of similar goods tend to be equalized by equilibrium exchange rates. This ideal model is hardly approximated in the real world, where tariffs, quotas, exchange controls, differential transport costs, fixed disequilibrium exchange rates, differential bargaining power, ignorance, and many other impediments to free trade exist. Consequently, one may find the same commodity selling at substantially different prices in different countries. Despite the flaws in this model of a capitalist trading system, the system has worked as postulated over most of the past century, though with less-than-perfect efficiency. Domestic prices of tradable goods have been interrelated through world markets; exchange rates have provided a guide to the relative values of different currencies and have been close enough to an equilibrium value for most countries that extensive controls have not been required to balance international payments.

The set of relationships just described does not fit the Communist nations. As noted in the preceding chapter, the internal prices of each country not only are not free prices which equate supply and demand but are further distorted from "rational" levels and relationships to each other by planners' practices regarding subsidies and excise taxes, and by adherence to a labor theory of value. From an international point of view, some order might be brought to this chaos if the price structure in each of the bloc nations were "irrational" in much the same way. Apparently this is not the case, even though irrationality stems from the same deep-seated causes in each country. In the words of three Polish economists: ". . . Because of the autonomous system of domestic prices in each country, an automatic and purely internal character of the monetary system and arbitrary official rates of exchange which do not reflect relative values of currencies, it is impossible to compare prices and costs of production of particular commodities in different countries."[1] The result is that both internally and internationally, prices do not convey to planners reliable information regarding either costs of production or value (usefulness) of products.

Clearly, there is no organic connection between the prices of tradable goods in the Communist countries. The question arises: at what set of prices, then, does international trade take place? The answer to this question is quite simple in the case of East-West trade. Since the trade of the Communist nations amounts to such a small part of the trade of their Western partners, they are forced to export and import at close to world prices. They are not unlike the average farmer or consumer to whom the market price must be taken as given. The case of intrabloc trade is less constrained. There has been in the Communist literature on foreign-trade pricing a persistent effort, since the formation of CMEA in 1948, to find some principles upon which a so-called "own" foreign trade pricing system could be based. Since the U.S.S.R. is the dominant trader in the Eastern bloc, its price structure has often been mentioned as a possibility. However, until Soviet prices become more rational, they would not be acceptable to the other Soviet bloc countries, or to the Soviet planners themselves for that matter. Consequently, the "own" price system is as chimerical today as it was twenty years ago. How then do the bloc nations trade with each other? So far, they have been able to find only one set of consistent relative values upon which mutual agreement was possible, namely, capitalist world prices, usually expressed in dollars or pounds. From a political standpoint, reliance on capitalist prices has not been a happy solution, and the search for an "own" price system will no doubt continue though with little chance of success.* Capitalist world prices are not used without adjustments; the actual practices will be described in the following chapter.

By this time, it should be clear that the exchange rates of the Communist nations do not function as market prices used, on the one hand, for comparing domestic prices between nations or, on the other hand, for achieving a balance in the balance of payments. Obviously,

---

*It has been reported that in East-West discussions at the United Nations in Geneva a bitter quarrel developed between the British and Soviet representatives. The British delegate angrily told the Russian delegate that he found it hard to take seriously the proposals of a representative of a group of nations which were unable to generate their own foreign trade price system. "How will you trade when the world revolution comes and there are no longer any capitalist prices?" the British delegate triumphantly asked. The Soviet delegate rose to his feet and said that the British delegate had raised a serious question, one that had been considered in the highest councils of his nation, and that it had finally been decided that when the revolution came, to leave one capitalist country outside the Communist camp.

there is no point in comparing irrational prices with each other; furthermore, if world prices are used for trading, conversion becomes unnecessary. Nevertheless, all the bloc nations do have exchange rates. The uselessness of these exchange rates for trading purposes can be demonstrated by reference to the Russian ruble. In 1956, the ruble was officially pegged at a value of $.25, or 4 rubles to the dollar. In 1956, the Soviet Union exported turpentine. At the official rate of 4 rubles to the dollar, every dollar's worth of turpentine exported was worth 4 foreign exchange rubles. Yet, the internal price of one dollar's worth of turpentine was 33 rubles. In effect, turpentine was exported at about one-eighth its internal price. To take another example, in the case of sawn lumber a dollar's worth of exports had an internal price of 11 rubles compared to a foreign exchange ruble value of 4. In the case of fuel oil, the domestic price was 18½ rubles. In effect, each of these groups of commodities was exported at a large nominal loss if the foreign exchange ruble price is compared with the domestic price. In contrast, fire brick was sold at a 100 percent profit, a dollar's worth having an internal price of 2 rubles and a foreign exchange price of 4 rubles. Fire brick was, however, an exception; most exports were sold at a nominal loss because the ruble was highly overvalued in 1956 and should have been pegged at about $.10 instead of $.25. The counterpart, with overvaluation, of nominal losses on most exports should be profits on most imports, and this turns out to be the case. For example, in 1956 a dollar's worth of nonferrous metal imports with a foreign exchange ruble cost of 4 rubles had an internal price of 28½ rubles. The same foreign exchange cost of grain was priced internally at 9.6 rubles, of cement at 12½ rubles, etc. From these figures, it is clear that if the exchange rate were a real price, the Soviet Union would have had almost no incentive to export but a strong incentive to import, thus running a serious deficit, the problem which faces all nations with overvalued currencies. In fact, Soviet exports and imports are always nearly balanced.

What, then, is the function of an exchange rate under these bizarre conditions? Why bother with an exchange rate at all? Actually, the exchange rate serves two functions. First, if tourists, the foreign press, embassy personnel, etc., are to have a reasonable amount of freedom, they must be able to purchase the local currency (at some exchange rate) and to spend it freely on consumers' goods and services. The alternatives are either to restrict tourists' freedom of movement severely or to sell goods and services in local and foreign currencies widely. Because the exchange rate used by foreign travelers and residents is a real price at which transactions actually take place, it should be relatively realistic; that is to say, it should roughly equate local and foreign prices. Since official exchange rates of the Communist nations have often been far out of line, most of them have had special tourist and/or diplomatic exchange rates for foreigners. In the U.S.S.R. in 1956, for example, the tourist rate was 10 rubles to the dollar in comparison with an official rate of 4 rubles to the dollar. The tourist rate for the Polish zloty was only one-sixth of the very much overvalued official rate.

The second function of the exchange rate (and we refer here to the official exchange rate) is simply to serve as a unit of account so that the Communist nations can present a balance of trade or payments in their own currencies. Since trade is conducted in terms of Western prices and currencies, an exchange rate is necessary if balance of payments in "own" currency is to be possible. The desire to present a balance of payments in "own" rather than in Western currencies is almost entirely politically motivated—a matter of prestige—for the figures which result often have little relationship to internal prices as the figures presented above with regard to turpentine, lumber, and so forth suggest. In fact, in order to include foreign trade activities in the gross social product, the commodities traded must be revalued at domestic prices. This results in a different foreign trade balance from the one that is published. In 1959, the U.S.S.R. for once published both trade balances, showing a surplus of 300 million rubles in foreign trade prices and a deficit of 3.8 billion rubles in domestic prices! Clearly, conversion of foreign trade data into foreign exchange rubles, zlotys, etc., at official exchange rates is useless for purposes of national income accounting and simply amounts to converting trade weighted by world (dollar, pound) prices nominally into Communist currency; it does not weight (value) this trade by Communist internal prices, however.

The irrelevance of the official exchange rate can be demonstrated in still another way. East-West trade is conducted in dollars or pounds or other Western currencies. If trade is not balanced, the surpluses and deficits are always settled in Western currencies, never in Communist currencies, for reasons which will become clear later (see Inconvertibility and Bilateralism). Since there is no exchange of Western for Communist currencies, there is no need for an exchange rate. Intrabloc trade is conducted in world prices also. However, surpluses and deficits are not allowed to develop; trade is bilaterally balanced to a very fine degree. Hence, payments are usually unnecessary. Where a trade balance is not achieved over the normal annual accounting period, the provision is usually for the imbalance to be worked off by excess shipments of goods from the deficit to the surplus country in the subsequent period or by payment of Western currencies or gold. Again, there is no need for an exchange rate. The fact is that the Communist currencies are all completely inconvertible and can serve neither as a medium of exchange nor store of value in international trade. They are used for prestige reasons, as noted above, as a unit of account and not a very useful accounting unit at that.

Until about 1970, most nations viewed their exchange rates as symbols of masculinity and preferred not to devalue unless absolutely necessary. As the dominant nation in the Soviet bloc, the U.S.S.R. has shown a similar sensitivity with regard to the ruble. After CMEA was formed in the late 1940s and intrabloc trade expanded rapidly, Soviet writings stressed the future role of the ruble as the key currency in this trade, just as the dollar and sterling were the key currencies in Western trade. At this time, the ruble was officially valued at $.1887, or 5.3 rubles to the dollar. At this rate, it was overvalued. Nevertheless, on March 1, 1950, the ruble was revalued upward to $.25, or 4 rubles to the dollar. The only explanation of such a move is that it was done for reasons of prestige. This explanation is fortified by the official statement that henceforth the ruble was to be "transferred to the more stable gold standard" and no longer to be defined in terms of dollars. At that time, of course, with the so-called dollar shortage at its peak, dollars were certainly as good as gold, if not better. Basically, the whole operation was nothing more than a gesture, since the exchange rate served no significant function anyway.

The ruble remained technically overvalued (by about 100 percent) throughout the 1950s. Then in 1961, in terms of existing prices it was devalued from $.25 to $.111 cents, a devaluation of roughly 55 percent. Simultaneously, however, all internal prices, wage rates, rents, etc., were reduced to 10 percent of their previous value, that is to say there was a tenfold reduction in all internal prices. Given this price reduction, the ruble was technically worth not $.111 but rather $1.11. That is to say, instead of a 55 percent depreciation, the ruble was appreciated from $.25 to $1.11 (in Soviet terms, the gold content rose from .222168 to .987412 grams), a 444 percent increase in value. It would seem that the only reasons for having the tenfold reduction in internal prices at the same time that the value of the ruble was changed were the political ones of making a currency depreciation look like an appreciation and raising the value, or gold content, of the ruble above that of the dollar.

It is worth noting at this point that the changes in the value of the ruble just noted had absolutely no effect on Soviet foreign trade. This is to be expected in view of the fact that the exchange rate is not a real price. If it were, the depreciation of January 1961 would have increased exports and reduced imports. In fact, while exports rose, it was by no more than can be explained by "trend"—from 5 to 5.4 billion rubles; imports, instead of declining, rose by even more from 5.2 to 5.8 billion rubles.

While the manner in which the depreciation of 1961 was conducted was politically inspired, the depreciation was designed to eliminate overvaluation so that internal prices would be more closely equated with external prices by the new value of the ruble. This was also true of the enormous depreciation of April 1, 1936, which lowered the value of the ruble from $.8712 to $.1992. Among other things, the relatively realistic official exchange rate of 1961 allowed the U.S.S.R. to discontinue its tourist exchange rate. It was also designed to eliminate the enormous subsidies which had to be granted to most export organizations because they were required to sell products abroad at so much below internal prices and the enormous profits of the import organizations which were able to procure products from abroad so cheaply in comparison with internal prices. Even though the state budget authorities expeditiously doled out subsidies and collected excess profits, the situation was viewed as undesirable because, in the face of such distortions, it was difficult to get the FTOs to strive for efficiency. Why try, for example, to buy a product abroad at a price 10 percent lower when your profit will be around 200 percent anyway?

Aside from politics, the major reason then for devaluations, which are designed to bring exchange rates into "purchasing power parity" in the Communist nations, is to foster economizing behavior on the part of the foreign-trade combines. This is a very modest role compared to that of Western exchange rates, which are real prices and largely determine the relative level and structure of exports and imports, hence the balance in payments. Levels and structure of exports and imports, and the balance in payments, are largely determined by direct controls in the Communist nations.

FOREIGN TRADE EFFECTIVENESS INDEXES

To say that Soviet bloc exports and imports are determined by direct controls largely begs the question. The interesting question is *how* those who manipulate the controls actually determine what and how much is to be exported and imported in a situation of disequilibrium prices and exchange rates. In the early days of CMEA many scholars believed that each Soviet bloc nation attempted to industrialize as rapidly as possible and, in the process, exported any surpluses which happened to develop, using these to pay for the imports necessary to eliminate unforeseen bottlenecks. This is basically an error theory of international trade since, presumably, if the method of material balances had assured perfect balance for all commodities, neither exports nor imports would be necessary, nor would they serve a useful function. Undoubtedly, some foreign trade is and always has been explained by planning errors and, in fact, foreign trade certainly performs a very valuable rescue function along these lines because of the immense difficulties of coordination that face central planners. But certainly only a small part of the total trade flows are explained in this way. The Soviets, for example, have always produced surpluses of grain, petroleum, and lumber, and exports of these commodities are built into the material balances. The situation is similar with regard to Bulgarian tobacco, Polish hams, and Czech machinery. These are commodities in which trade has been "traditional" and assumed to be advantageous, although often mistakenly so (e.g., Soviet grain exports). Traditional exports and imports are a second major class of Communist foreign trade flows. In both error-induced and traditional exports and imports, the chances are that trade is profitable, although, as just noted, the economic basis of some traditional trade flows may need reexamination.

For the rest, the case is not so clear. Given distorted prices and exchange rates, planners often find themselves without a rational basis for deciding what should and should not be exported or imported. In an effort to cope with this problem, a number of devices have been developed. In the mid-1950s, Polish and Hungarian planners each developed sets of what are called notional exchange rates to facilitate decision making. These exchange rates were designed to overcome simultaneously the distortions of internal prices and exchange rate. Thus, while the official exchange rate for the Polish zloty was 4 to the dollar, the rates for exports and imports in general were 16 and 40 zlotys to the dollar respectively. These rates were a recognition of both the overvaluation of the zloty and the need to keep down imports (hence its more devalued rate) for balance of payments reasons. Because internal prices were distorted so selectively, many commodity groups had their own special notional rates. Thus, trade decisions on brown coal were based on a notional exchange rate of 4 zlotys to the dollar, because the internal price of brown coal was considered to be extremely low. In contrast, food products, which were priced high internally because of excise taxes, had a notional exchange rate of 36, and cotton and silk fabrics, apparently with extremely high internal prices, were assigned rates of 200 zlotys to the dollar. Most notional rates fell between these limits. The situation in Hungary was similar. While the notional rate system probably led to some improvement in foreign trade planning, there is some question as to whether it provided a basis for completely rational decision-making. The question arises because it seems dubious that the planners had enough information to establish fully realistic notional rates.

Over the past decade, most of the effort to rationalize foreign-trade decisions has gone into the development of so-called foreign trade effectiveness indexes. Dozens of these indexes exist and are used in Eastern Europe. They are similar to ones used by many less developed capitalist countries for the same purpose. Basically, they attempt to answer the following questions. In the case of exports, which domestically produced commodities will earn the largest amount of foreign exchange per ruble (zloty, lev) of expenditure of domestic resources? In the case of imports, which commodities will save the largest amount of domestic resources per dollar of foreign exchange expended? The following very simple export effectiveness index is illustrative:

$$E = \frac{C - i}{P_f - i_f}$$

where E is the export effectiveness index, C is the internal cost or price of the commodity, i is the domestic value of imported goods embodied in the export, P_f is the selling price of the export in foreign exchange, and i_f is the foreign exchange cost of the import content of the export. Suppose, for example, that commodity A has a domestic cost of 100 rubles and sells abroad for \$190, and that i is 20 rubles and i_f is \$30. In this case, E is .5, which means that a ruble's worth of exports of A earns 2 units of foreign exchange. Suppose commodity B has an $E = .4$. This would mean that one ruble's worth of exports of B earns 2½ units of foreign exchange. Clearly, it is more advantageous to export B. In this way, all commodities can be scaled and an attempt made to market those with the lower ratios.

The following formula illustrates the operation of import indexes. Let

$$M = \frac{P_d}{P_f}$$

1367559

where M is the import effectiveness index, P_d is the domestic price of the imported commodity, and P_f is its cost in foreign exchange. Suppose commodity C has a domestic price of 125 rubles and can be imported for \$100, whereas commodity D has a price of 150 rubles and an import cost of \$75. The import effectiveness ratios are $E_c = 1.25$ and $E_d = 2.0$. Clearly, the importing nation gets more value per dollar of foreign exchange from importing commodity D. Using this technique, all commodities can be scaled and the nation should concentrate its expenditures of foreign exchange on those commodities with the higher ratios. In fact, it can be seen in a moment that M and E are really identical measures and that all produced and consumed commodities can be put on a single scale with those at the upper end being imported and those at the lower end being exported. If all goods were tradable and there were no transport costs, everything above a certain ratio would be imported, everything below it would be exported, and that ratio which balanced trade would be, in effect, the equilibrium exchange rate. In practice, limiting export and import ratios are often established below and above which, respectively, exports and imports are allowed. These ratios are set with a view to balancing trade.

One of the major problems with the two simple indexes just set forth is that "effectiveness" is based on distorted internal prices. In the U.S.S.R., an attempt to solve this problem has led to the establishment of some 250 price adjustment coefficients for broad groups of commodities which presumably adjust prices to a "full cost" basis. In other countries, the indexes themselves include a term in the numerator which subtracts excise taxes and adds subsidies back in. While helpful, it seems doubtful that these devices are completely successful in establishing rational prices, because the distortions have existed for so long and are so deeply embedded in the whole economic structure.

Another problem with the effectiveness indexes and also with the notional exchange rates is the fact that each Communist nation faces not just one generalized world market but rather more than a dozen segregated markets. This is a result of the fact that each bloc nation trades strictly bilaterally with every other bloc nation and with some underdeveloped nations as well. While it is true that some approximation of world price is used in trading with all nations, the commodity mixes differ substantially between nations. For example, a nation may find that with one trading partner it is able to export commodities with an average E of .3 and import commodities with an average M of 2.5, whereas with another partner the corresponding figures are .2 and 1.3. Obviously, its balance of trade picture will be different in the two instances, with a relative tendency toward an import surplus in the former and export surplus in the latter. This type of situation has led to the development of still another set of coefficients called "coefficients of the relative desirability of foreign currencies," which amount to the establishment of different notional exchange rates for different trading partners. The major distinction here has been between intrabloc and East-West trade. In both the Czech and the Hungarian estimates (for the late 1960s), the dollar (representing advanced Western currencies in general) was valued at a significantly higher exchange rate than the ruble in comparison with the official exchange rates.

Many other techniques for trading rationally are being worked on in the various Communist countries but most of these are too complicated mathematically to be described here.[2]

Commercial Policies and Balance of Payments Problems

TARIFFS AND MOST-FAVORED-NATION PROBLEMS

State ownership of industry and control of agriculture, along with the state monopoly of foreign trade operations, eliminates the need for tariffs by Communist nations. The planners decide what is and is not to be imported when the annual plan is established, and these decisions constitute implicit quotas. Foreign suppliers have no means of competing with domestic industries, and tariffs are therefore unnecessary for protection. Tariffs are also unnecessary for revenue-raising purposes since the greater governmental power of one-party systems makes it much easier to collect the funds necessary to finance public expenditures. Finally, tariffs only make sense under circumstances in which they affect the price at which imported goods are sold domestically. Under the Communist system of planned and fixed prices, this is not the case.

Over the past ten years, most of the Communist countries have introduced two- and sometimes three-column tariffs. These tariffs are not protective in the sense of protecting domestic industry, nor are they revenue raising, nor are they allowed to affect the internal prices at which the imported products are resold domestically. Their sole purpose is to serve as a bargaining device in negotiations with Western powers for most-favored-nation (MFN) treatment. Most-favored-nation clauses in agreements among nations have as their objectives the increase of trade by reducing the use of protective devices like tariffs and quotas, and also to guarantee nondiscriminatory or equal treatment in the application of trade barriers among nations. Two nations which sign a most-favored-nation clause agree, in effect, to reduce the various impediments (tariffs, quotas, etc.) to each other's exports to the lowest level that is applicable to the exports of any third nation. The difficulty facing the centrally planned economies desirous of being granted MFN treatment by Western nations is that their own trade impediments are "implicit," that is, they do not have explicit tariffs or quotas which can be reduced in reciprocation. The two- (and three-) column tariffs were introduced to get around this difficulty. The lower of the two columns of rates is reserved for nations which grant MFN treatment, the higher column for those nations which do not. The foreign trade organizations have an incentive to import a commodity from a nation subject to the lower column of tariff rates because the tariff is, in effect, paid out of their profits and affects their bonuses.

Suppose, for example, that the FTO is authorized to import commodity A, which has a domestic price of 150 rubles. It can buy the product for 100 rubles from country X, which does not grant MFN treatment and which pays a 30 percent tariff, or from country Y, which does grant MFN, for 110 rubles and a 10 percent tariff. If the FTO buys from X, it nets 20 rubles (150-100-30); if it buys from Y, it nets 29 rubles (150-110-11); so it buys from Y. At first glance, this system seems equivalent to an MFN system under free market conditions. For two major reasons, however, it is not. First of all, the example only applies in cases in which the FTOs have some choice. They do not have any choice in intrabloc trade, which comprises the bulk of their transactions. This trade is planned in advance under the bilateral trade agreements, and all the Soviet bloc nations are assumed to grant each other MFN treatment. Second, a major effect of tariff reduction under market conditions is to reduce the domestic price of the imported product. This increases the volume of trade and enables the exporter to compete more effectively against domestic producers. Here, as we can see, the domestic price of imported goods is not changed and the volume of trade is not affected. All that happens is that the distribution of a given volume of trade is altered. Clearly, the use of double-column tariffs by the Communist countries is not in harmony with the spirit of MFN clauses and does not work toward their objectives of increasing world trade in a nondiscriminatory way.

In practice, some of the Communist countries have agreed to increase by a certain percentage their imports from countries which grant them MFN treatment. This device and its implications will be discussed in Chapter 4.

DUMPING

The Communist nations have been accused of dumping on numerous occasions since World War II, a charge the U.S.S.R. was also frequently subjected to in the prewar period. Dumping usually means exporting products at a price below the domestic cost of production or domestic price. A dumping charge is typically not brought against an exporter unless his price is also below the domestic price of the importing nation. Basically, the objection to dumping is that it constitutes unfair competition. If an exporter is able to sell a product abroad at less than the importer's domestic price and still make a profit, the competition is viewed as fair. If, by fair competition, an exporter is able to take over the domestic market, this is all to the good, since the loss to domestic producers is more than compensated for by the gains to the domestic consumers. On the other hand, loss of markets to exporters who are dumping is not so compensated over the long run, since the dumpers cannot sell at a loss indefinitely. In the national interest, then, most nations protect their enterprises from disruptive dumping by levying countervailing tariffs against imports suspected of being sold at a loss. These tariffs are designed, at the least, to raise the price of the dumped product to the level prevailing in the domestic market and, in theory, should raise the price to the level at which the product would sell if no loss were sustained.

Because it is so difficult to identify true dumping by a CPE, some Western capitalist nations have gone beyond the use of countervailing tariffs. In a number of East-West trade agreements, including the subsequently annulled U.S.-U.S.S.R. Trade Agreement of 1972, it has been specified that any export which causes distress to enterprises in the importing nation will immediately be withdrawn. This is a fairly extreme measure and effectively prevents an exporter from competing successfully with domestic enterprises which produce the same or similar products.

There are at least two basic reasons why it is difficult, and often meaningless, to apply the Western concept of dumping to the Communist countries. First, because of the irrationality of internal prices in the Soviet bloc, along with the fact that exchange rates often do not reflect the purchasing power parity of the bloc currency, it is usually impossible to determine whether the commodities in question are being sold below production cost or below the domestic market price. For example, before the ruble devaluation in 1961, the U.S.S.R. exported practically everything at a nominal loss, as the examples cited earlier suggest. This was true of all Soviet bloc currencies before 1961 and is still true of some. The second reason for questioning the dumping concept has to do with the existence of the foreign trade monopoly and the fact that export and import decisions are not always independent of each other, as is the case in the West. Hence, as we pointed out above, the price at which a state trader sells an export may not always be viewed as the foreign exchange earned but, rather, the value in domestic currency of the import purchased with the foreign exchange. Would it be proper to accuse a state trader of dumping who exported a product at 50 percent of cost but used the currency earned to buy a product abroad at 25 percent of domestic cost?

BALANCE OF PAYMENTS PROBLEMS

The Communist nations usually show a balance in their international accounts. This is a result of strict state control over foreign trade operations. There is little doubt, however, that if trade were freed, deficits would rapidly develop unless the terms under which trade is conducted were substantially altered by, say, currency devaluations. Given present terms of trade, several factors are responsible for balance of payments pressures. First, as noted above, the domestic economies of the Communist nations are characterized by over-full employment planning and repressed inflation. This results in persistent unsatisfied demand which, if released, would reduce exports (as domestic users compete with foreign buyers for exportables) and increase imports. Alternatively, internal prices would rise, if freed, thereby having the same effect. Second, most countries that pursue a goal of rapid growth and industrialization find that there is a tendency to develop import requirements more rapidly than exports. This has been true of the less developed nations of the world and has also been true of the Communist nations. In particular, with the exception of the U.S.S.R., the Communist countries of Europe, in their drive to industrialize, have tended to generate serious raw material shortages which have had to be met through imports, mainly from the U.S.S.R. Third, the growth of exports has suffered because of the prevalence of sellers' markets internally, a consequence of over-full employment planning. Because they are faced with sellers' markets, the managers of Soviet bloc enterprises have very little incentive to either produce high-quality products (always important in world markets) or to adapt and sell their products abroad. Until the late 1960s, quality was also neglected because the major enterprise goal was a quantitative target, not sales or profits. Quality was often sacrificed to quantity. The importance of these factors is still further aggravated by the fact that producing enterprises do not usually deal directly with foreign buyers but rather through the intermediation of the foreign trade combines. Lack of concern by producing enterprises with quality probably explains in large part the predominance of raw materials and relatively homogeneous products and the relatively small role of manufactured products in the exports of the Communist nations to the West. Among

40

themselves, however, they do trade low-quality manufactured products much to the dissatisfaction of all parties concerned. Fourth, for reasons to be discussed in more detail in Chapter 4, the Communist nations are poor at industrial innovation, diffusion, and imitation of foreign innovations. This is primarily because of the factors (discussed above) which have been responsible for the general lack of quality in manufactured products. To these can be added the lack of communication between R & D organizations and the industries and enterprises they are supposed to serve. The result is that the CPEs export fewer products embodying new technology or imitative of other nations' technologies (like Japan) than comparable capitalist nations. Excess demand for products embodying new technology (and new technology itself) has generally been viewed as an important contributor to Communist bloc balance of payments problems over the past ten years.

The disadvantages just noted would not prevent a nation from achieving balance of payments equilibrium under capitalism. Except under extraordinary circumstances, deficits can be cured by currency devaluation. Unfortunately, this mechanism is not available to centrally planned economies because they do not have exchange rates which function as real prices, nor are their currencies used in international trade. A change in the official exchange rate has absolutely no effect on trade or on the prices at which products are traded, the latter being based on world prices. Why do the socialist nations not simply export at below world prices as a substitute for exchange rate depreciation? This is possible in cases where the importing nation does not produce competitive products. Otherwise, however, the Communist nations are subject to anti-dumping and, in the case of the United States and some Western European nations, to market disruption laws and agreements. The stringency with which these laws are applied to the Communist countries is a result of the great difficulties, noted above, of proving or disproving dumping charges where internal prices are irrational and exchange rates do not function as real prices.

Finally, balance of payments pressures and even crises have resulted from unforeseen catastrophes, both internal and external. In the late 1920s and early 1930s, the U.S.S.R. planned for heavy imports of machinery and equipment with which to launch the first Five-Year Plan. These were to be financed by exports, primarily of agricultural products. The world depression drove the prices of Soviet agricultural products down to less than two-fifths of their previous level, whereas the prices of machinery and equipment fell by only one-fifth. In order to maintain the plan, food exports had to be increased still further in the face of famine and starvation for the Russian people, and credits at high rates of interest had to be negotiated. Other Soviet balance of payments crises occurred in the 1962-63 period, in 1972, and in 1975, as a result of the disastrous crops in those years. Hungary experienced a crisis as an aftermath of the 1956 uprising; so did Czechoslovakia, largely as a result of the overinvestment-induced depression in 1962-63. All the Eastern nations except the U.S.S.R. and Rumania face balance of payments crises beginning in 1975 because of the sharp increases in gas, oil, food, and other raw material prices.

Inconvertibility and Bilateralism

A notable characteristic of Communist foreign trade is that all currencies are inconvertible, and intrabloc trade, as a result, is bilaterally balanced between every pair of nations. Inconvertibility and bilateralism are explainable in terms of the hidden balance of payments pressures noted above, which result from over-full employment planning, repressed inflation, rapid growth, and so forth. If a nation is in balance of payments difficulties for the reasons noted, foreigners eventually become unwilling to hold its currency because at existing prices and exchange rates its prices are too high and products insufficiently attractive. Outstanding currency balances begin to sell at a discount and eventually the nation is forced either to devalue or to place controls on imports. The act of controlling imports forbids residents to convert domestic currency into foreign exchange or gold with which to buy abroad. This is called resident inconvertibility. Conversions are only allowed for necessities and are equal to the amount of current earnings of foreign exchange through exports. The result is, of course, balanced trade—often bilaterally balanced. This kind of inconvertibility and bilateralism is common to capitalist and Communist countries.

The Communist countries suffer from an even more serious form of inconvertibility unique to central planning with direct controls; it has been dubbed "commodity inconvertibility." Commodity inconvertibility is independent of currency inconvertibility and would exist even if balance of payments pressures did not exist. Commodity inconvertibility means that foreigners (except tourists) are not allowed to shop for imports indiscriminately in the domestic markets of the Communist nations. Basically, they are restricted to those products offered by the FTOs as established in the annual plans, most of which have already been preempted in one of the foreign trade agreements. There are two major reasons for this form of restriction on potential buyers. First, unplanned purchases by foreign importers would disrupt the carefully drawn fabric of the plan implemented by balances and other direct controls. Second, given irrational internal prices, importers might purchase commodities at prices far below the real costs of production (for example, heavily subsidized commodities). For these reasons, the Communist countries do not allow foreigners to hold their currencies (or to convert them freely into goods). Even if they did allow their currencies to be held externally, there would not be any takers because of the great uncertainties as to what the money could buy, if anything, and at what price.

Under these circumstances, it is not surprising that intrabloc trade is rigidly bilaterally balanced. No Soviet bloc nation is willing or legally able to hold the currency of any other Soviet bloc nation. To the extent that Soviet bloc countries have reserves of gold or convertible foreign exchange earned by payments surpluses with Western nations, they can run deficits with each other. But convertible foreign exchange and gold have so much higher a value when used to import from the West that they are rarely expended to finance intrabloc deficits. The rigid bilateralism which characterizes intrabloc trade is viewed as a serious handicap, and many unsuccessful attempts have been made to find ways to multilateralize trade. Unlike the more common variety of currency inconvertibility, which can be eliminated simply by devaluation, commodity inconvertibility requires a drastic change in planning techniques. In effect, the Communist countries will have to establish the conditions for decentralized market planning and rational pricing if they are ever to get rid of commodity inconvertibility and rigid bilateralism.

Adjustment Mechanisms—Relationships Between Trade and Internal Policies

In a classical free market system of nineteenth-century vintage, the interactions between the foreign trade and domestic sectors of the economy were much more intimate than they are today. Not only did foreign trade increase the national product by taking advantage of division of labor, but the state of the balance of payments was reflected in the levels of unemployment and prices. Given the fact that most nations were on the gold standard and therefore had fixed exchange rates, a deficit in the balance of payments of any magnitude and duration was bound to lead, eventually, to rising unemployment and falling income and price levels. This would occur, of course, because too much demand was directed at foreign as opposed to domestic products. The decline in employment, income, and price levels served as an adjustment mechanism and tended to eliminate the deficit. As employment and income fell, imports also fell, and as internal prices fell, exports increased and imports declined.

The mechanisms described above have very little scope for operation among post-World War II capitalist nations. This is because most nations have adopted objectives whose achievement forces them to prevent the operation of market forces as described above. The major objectives along these lines are the commitment to full or near-full employment, economic growth, and the maintenance of stable price levels. In addition to government policies, price levels are prevented from falling by changes in the attitudes and organization (unions) of labor and of industry. As a result, equilibrium in the balance of payments had to be achieved in other ways. Among these were extensive governmental assistance by surplus to deficit nations; creation of the International Monetary Fund; invention of special drawing rights, a kind of paper gold (SDRs); more frequent changes in exchange rates; the widespread adoption of floating rates since 1971; and more refined use of the combination of fiscal and monetary tools to achieve internal and external balance simultaneously. All these devices work through the market system. Where, for one reason or another, these devices have been inadequate or inappropriate for achieving foreign trade balance, balance has been "forced" by commodity and exchange controls. A mechanism of adjustment to the enormous disequilibrium which resulted from the rise in petroleum prices in October 1973 has yet to be found.

Communist foreign trade is almost completely devoid of market adjustment mechanisms. As we have seen, foreign trade prices are completely divorced from domestic prices; exchange rates are not a real "price" but simply a unit of account; full employment of labor and other resources and stable prices are iron-bound objectives, achieved directly and not subject to market influences. Balance in payments is achieved by direct controls and, under the circumstances outlined, would have to be, since no other avenue for adjustment exists. The degree to which "balance" is "forced" is therefore probably greater in the trade of centrally planned economies than in the trade of any capitalist nations.

The Real Cost of Aid

Most of the advanced nations of the world make loans or grants to the less developed nations. The grants are gifts (or what might be called aid in the purest sense, since they need not be repaid). The loans, although they have to be repaid, also often contain a grant or aid element since the rates of interest charged are usually concessionary, that is, below the market rate. The question is, What is the "real" cost to the donor countries of giving "aid" and is there a difference between the systems on this count?

In assessing the real cost of aid—or of loans for that matter—at least two factors should be considered. First, the granting of aid should be considered a real cost from a societal point of view only if the nation is thereby deprived of using the resources exported for domestic purposes. While at first glance it would seem self-evident that the export of any commodity is an act which deprives the nation of the use of the good, this is not generally the case. It is only true if the nation is at full employment. If there are unemployed resources, including labor and plant and equipment, then aid exports can be viewed as having been produced with these unemployed resources. Or, to put it another way, as long as unemployed resources are available, no domestic consumer need be deprived of anything because aid has been extended to another nation. Second, if a nation is deprived of resources by the extension of aid or of loans, it has become customary, at least in theory, to value the cost to that nation at its domestic rate of return on capital. That is to say, it is assumed that the resources exported could have been invested domestically and provided the going rate of return on capital.

The differences between capitalist and Communist countries used to be substantial on both counts. As we have noted, over-full employment planning has meant that aid extended by Communist governments has reduced the product available for domestic use by 100 percent. This has not been the case in all capitalist countries all the time. In 1957-58, for example, when 7½ percent of the American labor force was unemployed, extension of aid hardly prevented the United States from achieving domestic goals. This has been true for the United States in other years, though to a lesser extent, and for the nations of Western Europe at one time or another. Since the mid-1960s, however, most of the Western nations, including the United States, were either so close to full employment or so beset by inflationary pressures that it was difficult to extend aid without cutting back elsewhere in the economy or aggravating inflation.

In the 1950s the rate of return on capital in the Communist nations must have been much higher than among the Western European nations. In terms of planners' investment and growth objectives, and given the low standard of living in most of Eastern Europe, capital was extremely scarce and the implied rate of interest was viewed by most economists as very high. Taking this factor into account would lead one to argue that extension of aid or loans by the Communist countries was indeed more expensive in terms of foregone internal economic growth than was the case in the Western capitalist nations. More recently, the growth rates in Eastern Europe and the U.S.S.R. have declined despite continuing very high rates of investment, implying a sharply declining rate of increase in the productivity of capital. At present, there probably is very little difference between the systems on this count, if, in fact, the rate of return on investment is not higher in some capitalist nations.

Foreign Trade Behavior Under the Recent Reforms

With the possible exception of Hungary (to be discussed later) the foreign trade reforms in Eastern Europe and the U.S.S.R. have not involved a significant modification in the foreign trade behavior of these countries as outlined in the preceding pages. As noted in the final section of Chapter 1, the reforms have served primarily to rationalize central planning rather than to introduce methods and institutions of decentralization and use of market instruments, and this has largely determined the kind of foreign trade reforms which have been implemented.[3]

Much of the effort in the reforms has been to reduce the insulation of domestic producers and consumers of internationally traded products from foreign markets. To this end, a number of the Eastern European nations (e.g., East Germany, Poland, Hungary) have allowed some producing enterprises to deal directly with foreign enterprises without the intermediation of FTOs. The number of such enterprises, however, is still very small. Somewhat less dramatic attempts have been made to provide a closer link between the producing enterprise and the FTO and thereby to achieve something of the same benefits without losing the instrument of control over trade which the associations provide. In the U.S.S.R., for example, representatives of some producing enterprises are put on the payroll of the FTO; in Poland, some FTOs have been subordinated to their industrial ministries; in Czechoslovakia, the FTOs are now set up as joint stock companies with producing enterprises participating in their management and profits. All these devices improve communications and information in international trade and in that sense increase efficiency somewhat. However, they in no way change basic behavior, that is, state trading, trade agreements, and the general subordination of foreign trade to the overall central plan. Still closer ties with foreign enterprises have resulted from the numerous cases of joint ventures and joint cooperation agreements which have sprung up on both East-East and East-West fronts since the mid-1960s. These are more in the nature of investment agreements with joint production and marketing arrangements than ordinary trade deals. And while the concept is quite radical for nations in which industry is nationalized, the activities of these ventures are still included in the central plan. The radical feature, ideologically speaking, is the fact that several of the Eastern nations (e.g., Rumania, Hungary) are allowing Western enterprises to own up to 49 percent of the equity in these ventures, discussed in more detail in Chapters 3 and 4.

Another reform designed to encourage producing enterprises to sell abroad, but again involving no fundamental change, is the linking of profits and bonuses to export earnings. Enterprises have been given a share in the profits on exports (Czechoslovakia) and also have been allowed to keep part of their foreign exchange earnings for their own imports (Poland, East Germany).

The price reforms which have taken place in Eastern Europe have also not gone far enough to change foreign trade behavior. With prices somewhat rationalized, it has been possible to unify many of the commodity-by-commodity exchange rates and thereby simplify the task of the planners. Price reforms have also made it more meaningful to allow enterprises to share in the profits from foreign trade. Poland has even gone so far as to establish a dual exchange rate system, with one rate applicable to the socialist nations, the other to the capitalist nations. These rates are used, as a first approximation, in an attempt to calculate the profitability of foreign trade. However, neither Polish prices nor those of the other CPEs are "rational" enough to be relied upon fully for this purpose. Internal prices are still divorced from world prices, tariffs have no real impact on prices, exchange rates are still more in the nature of accounting units than real prices, and currencies remain inconvertible.

Hungary has moved further toward adopting market mechanisms in foreign trade, the counterpart of its more radical internal economic reform. Since its reform is in constant state of evolution, it is difficult to describe it precisely at any one time. As with the case of enterprises that produce exclusively for the domestic market, the enterprises which produce for external markets usually have targets suggested to them by the economic authorities. But these targets do not have the force of law as in the other Eastern nations; rather they are "indicative," that is, suggestions by the authorities, as in the case of French planning. However, while the authorities do not insist that plans be realized, they use a number of market and financial instruments (inducements) to push or pull the enterprises in the desired direction.

Unlike the other Eastern nations, the Hungarian production enterprises or FTOs make their trading decisions, in first approximation, by comparing their costs and prices with foreign costs and prices. The Hungarian internal price reforms were designed in theory to link their prices with world prices and, as noted in Chapter 1, internal prices were to be free. The link between internal and external prices is not as simple as it is in a Western nation, however, because prices were not completely freed, partly because of inflationary pressures, partly because the prices set are not as yet completely rational, and partly because the Hungarians conduct their foreign trade with two quite distinct trading blocs, East and West. The latter problem is taken care of by having, as in Poland, not a single unified exchange rate but one for each bloc. In 1968, the forint was valued at 60 to the U.S. dollar (representing Western currencies) and 40 to the U.S.S.R. ruble (representing Eastern currencies). That is to say, despite the fact that the ruble was officially valued at $1.11, it was valued at only two-thirds of the value of a dollar for Hungarian foreign trade purposes. This made sense since it is generally considered that prices in intrabloc trade are higher than in Western trade for similar goods. It also serves to discourage imports from and encourage exports to the West, where the Hungarians have balance of payments problems.

A second link between internal and external prices are customs tariffs on goods from the West and special import-turnover taxes on goods from the East. The latter are designed to reduce the disparities between the prices of goods bought from the East and Hungarian internal prices. There is no real link between these prices since other Eastern prices are still quite irrational; the former are probably instituted partly to discourage imports from the West and partly for use in bargaining over MFN status. The third link consists of taxes and subsidies (or tax refunds) by the state to trading enterprises.

These three links are sufficiently complicated so that there must be considerable doubt regarding the true organic connection between Hungarian prices and world prices. First of all, there is no real relation between Hungarian prices and Eastern prices, and it is the function of the import-turnover taxes simply to bridge this gap on a commodity-by-commodity basis. Since trade with the Eastern bloc constitutes most of Hungary's trade, this is a substantial exception. Second, the major function of the third link—taxes and subsidies—is to eliminate any further disparities between internal and external prices including trade with the West. This is one way of interpreting their use.

Another way of looking at these links, suggested earlier, may be more instructive. The Hungarians have established "indicative" plans for enterprises with foreign trade potential. The various links, especially the third, between internal and external prices are the devices used to induce the enterprises to fulfill these plans. The first two links take account of East-East vs. East-West trade, the differences in prices between the blocs, relative desirability of products, and, in the case of the import-turnover tax, the irrationality of other Eastern nations' prices. However, suppose that the Hungarian government has concluded a trade agreement with Bulgaria which envisages a large export of shoes to Bulgaria at a fixed price. Suppose the enterprise, upon examining alternative possibilities, discovers that it can sell the shoes in some other market (at home, or to Belgium) at a higher price. Because the Hungarian government is committed to the sale to Bulgaria but cannot order the enterprise to make the sale, it "induces" the sale by granting the enterprise sufficient subsidy. This kind of device is, in truth, a link between internal and external prices, but the prices which are linked are also distorted. Furthermore, the transaction involves trade discrimination.

While it is to be hoped that the Hungarians are moving in the direction of greater rationalization and true reliance on market mechanisms, it should be recognized that if there are enough artificial links between internal and external prices, then the link becomes meaningless in a market sense. This is why I think it is fair to say that, while considerable liberalization of the foreign trade mechanism may have occurred in Hungary, many of the behavioral characteristics of the foreign trade mechanism, described earlier, still hold for Hungary. Exchange rates may perform some of the functions of real prices, and tariffs may also have a price-setting function. Nevertheless, the forint is still as inconvertible as ever, and trade with other Soviet bloc nations must still be conducted on a rigidly bilateral basis.

Perhaps the real problem facing Hungary is the fact that it is still an integral part of the Eastern bloc and must continue to conduct the bulk of its trade with that bloc. This involves trade agreements with the Eastern bloc nations, which have irrational prices and which insist on bilateral balance. Under these circumstances, it is almost impossible for the Hungarians to leave their own foreign trade to the "market" and to make the required institutional changes. They have also been handicapped by severe inflationary pressures which have prevented the freeing-up of internal prices. Until these pressures are reduced and enterprises are totally free to choose their foreign trade opportunities without the intervention of so many "links," true convertibility, real tariffs, and multilateral trade will not be realizable. As long as trade with the East is so dominant a part of Hungary's trade, and as long as the other Eastern nations lag in their reforms, the situation is not likely to change significantly.

Chapter 3

Intrabloc Economic Relations

The remaining chapters of this book deal with political and economic relations among the Soviet bloc nations and between Soviet bloc and advanced and developing non-Communist nations, respectively. Before proceeding to a discussion of intrabloc relations, we shall first set forth briefly some of the tools of analysis: a paradigm of some of the expressions of and interrelations between political and economic forces, two models of economic integration, and a statement of the conditions under which economic warfare is likely (or not likely) to be effective. Other economic and political concepts are developed as they are used. The term *political* is often used here and in subsequent chapters to stand for all noneconomic factors and military, strategic, and diplomatic objectives.

Having presented our conceptual framework, we will then turn to a discussion and analysis of the course of events in intrabloc economic relationships. The initial period, from the end of World War II until about 1955, is one in which Soviet exercise of raw political and military power is quite uninhibited. The major events of this period are: the forced restructuring of the trade of all CMEA members away from the West and toward each other, particularly the U.S.S.R.; the economic exploitation of Eastern Europe by the U.S.S.R.; and the break with and embargoing of Yugoslavia. The picture changes substantially with Khrushchev's accession to power, especially after the Polish and Hungarian uprisings in 1956. No longer possessed with the almost absolute power of a Stalin, the U.S.S.R. became slightly less authoritarian in its economic relations with the other nations of Eastern Europe. For political and economic reasons, Khrushchev attempted in the mid-1950s to activate CMEA, which had been a dead letter since its formation in 1949; the Warsaw Treaty Organization was established at roughly the same time. The political and ideological break with China around 1960 led to extraordinary economic measures again: the partial embargoes on China and Albania. Further attempts in the early 1960s to make CMEA more effective in integrating the economies of the Eastern nations were blocked over the political issue as to whether CMEA should be given supranational power, presumably under Soviet domination. The debate over supranational power vs. national sovereignty is explored in depth for its implications for a host of economic issues. It was and certainly still is one of the crucial political and economic issues in intrabloc relations. The Brezhnev-Kosygin era represented more of a continuation of the Khrushchev era than the Khrushchev era did of the Stalin era. However, the economic reform movement begun in the early and mid-1960s ran into a major constraint when its political and intellectual consequences in Czechoslavakia led to the invasion by Warsaw Treaty Organization troops in August 1968. Détente with the West was another new development with major implications for intra-CMEA economic and political relationships. A mammoth *Comprehensive Program* to promote intrabloc economic integration was introduced in 1971 and provides something of a counterweight to the forces of East-West détente. At present, it is not clear which way the scale is tipped.

Concepts: Theory

POLITICAL AND ECONOMIC POWER

Interrelationships between economic and political (military, strategic, diplomatic) variables are complicated and difficult to envisage. Chart 3.1 presents a paradigm for some of these interrelationships. It must be stressed this is only a very simple representation of the complexity of reality. Furthermore, Chart 3.1 views the interrelationships among economic and political factors primarily from the standpoint of nations which initiate activity, not from the standpoint of nations on the receiving end, although in most instances the forces affecting the behavior of the latter are easily inferred.

Chart 3.1 is based on the assumption that a nation can have economic power and/or political-military power. While the economic

CHART 3.1

Interactions Between Uses of Economic and Political Power

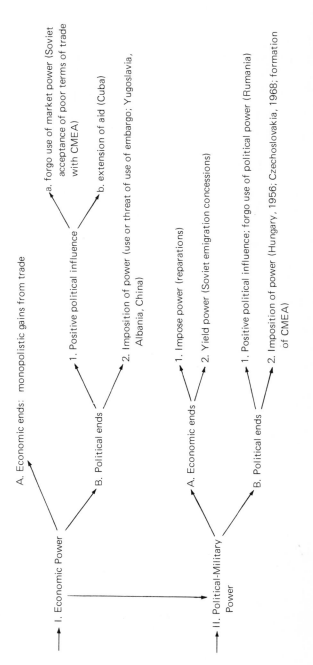

I. Economic Power

A. Economic ends: monopolistic gains from trade

B. Political ends

1. Positive political influence

   a. forgo use of market power (Soviet acceptance of poor terms of trade with CMEA)

   b. extension of aid (Cuba)

2. Imposition of power (use or threat of use of embargo; Yugoslavia, Albania, China)

II. Political-Military Power

A. Economic ends

1. Impose power (reparations)

2. Yield power (Soviet emigration concessions)

B. Political ends

1. Positive political influence; forgo use of political power (Rumania)

2. Imposition of power (Hungary, 1956; Czechoslovakia, 1968; formation of CMEA)

and political-military powers may be quite independent of each other, it is nevertheless assumed that economic power or lack of it can have a direct impact on political-military power (although the reverse is not true, except as in section II.A of Chart 3.1). What is economic power? By economic power, we mean two things. First, there is classical monopolistic (monopsonistic) market power in which a seller (buyer) has enough control over supply (demand) to influence the terms on which a transaction takes place. The U.S.S.R. is such a buyer and seller in intrabloc trade; the Middle East oil producers have monopolistic (oligipolistic) power and have exercised it. Obviously, influencing the terms on which a transaction takes place includes depriving the other party of the possibility of a purchase or sale at going prices—or in extreme cases at any price. Second, economic power may stem from affluence or, even in the absence of affluence, from government ability to control large flows of resources. No attempt is made here to define political (diplomatic) or military power, except to note that much political power in intrabloc relations derives from Communist party control over the various governments of Eastern Europe and the U.S.S.R., whereas military power is rooted in the Red Army.

If a nation has economic power, it can use it in two ways. First, it can use its monopolistic power in the market framework to obtain somewhat larger gains from trade than would be possible if it were a small buyer-seller (Chart 3.1-I.A.). It buys at lower and sells at higher prices than the pure competitor. The recent rise in the price of petroleum represents an extreme use of such monopoly powers on the part of the Middle East and other oil producers. Second, it may use its economic power for the achievement of political ends (Chart 3.1-I.B). If it is trying to gain favor with another nation, at least two courses are open. On the one hand, it can trade at competitive or "fair" prices, not taking advantage of its normal market power (Chart 3.1-I.B.1.a). This certainly has been Soviet policy, at least since 1956, as we shall see later. On the other hand, it can also gain favor by extending economic assistance, which is usually a function of relative affluence (Chart 3.1-I.B.1.b). Aid to the less-developed countries by East and West falls into this category. In both of the preceding situations, that is, forgoing the use of market power and the extension of aid, the process may be viewed as a trade-off of economic gains for some form of noneconomic gain. The recent application by the United States of so-called linkage politics is another case in point. Our dismantling of economic barriers against the U.S.S.R. has been linked to an overall détente which included cooperation (or noninterference) with the settlement of the war in Vietnam, the SALT agreements, and freer emigration from the U.S.S.R., particularly for Jews.

Economic power can also be used negatively by a nation in order to impose its will on or to punish another nation (Chart 3.1-I.B.2). These objectives are achieved by use of embargoes, threatening an embargo, denying MFN status, and so forth. Such exercise of power has been used frequently in recent history: by the United States against all Communist nations; by the U.S.S.R. against China, Albania, and Yugoslavia; by the Middle East oil producers against Europe, Japan, and the United States; and so forth. All the kinds of action noted constitute economic warfare and are not usually undertaken unless political relations are very strained. Two nations must be economically inter-dependent before one can directly practice economic warfare against the other. Indirectly, however, a politically and economically strong nation can induce (force) its allies to join ranks with it. The U.S.S.R. had the support of Eastern Europe in its boycott of Yugoslavia and the United States had the support of the NATO countries in its economic warfare against the Communist bloc. The conditions favoring successful economic warfare are described below.

A nation which has and chooses to exert its political-military power may use its power for economic and/or political gains. The classic case of use of political-military power for economic gain is war reparations (Chart 3.1-II.A.1). The U.S.S.R. collected reparations after World War II from the nations of Eastern Europe which had been allied with Germany. A (relatively weak) nation can also use its political power for economic gain in a negative way by surrendering (exchanging) some of it, that is, by making political concessions (Chart 3.1-II.A.2). Western Europe exchanged controls over its trade with the U.S.S.R. and Eastern Europe for Marshall Plan assistance after World War II; the U.S.S.R. recently made changes in its emigration policy in an effort to secure Congressional ratification of its commercial treaty with the United States; and developing nations are often optimistically expected to exchange "loyalty" for economic assistance.

War is an extreme example of the use of political-military power for political or economic ends. In recent history, the Soviet interventions in

Hungary in 1956 and Czechoslovakia in 1968 and the American interventions in Guatemala and the Dominican Republic are among the many which fall into chart category II.B.2. While we have not done so in Chart 3.1, category II.B.2 could have been divided into two kinds of political objectives, those dealing with political institutions and those dealing with economic institutions. Soviet intervention in Hungary in 1956 was an example of the former, whereas enforced maintenance of the very high level of intrabloc (as opposed to East-West) trade is an example of the latter.

A nation can also choose not to use its political power coercively and thereby reduce irritation and achieve a measure of what might be called positive influence (Chart 3.1-II.B.1). The U.S.S.R. has frequently taken this course in intrabloc relations. A major example has been its unwillingness to intervene and impose its will on the often dissident Rumanians.

This completes the paradigm which, it is hoped, will be useful in organizing thoughts about the interrelationships between economics and politics as they are intermingled in Communist international relations.

ECONOMIC INTEGRATION MODELS

There are two economic integration models. The first, which deals with commodity trade, is called a customs union model. When nations form a customs union, they reduce trade barriers among themselves while maintaining them against the rest of the world. A customs union is a first step in the direction of economic integration. Economic integration involves, in addition to freer flows of commodities between nations, the reduction of barriers to flows of factors of production—primarily labor and capital. It also involves any other measures which are required and might be taken to encourage the development of a "common market" in participating countries. We have separated the customs union analysis from economic integration proper, primarily because Western economic theory has been developed in such a way that it is possible to analyze the effects of integration more incisively if commodity and factor flows are dealt with separately. It is important to set forth these two basic models in some detail for three reasons. First, they provide a framework for assessing the possible economic gains and losses from the close economic association assumed by the Eastern nations. Second, since these two models are framed mostly in terms of market forces, we are provided with a basis for further evaluating (beyond the analysis of Chapter 2) the efficiency of socialist economic institutions in economic relationships among nations. Third, the models facilitate an understanding of some of the political forces and institutional changes which may be involved in implementing and maintaining such a close economic association.

The Customs Union Approach

When a group of Western nations forms a customs union, they reduce or remove the tariffs and other trade barriers on trade with each other, at the same time maintaining their barriers to trade with outsiders. This naturally causes an increase in trade among the customs union members. It is important to distinguish between the two major causes of the increase in member trade.

First, trade increases because with barriers among members reduced, products which had previously been produced domestically can now be imported more cheaply. This is called trade creation because it involves a net increase in the amount of trade in the world, that is, a substitution of foreign trade for domestic production between members of the union. Trade creation benefits the participants and hurts no one: one country imports at a price below its domestic cost of production; the partner country exports more; outsiders are unaffected.

Second, trade among members increases at the expense of nonmembers. With barriers reduced among members but maintained against outsiders, members are able to outcompete outsiders. There is no net increase in trade but rather a diversion of trade to members, away from nonmembers. Since there has been no increase in trade, there can be no overall gain from trade diversion unless it leads to more efficient production. In fact, however, there is a loss to world income as a whole, because the favored member country is enabled to specialize at the expense of the more efficient nonmember. We know that the nonmember is more efficient because he was able to outcompete the member before the customs union was formed, when both were subjected to the same trade barriers. The importing country loses, since it now buys from a less efficient producer.* The nonmember nations also lose since

---

*The consumers in the importing nation pay a lower price for imported products, because the tariff on them has been removed or reduced. However, the

their exports have been reduced. The only gainer from trade diversion is the member nation to whom the trade has been diverted, and this gain is at the expense of other nations.

These then are the bare bones of static customs union analysis. (We look at the dynamic factors later.) To the extent that a customs union leads to trade creation, it is good (from an economic standpoint); to the extent that it leads to trade diversion, it is usually bad. The important question, then, is: When is a customs union apt to lead to trade creation and when to trade diversion? A partial answer to this question is along the following lines:

Trade creation is more likely to occur, the higher the trade barriers were to begin with. This is because: the higher the trade barriers the greater the number of protected domestic industries—and the greater the number of protected industries, the greater the possibility of creating trade by removing protection; and the higher the trade barriers, the greater the cost differentials between industries in different countries producing the same product—and the greater the cost differentials, the larger the potential gains from removing trade barriers on any product.

Trade diversion is less likely (and trade creation more likely) to occur, the more trade the nations forming the union had with each other before the union, and the larger the group of nations included in the union. These are important though quite obvious propositions. Clearly, if the nations forming a union conducted most of their trade with each other before the union, very little trade remains to be diverted. Equally clearly, the more nations included in the union, the fewer remain from whom trade may be diverted; in fact, if all the world joins the union, there can, by definition, be no trade diversion.

The potential gains and losses just discussed are static. So-called dynamic benefits of customs unions flow from economies of scale and increased competition resulting from union. Presumably, the union increases the size of the external markets available to the partners and thereby allows larger-scale production, with consequent reduced costs.

---

cost to the nation (and therefore ultimately to the consumer, as well) must be measured by the price without the tariff (which is, in effect, simply a sales tax levied by the government on imports). But the price without tariff is higher from the member than from the nonmember since the latter is more efficient.

Furthermore, lowering one's trade barriers to partner nations puts competitive pressure on formerly protected industries, forcing them to produce more efficiently. In both instances, investment and innovations are encouraged. Many scholars feel that the dynamic benefits of a customs union are more important than the static. Unfortunately, neither are easy to measure quantitatively. As we shall see below, however, the qualitative conditions for a successful customs union are so poorly fulfilled by the Soviet bloc nations that it is safe to infer that CMEA is a losing proposition in economic terms. This brings the political motivation behind its establishment into clearer perspective.

Economic Integration

In the ideal model, economic integration can be defined as a situation in which prices of all similar goods and all similar factors in two regions are equalized, thereby making them, in effect, one region or market. To the extent that inequalities exist, goods and/or factors flow from the lower to the higher price part of the region until equality is achieved. In theory, when these equalities have been achieved, perfect allocation of factors will have been reached and just the right combination of goods will be produced. The creation of a single market out of two distinct regions implies that greater specialization will exist and, wherever possible, economies of scale will be realized.

From an operational standpoint, economic integration is usually defined in terms of the techniques used to try to achieve it. These would be, first of all, the removal of all barriers to commodity trade (customs union) and to the unrestrained flow of factors of production (principally labor and capital). Second, integration also requires a harmonization of the internal policies of the governments involved. Otherwise factors or goods will flow from one nation to another, not because of price differences, but because of, say, better unemployment benefits, lower taxes on profits, lower sales taxes, and other distorting factors. Even if there were perfect harmonization of internal policies and unrestrained flows of goods and factors, ideal integration would not be achieved because of transportation costs between countries, impossibility of moving land and some other resources, and differences in languages, customs, and climate. These factors also make it impossible to achieve ideal economic integration even within one country, especially a large one like the United States or the U.S.S.R., or a nation composed of many diverse peoples, such as Yugoslavia. It is sobering to consider that in 1950 the per capita income of the East South Central region of the United States was five-eighths that of the national average and only half that of the Pacific region. The differences between northern and southern Italy are just as great and those among the provinces of Yugoslavia even greater. With differences within nations of such magnitude, the practical goals of international integration must be scaled accordingly.

Integration Under Central Planning

While most of our evaluation of the measures taken to implement a customs union and integration under CMEA has to await a presentation of the historical facts (see below), some preliminary comments are possible on the basis of the differences which exist between free market and central planning institutions.

In attempting to achieve integration, the centrally planned economies have advantages and disadvantages vis-à-vis capitalist nations, the disadvantages outweighing the advantages. A major disadvantage is chronic inconvertibility of currencies. Inconvertibility leads first of all to strict annual bilateral balancing of trade between bloc nations. Generally speaking, the most profitable levels of free trade involve surpluses and deficits with different trading partners which are balanced off against each other, that is, multilateral trade. If surpluses and deficits are not allowed, then the deficit nation must either reduce its imports or the surplus nation must be willing to take goods in payment which it really does not want or could get elsewhere at a lower price. That is to say, trade must either be reduced or uneconomic trade must be engaged in. The relatively lower trade participation ratios of the centrally planned economies probably reflect, in part, the reduction of trade for bilateral balance. But much uneconomic trade is also engaged in as well. The U.S.S.R., for example, had to scrape the bottom of the barrel in order to help China finance its imports from her. Soviet imports consisted largely of lower priority consumers' goods and stockpiling of tin far beyond ordinary needs. Hungary is reported to have trans-shipped to other nations as much as 15 percent of her imports, an expensive and cumbersome device for introducing some multilateralization into her trade. A Polish economic journalist reports the following examples of uneconomic trade for Poland:

> In a group of metal-working machines, for instance, 40 percent of all the machines exported possess exactly the same characteristics as those

we import and 87 percent of those we import have the same characteristics as our own . . . [also] prices paid by Poland for imported metal-
working machines are higher than those paid to her for exported
machines of types which are similar in quality and technical performance . . . . Similarly, import prices paid by Poland for bearings are
about 42 percent higher than the prices obtained for Polish bearings on
foreign markets.[1]

Bilateralism not only reduces the level of trade and results in some
uneconomic trade, it also distorts the pattern of trade and specialization. Under rigid bilateralism, nations do not necessarily buy in the
cheapest markets, thereby encouraging specialization according to
comparative advantage, but often from less efficient producers in order
to balance accounts bilaterally. Since trade is the major economic
contact between nations, the reduction and distortion of trade which
results from inconvertibility and bilateralism is bound to reduce the
potentialities of integration.

As noted in the previous chapter, the absence of rational internal
prices also reduces the trade of the Soviet bloc countries by creating a
considerable degree of uncertainty as to what should and should not be
traded. Techniques devised to overcome this handicap have not been
completely successful.

Inconvertibility and irrational pricing also impede and distort capital
flows among centrally planned economies, and for the same reasons as
cited in connection with trade flows. Capital flows eventually involve
transfers of goods and repayments, and these must be accomplished
within an otherwise bilateral balance framework, albeit over a longer
period of time than one year. Furthermore, if there is uncertainty
regarding the comparative advantage among existing industries, there is
bound to be even greater uncertainty with irrational prices in attempting to predict the comparative advantage ten years hence as a guide to
international investment. Other factors also impede investment flows.
The ideological objection to recognizing interest as a return on capital
has sharply reduced the incentive of Soviet bloc nations to invest in
each other's economies. The going rate on loans has been (through
1974) 2-3 percent and, given the chronic scarcity of capital, it is no
wonder that the flow of investment across borders has been slight, since
higher rates of return can be obtained by investing domestically.
Finally, of course, until very recently, it has been impossible for foreign
businesses or governments to own means of production in a Communist

country (just as private nationals are not allowed to do so), and this prevents the flow of whatever equity capital might otherwise have been induced to move. As Peter Wiles has put it, the centrally planned economies are "rather inclined to *capital autarky* [italics added]."[2]

One of the most important factors impeding integration among the Soviet bloc nations, in terms of both trade and investment, is the unwillingness of these nations to allow existing enterprises, industries, and sectors to be outcompeted and scrapped. Such behavior is also characteristic of capitalist nations, as evidenced by protective tariffs, quotas, etc. In explaining the difficulties of Comecon integration, an eminent Hungarian economist quoted a Swiss cabinet minister, speaking in 1957, as follows:

> The major problem does not lie in the commonplace fact that production of large series means a savings in costs, but in that who would manufacture the larger series, and who should renounce the former small series . . . . All the enthusiasm about the large series affords little consolation to the party who is forced to surrender his less profitable branches of economy to better suited zones or countries.[3]

The long battle over agriculture in the EEC is a dramatic case in point, with each nation resisting the sacrifice of its farm sector to the cause of the overall efficiency of the Common Market. While Western nations are generally sensitive to the survival desires of their private enterprises and will often intervene to protect them, particularly if they represent an important economic or political interest group, the centrally planned economies appear to be even more protective of state enterprises. In theory, this need not be the case; presumably, governments should be able to plan integration and change more efficiently and rationally, unencumbered by the lobbying of private profit pressure groups. Apparently, socialist governments are no more rational at planning integration than they are at avoiding pollution.[4]

However, there may be reasons both rational and irrational for their apparent madness. First, it is very easy for a centrally planned economy to absorb the costs or losses of an inefficient industry. Institutionally, this can be handled by simply raising the prices of the products in question or by granting budget subsidies to cover losses. And, given the irrationality of internal prices, it is difficult to distinguish between an inefficient industry and one that appears to be inefficient but really is not. Second, it is much more difficult for capital-poor nations than for capital-rich nations to allow forced obsolescence through international trade. A poor man keeps his automobile much longer than a rich one. On the average, the rich Western industrial nations replace 10 percent of their equipment every year; Czechoslovakia, one of the most advanced of the socialist nations, replaces only about 2 percent of its equipment every year.[5] The relative lower per capita GNPs of the Eastern nations, as reflected in capital scarcity, then, may provide a relatively legitimate obstacle to integration. Third, it is a fact that like so many other developing nations, those in Eastern Europe want to emphasize industry at the expense of agriculture and the development of a raw materials base. In this sense, it has been the national policy of each nation to pursue development which was competitive with, rather than complementary to, the development of other nations in the bloc. What this means, in effect, is that the nations of Eastern Europe could not (and perhaps did not want to?) agree on a path to integration, although in the early years, until at least the mid-1950s, this disagreement was more a form of omission than of commission.

From an overall standpoint, economic integration should benefit each nation involved. However, each specific act of integration is likely to benefit some nations but involve others in at least short-run losses, or to benefit some nations more than others. Nations are motivated, of course, to maximize their gains and minimize their losses, if possible. The process of negotiation may be long and complicated—perhaps fruitless—if each nation retains complete sovereignty over its destiny. Among market economies, integration can be implemented if nations agree to stop protecting domestic enterprises and industries even when absence of protection involves losses, when they remove trade barriers and agree to abide by the consequences. Under central planning, the process of integration can be expedited and assured of some success only if a supranational authority to make decisions is granted to some international agency. But the nations of Eastern Europe, particularly Rumania, have been unwilling, as we shall see, to give up their sovereignty, and this has been a major factor behind the slowness of the integration of the Eastern bloc and a source of continuing discussion and disagreement in Comecon.

ECONOMIC WARFARE

In the customs union and integration models, normal international economic relations exist under the influence of relatively stable rules, incentives, and parameters, largely within a given political framework. In the economic warfare model, an attempt is made to achieve ends, unachievable under normal economic and political relationships, by the use of economic pressures, mainly through the threat or act of ending gainful trade and investment between nations. Economic power is exercised here beyond the point which might be considered in the framework of normal commercial relationships (see Chart 3.1-I.B.2). Because economic warfare has played an important role in intrabloc and East-West relations, it is useful to set forth an economic warfare model. In intrabloc trade, economic warfare was used at different times by the U.S.S.R. to exert political pressures on Yugoslavia, Albania, and China. In East-West economic relations, the U.S.S.R., and to some extent Eastern Europe, has been on the receiving end of Western economic warfare. In fact, economic warfare policies dominated the U.S. approach to the Soviet bloc for the first twenty years after the end of World War II.

The economic warfare model is simple, obvious, and well known. Its basic idea is that the amount of economic pressure which one nation can exert on another, whether for political ends or simply as punishment, is a function of the economic dependency of the second nation on the first. Economic dependency is a function first of all of the importance of trade and aid to the nation in question. Obviously, a nation like the United States, which trades only 5 percent of its GNP and receives no net foreign aid, is much less susceptible to economic pressures than a small nation which trades 30 percent of its GNP and depends on foreign aid for half its investment. Second, the economic dependency relationships between two nations depend also on the relative importance of the first nation in the trade of the second. Clearly, a nation which buys 50 percent of the exports from and supplies 40 percent of the imports to a second nation is in a stronger position to exert pressures than another nation where the percentages are each 10. Even where the percentages are high, dependency is not strong if alternative buyers and lenders stand waiting in the wings to deal on similar terms. Third, the nation "waging" economic warfare is freer to exercise its power the less dependent it is on trade and the less important to its trade is that with the target nation.

Fourth, the character of the trade is also relevant. A nation which imports inputs (machinery, raw materials) from another will be more susceptible to pressure than one which imports final outputs (consumers' goods). There are several reasons why this is so. Loss of inputs disrupts the productive process in a country and causes total losses to the economy which may be much greater than the value of interrupted imports per se. Inability to import crucial inputs like petroleum could quickly bring any advanced nation without domestic supplies to its knees. Imports of machinery and equipment are much more specialized than consumers' goods and therefore harder and more expensive to replace. It is very easy to substitute one consumers' good for another, but not always easy to substitute the machines of one supplier for those of another. Related to this, disruption of trade may mean the disruption of the supply of spare parts of a very large stock of capital goods, spare parts which cannot be quickly and easily replaced from other sources. It was a matter of years before the Russians were able to replace the spare parts for the American-built Cuban transport system. These principles apply to all economies, free market or planned. Several forms of economic warfare are peculiar to market economies. Thus, centrally planned economies are not concerned with dumping, competitive exchange depreciation, tariff wars, etc.[6]

There are special factors in intrabloc trade which make nations particularly susceptible to economic warfare, particularly by the U.S.S.R. As we saw in Chapters 1 and 2, central planning by direct controls is a particularly rigid mechanism; foreign trade, in the first instance, is avoided partially in order to minimize disturbances to the mechanism which originates in trade. A loss of imports, particularly of inputs, can have serious repercussions on the domestic economy. The fact that over-full employment planning generally prevails further exacerbates this situation. In addition, the use of foreign trade monopolies gives the aggressor nation a flexible instrument for manipulating trade if necessary, regardless of costs.

In terms of our model, the U.S.S.R. is particularly suited to exerting economic pressures on Communist bloc nations, with the possible exception of China. It is a large, self-sufficient nation like the United States, with a low trade-dependency ratio. The other Communist bloc nations, with the exception of China, have high trade-dependency ratios. Furthermore, the U.S.S.R. has been the largest trading partner of every other Eastern bloc nation for most of the period since World War II. Most of the products supplied to these nations by the U.S.S.R. are inputs rather than final products, either machinery and equipment or raw materials. So, for example, Hungary relies largely on Soviet ore and coke for its steelworks at Sztalinvares and Poland depends on Soviet ore at Nova Huta.[7] Both plants are poorly situated to import supplies from third nations. For many years Western export controls on shipments to the Soviet bloc further reduced the possibility of importing from third nations. Finally, not only is the Soviet Union the major market for exports of other Eastern nations, but these nations have adapted their industries, in many instances, to produce goods specifically designed to meet Soviet demands. (This point applies especially to the G.D.R. and Czechoslovakia.) Most of these products are unsalable in the West. Since other Soviet bloc nations provide poor markets for sudden and unplanned exports, it is clear that a trade embargo imposed by the U.S.S.R. would cause substantial losses on this count.

The major instances of use of economic warfare in intrabloc relationships have been with Yugoslavia, 1948-1953 and 1957-1961; Albania after 1961; and China after 1959.[8] These will be discussed in some detail below.

From World War II to Stalin's Death (1953)

The formation of the so-called Soviet bloc of nations after World War II was an essentially political act. By 1948, Communist governments with leaders loyal to the U.S.S.R. had taken power throughout Eastern Europe: in Albania, Bulgaria, Czechoslovakia, East Germany, Hungary, Poland, Rumania, and Yugoslavia. The U.S.S.R., which had stood virtually alone with only the Mongolian People's Republic as its ally before World War II, had succeeded in its major objective of surrounding itself with nonhostile governments. Moreover, to the East, the Chinese Communists took power from Chiang Kai-shek in 1949.

These political changes involved major economic realignments. Political insulation did not necessarily or logically require economic insulation. The Soviet political and military presence in Eastern Europe was undoubtedly adequate to maintain control. There is evidence that Stalin did not initially plan to isolate Eastern Europe and the U.S.S.R. economically from the West. However, as the Cold War developed and it became clear that Soviet trade with the West would not be expanded, a decision must have been made to develop a "second world market" and to use economic relations with Eastern Europe to further Soviet purposes. First, Eastern Europe was to provide, for the first time, a group of friendly nations with which the U.S.S.R. could have normal trade relations. Before World War II, Soviet trade had shrunk to a fraction of 1 percent of GNP in a hostile capitalist world. Second, Eastern Europe also provided the U.S.S.R. with a group of nations that were under its domination and from which more than the normal gains from trade might be extracted, including reparations. Finally, to the extent that Eastern Europe became economically dependent on the U.S.S.R., the U.S.S.R. had at its disposal an economic lever to support its political and military controls over those nations.

The U.S.S.R. had almost no economic ties with the nations of Eastern Europe or China before World War II. In fact, Germany was the major focus of the trade of Eastern Europe, especially in the late 1930s, taking from one-fifth of the goods of Czechoslovakia and Poland to half of those of Bulgaria, with Rumania and Hungary in between.[9] The defeat and collapse of Germany in 1945 left a vacuum which was, within a few years, largely filled by the U.S.S.R. Immediately after the war a number of the Eastern European countries did receive aid from the West (e.g., UNNRA aid to Poland and Yugoslavia). Commercial relationships with the West were hampered, however, by the political uncertainty which prevailed in most of these nations at this time, compounded by the fact that the whole area was already in the Soviet sphere of influence, and the Cold War had already begun. Commercial relations with the West were also hampered by the great economic dislocation which characterized the Eastern nations. In many of them economic life was at a standstill, inflation raged, and war destruction was universal. It was one thing to grant aid to such countries; it was another to find a reasonable basis for commercial trade and investment. The U.S.S.R., strongly motivated by political considerations, moved into the gap left by Germany and the West and rapidly developed trading relationships with the Eastern nations. After 1949-1950, the choice for them was trading with each other and the U.S.S.R., or largely forgoing trade. The ex-enemy countries (East Germany, Hungary, Rumania, and Bulgaria) had very little choice in the matter. The Russians had occupied these countries, collecting reparations and maintenance payments for their troops, removing German and Italian plants and equipment, and establishing and running jointly owned enterprises. Russia's influence in the other Eastern nations was hardly less effective. By 1948, all the countries of Eastern Europe had Communist governments which had begun to practice central planning and were striving for rapid industrialization and self-sufficiency along the lines of the Soviet 1930s model.

On January 25, 1949, a major organizational development occurred with the establishment of the Council for Mutual Economic Assistance. CMEA was actually the first international organization of the Eastern nations, the Cominform established in September 1947 having linked Communist parties rather than governments. At least three reasons have been advanced for the formation of CMEA. It has been seen as the economic counterpart of the Cominform. It has also been viewed as a rebuff to Yugoslavia, which had broken with the U.S.S.R. and was excluded from the organization. Finally, all observers agree that the major impetus to the formation of CMEA was a need to respond to the Marshall Plan (see Chapter 4), the concomitant development of the Organization for European Economic Cooperation (OEEC, now OECD), and to the division of Europe into two political camps. The communiqué of January 22, 1949, which announced the formation of CMEA, said in explanation that "the Governments of the United States of America, of Great Britain, and of certain Western European states had boycotted trade relations with the countries of people's democracy and the U.S.S.R. because these countries did not consider it appropriate that they should submit themselves to the dictatorship of the Marshall Plan, which would have violated their sovereignty and the interests of their national economies." More positively, the communiqué goes on to say that CMEA was formed: "To establish . . . wider economic cooperation between the countries of people's democracy and the U.S.S.R. . . . on the basis of equal representation and with the task of exchanging economic experience, extending technical aid to one another, and rendering mutual assistance."[10]

The establishment of CMEA was followed by a series of meetings at which long-range plans were discussed, documents on technology and investment were exchanged, and many proposals for collaboration were advanced. Trade among the nations involved and with China did increase very rapidly until 1953. For the most part, however, the increase could not be attributed to any special form of collaboration or integration as a result of CMEA. Rather, it simply represented the natural increase in trade to be expected as the various Soviet bloc nations recovered from the war and began to grow, with the increase concentrated, for political reasons, entirely within the socialist camp, and trade with the West actually declining absolutely.[11] This increase, furthermore, was inhibited by the fact that each nation planned its industrial development with little or no regard for the plans of the other nations. Referring to this period a Soviet economist has written:

> The initial form of coordination, or the first stage of economic cooperation among the countries, was the planned exchange of the relatively surplus output through foreign trade channels. For this purpose, bilateral agreements were concluded, as a rule for one year, each country thus ensured the balancing of its economy. But this was done for a limited period, and not infrequently the balancing was obtained through casual ties that were not always economically rational.[12]

This statement makes very clear the low level of economic cooperation which existed: "planned exchange of . . . surplus output" suggests that plans themselves were not geared to each other *ex ante* but that the disproportions between domestic supply and demand in each country were adjusted *ex post* via external trade; that bilateral rather than multilateral exchange was practiced; that such coordination as existed was on a year-to-year basis rather than long-run; and that CMEA exerted no supranational coordinating authority. For more than a decade this situation was changed in numerous details but not in substance.

While CMEA as an institution did little to facilitate trade in the early years, intrabloc trade rapidly came to dominate the total trade of each member nation. It is important to consider what the change in trading patterns meant, economically, to the nations of Eastern Europe. It is clear that the formation of Communist governments in Eastern Europe represented the exercise of Soviet political-military power for political-military objectives. It is also clear that the collection of reparations and establishment of exploitative joint stock companies in former enemy nations was an exercise of political-military power for economic ends, however justified such reparations may have been. Did the Eastern nations lose or gain from having had to trade with each other? Did the gains from intensified intrabloc trade more than offset the losses from trade diversion? If the answer is yes, then the intrabloc trade can be looked upon as one factor, at least, which served to mitigate the harshness of the political changes which had occurred; if the answer is no, then the increase in intrabloc trade can be viewed as a further exercise in political power by the U.S.S.R. To some extent, of course, the shift in trade patterns was due to the controls erected by the Western nations (see Chapter 4); but it was also due in part to Stalin's politically and economically motivated interest in establishing an insulated world socialist market.

APPLICATIONS OF CUSTOMS UNION ANALYSIS

What kind of customs union is the Soviet bloc? It is not a customs union in any formal sense, of course, but like a Western customs union, it takes measures which increase trade among members and reduce (relatively) trade with the rest of the world. In 1938, trade between the nations of Eastern Europe and the U.S.S.R. amounted to about 15 percent of their total trade, most of which was with Germany. The U.S.S.R. had virtually no trade at all with Bulgaria, Hungary, Poland, and Rumania, and only 2 percent of Czechoslovakia's trade. By 1950, intrabloc trade exceeded 60 percent of the total; by 1953, it amounted to almost 80 percent. As the figures in Table 3.1 demonstrate, trade with the U.S.S.R. accounted for the largest part of the change in trading patterns. While the percentage of intrabloc trade declined gradually over the next twenty years, it still constitutes, on an average, close to 60 percent of the trade of member nations (Table 3.2).

TABLE 3.1

Soviet and East European Imports, 1938, 1950, 1953
(in percent of total)

	1938	1950	1953
Eastern European imports from Eastern Europe	15.7	31.1	30.7
Eastern European imports from the U.S.S.R.	1.6	33.9	41.2
Total East European imports from CMEA	17.3	65.0	71.9
Soviet imports from Eastern Europe	5.5	59.1	61.0
CMEA imports from all socialist nations		70.2	78.7

SOURCES: 1938: derived from the League of Nations, *The Network of World Trade* Geneva, 1942; 1950, 1953: derived from Paul Marer, *Soviet and East European Foreign Trade, 1946-1969* (Bloomington: Indiana University Press, 1972), pp. 24-34.

TABLE 3.2
Intrabloc Trade
(percent of total)

COUNTRY	YEAR	U.S.S.R.	REST OF CMEA	TOTAL CMEA	NON-CMEA
Bulgaria	1950	67.1	21.3	88.4	11.6
	1960	52.8	27.6	80.4	19.6
	1971	53.7	21.7	75.4	24.6
	1973	53.3	21.7	75.0	25.0
Czechoslovakia	1950	27.4	27.1	54.5	45.5
	1960	34.4	29.4	63.8	36.2
	1971	32.8	31.4	64.2	35.8
	1973	30.8	29.7	60.5	39.5
East Germany	1950	39.7	32.6	72.3	27.7
	1960	44.9	22.7	67.7	32.3
	1971	38.3	29.1	67.4	32.6
	1973	33.7	29.7	63.4	36.6
Hungary	1950	26.8	34.6	61.4	38.6
	1960	31.1	32.0	63.1	36.9
	1971	34.1	29.8	63.9	36.1
	1973	33.7	26.7	60.4	39.6
Poland	1950	26.8	31.6	58.4	41.6
	1960	31.2	25.4	56.6	43.4
	1971	35.7	26.2	61.9	38.1
	1973	28.0	25.0	53.0	47.0
Rumania	1950	55.4	27.8	83.2	16.8
	1960	39.7	27.2	66.9	33.1
	1971	24.8	22.4	47.2	52.8
	1973	21.0	21.4	42.4	57.6
U.S.S.R.	1950	—	—	57.4	42.6
	1960	—	—	53.0	47.0
	1971	—	—	56.2	43.8
	1973	—	—	54.0	46.0

SOURCES: 1950, 1960, 1971: Z. Fallenbuchl, "East European Integration: Comecon," in Joint Economic Committee, Congress of the United States, *Reorientation and Commercial Relations of the Economies of Eastern Europe* (Washington, D.C.: Government Printing Office, 1974), p. 82; 1973: *Handbook of Economic Statistics, 1975* (Washington, D.C.: Central Intelligence Agency, August 1975), pp. 54, 58.

NOTE: Total CMEA trade as a percentage of world trade can be calculated from Table 4.1.

These figures can be put into perspective by comparison with the experience of the original six nations of the European Economic Community (EEC). In 1958, the year before the first steps toward a common market were put into effect, the six EEC nations conducted 30 percent of their trade with each other. By 1970, this percentage had risen to roughly 48 percent. Some small additional increase may occur, of course, as economic trade barriers are eventually eliminated completely, but it is unlikely that CMEA percentages will be approached.

In terms of the static customs union framework presented above, it seems evident that the nations of the EEC stood a better chance of forming an advantageous customs union than did the nations of Comecon or the socialist nations as a whole. We refer to the fact that the EEC nations conducted about 30 percent of their trade with each other before forming a customs union, in comparison with approximately 15 percent for the socialist nations. Furthermore, even though the EEC nations reduced barriers among themselves, they also reduced, though to a lesser extent, barriers between themselves and nonmembers, thereby lessening the possible incidence of trade diversion. The major empirical study[13] of trade creation and diversion in the EEC shows that total trade of EEC members grew faster after the Treaty of Rome went into effect, suggesting trade creation. Furthermore, while intramember trade grew even faster than total trade, this was not significantly at the expense of nonmembers, with whom trade continued to grow at virtually the same pace as before.

It is impossible to estimate quantitatively the extent of reduction of barriers among members and against nonmembers in the case of the socialist nations because, as noted in Chapter 3, trade barriers imposed by socialist nations take the form of implicit quotas which flow out of planning decisions. Another factor confusing any attempt at systematic analysis is the fact that the redirection of trade among the socialist nations took place simultaneously with the internal reorganization from capitalism to central planning (as well as the recovery from World War II), and it is impossible to separate the effects on trade of the introduction of nationalization and central planning from those resulting from the "customs union." Nevertheless, the changes in the country structure of trade have been so drastic as to leave no doubt about the changes in barriers which would have been observed had explicit tariffs or quotas been used as policy instruments. Recall that in the prewar period, the socialist nations conducted about 15 percent of their trade with each other, 85 percent with others, and that the ratio of these percentages was approximately 75/25 by 1953. It seems clear that this switch in percentages must largely reflect trade diversion. Suppose, to take an extreme example, that the formation of a socialist customs union (elimination of trade barriers) had led to a doubling of their trade through "trade creation." In this case, all other things being equal, total trade would have risen by 15 percent (from 15/100 to 30/115), and intrasocialist trade would have been 26 percent (i.e., 30/115) of the total. A tripling of intrasocialist trade through trade creation would have raised the percentages to only 35 percent (45/130). It seems clear from these improbably optimistic examples that percentages like 60 and 80 percent must be due not to trade creation but primarily to trade diversion. In fact, the implied trade diversion is of such an extraordinary magnitude that it could not have occurred simply as a result of the removal of trade barriers among the socialist nations. More likely than not, it reflects a large increase in implicit barriers to trade with capitalist nations. East-West trade barriers were complemented, of course, by general West-East barriers. Such large-scale trade diversion implies substantial losses relative to what would obtain if trade were nondiscriminatory. For the socialist nations were forcing themselves as well as being forced by the West to purchase most of their imports in relatively high-cost markets. In fact, the very large percentage of intrabloc trade has led some observers to suggest that perhaps some of that trade is uneconomic, a matter of "taking in each other's washing." This position can be supported with citations from the Communist bloc literature. Some uneconomic trade is bound to result, of course, from the need to balance trade bilaterally with each partner—rather than extend involuntary credit, the surplus nation will take whatever it can get in commodities in order to achieve balance. All in all, the formation of a socialist world market must have reduced substantially the gains to be had from trade, at least in the short run.

What about the dynamic benefits from the customs union, such as economies of scale and the incentive to efficiency from increased competition? Neither factor is likely to have provided offsetting gains to the CMEA nations. While intrabloc trade increased, it did not increase as much as East-West trade decreased, so that all the Eastern bloc nations, with the exception of the U.S.S.R., ended up trading a smaller percentage of their GNPs than before. According to one authority, the percentage of potential trade reached by the CMEA nations in 1955 varied from 28 percent in the case of the U.S.S.R. to 50 percent in the case of Hungary.[14] In effect, the Eastern nations, as a group, were forced to become more self-sufficient, to produce a greater variety of goods for themselves and each other and therefore to specialize less and have fewer economies of scale.* These same facts spell less competitive pressure, since after World War II there were fewer rather than more foreign exporters able to enter the markets of the Soviet bloc nations, and those excluded were usually the more efficient. Even more important, however, is the fact that by its very nature Stalinist-type central planning does not allow unplanned competition with domestic industries. In effect, it allows no competition. It is rare indeed for socialist nations to phase out existing enterprises or industries deliberately regardless of how inefficient they are. Under socialism virtually every enterprise is a "Lockheed."

To sum up: customs union analysis leads us to infer that the sharp shift from East-West to intrabloc trade undoubtedly imposed large economic losses on all the Eastern European nations, including the U.S.S.R., in the sense that all the nations would have been much better off if they could have continued (or in the case of the U.S.S.R. begun) trading with the West. This brings into clearer relief the primarily political nature of the formation of the Communist trading bloc. The losses, it should be noted, were undoubtedly more serious to the smaller Eastern European nations than to the U.S.S.R. because the former depend so much more heavily on trade. Of course, once the political lines were drawn and the Cold War began in earnest, it made sense to expand intrabloc trade as a substitute, albeit a poor one, for East-West trade. This was especially true after 1949-1950 when the Western anti-Communist trade control-systems had been fully developed.

USES OF POLITICAL POWER IN ECONOMIC RELATIONSHIPS

While the nations of Eastern Europe were forced by a combination of Western controls and Soviet power to engage in intrabloc trade, it

*The decline in ratios of trade to GNP also suggests that no trade creation occurred, since trade creation, by definition, involves a rise in the ratio. However, a categoric inference is difficult to make because other factors were at work reducing the ratio, in particular the shift from capitalism to Communist central planning.

would be difficult to demonstrate that the terms on which trade generally took place were unfavorable. This issue will be discussed later. There are specific arrangements, however, in the case of some key commodities, and in the general area of reparations and joint stock companies, which do represent an exercise of political power for economic ends by the U.S.S.R.

The largest item by far is that of reparations from the former enemy nations, East Germany, Hungary, and Rumania. The Russians were, of course, legally entitled to reparations as a result of political settlements made after the war. It could also be argued that they were morally entitled to this kind of compensation since they suffered grievously during the war, both in human terms and in terms of war destruction. Questions must be raised, however, about the size of the reparations, particularly from East Germany, the way the reparations were collected, and the fact that while these transfers were being taken from former enemy nations, they were being taken from what had become fellow People's Republics.

The bulk of the reparations was paid by 1951, although some payments were made after that. Reparations took two forms: dismantled plants and deliveries of commodities. Estimates of the value of reparations vary considerably. One estimate is that the Soviets took $12 billion worth of plants and equipment and $4 billion worth of commodities from East Germany, with corresponding figures of $1 billion and $167 million from Hungary and $153 million worth of goods (mostly oil) from Rumania. In addition, an estimated $750 million worth of plants and equipment was removed from Manchuria.[15] In addition, Hungary had to make payments to Czechoslovakia and Yugoslavia, and Bulgaria to Yugoslavia.

The removal of plants and equipment from Germany by the U.S.S.R. was, according to all reports, an irresponsible undertaking. The transfer of whole factories is a difficult matter under the best of circumstances. Under the circumstances prevalent just after the war, it was clear that transfer would inevitably entail much waste and destruction. It is estimated by one authority that the gain to the Russians was no more than $4½ billion, or roughly one-third of the loss to the East Germans.[16]

Aside from the lost plants and equipment, the East Germans were saddled with large annual reparations in the form of commodity deliveries plus the support of some twenty divisions of Soviet troops, which may have cost in the neighborhood of $1 billion annually. The strain on the East German economy was so great that in May 1950, the Soviets agreed to halve the reparation debt, which left the Germans having to pay about $200 million annually for fifteen years in addition to troop maintenance costs. The East German rebellion of June 1953 led to a cancellation of reparation repayments (after almost $4 billion had been paid), return of about two-thirds of the factories that had been removed, and a reduction in troop maintenance costs. The latter were reduced again after the 1956-1957 unrest and finally eliminated in 1959. These events attest to the onerousness to the Germans of these various arrangements.

The Hungarians and Rumanians also found themselves very hard-pressed to make their reparation payments to the U.S.S.R., although their obligations were much smaller than the East German. As a result, a large part was likewise forgiven after several years. Both nations, however, were forced to sell valuable raw materials to the U.S.S.R. at bargain prices. The Rumanians are estimated to have subsidized the U.S.S.R. to the tune of some $150 million in low oil prices, and Hungary apparently shipped uranium ore to the U.S.S.R. at similarly disadvantageous terms. The outstanding example of this form of extortion is that of Polish coal. In 1956, after the Polish uprising, the Soviets agreed to pay Poland the equivalent of $626 million in compensation for the low price which had been paid all those years on imports of Polish coal. Coal was in very short supply throughout Europe in this period; as a result, the Poles lost a golden opportunity to earn hard currency, which undoubtedly would have had greater value for their economic reconstruction economy than the belated Soviet payment.

Finally, the U.S.S.R. exploited the nations of Eastern Europe through the establishment of joint stock companies.[17] Supposedly, these companies were to be financed half by the host nation and half by the U.S.S.R. For the most part, the U.S.S.R's share simply comprised captured German or other Western investments in the host territories. The evidence which has been made available strongly suggests that the U.S.S.R. ran these joint stock companies very autocratically and took far more than their fair share of the profits. The Yugoslavs were the first to complain publicly, which they did at the time of their break with the U.S.S.R. in 1948. Again, unrest among the

Eastern nations at the time of the German riots in 1953 and again in 1956 after the Polish and Hungarian uprisings led to the eventual dissolution of most of the companies. At first, the nations were required to buy out the Russian interest, but by 1956 most of these debts had to be forgiven. Again, the circumstances which surround the history of the joint stock companies make it clear that they involved exploitation of other CMEA members by the Soviet Union, a case of the use of political power for economic profit. It has been estimated that these companies cost East Germany, Hungary, and Rumania $200 million, $250 million, and $900 million respectively.[18]

ECONOMIC WARFARE AGAINST YUGOSLAVIA

While the U.S.S.R. used its political and military might to economic ends as indicated above, it also used its economic, as well as political, power for political ends against Yugoslavia in this period.

As we have pointed out, the U.S.S.R. held tight political, military, and economic control over the other nations of Eastern Europe in the first few years after the war. One Eastern nation—Yugoslavia—was unwilling "to become an obedient satellite"[19] of the U.S.S.R. at this time. Having come into power through its own resources, the Yugo-slavian Communist party viewed itself with more pride and indepen-dence than did the other satellite parties. By the end of 1947, Tito and Stalin had come into conflict on a number of economic and political issues. At the political level, the U.S.S.R. was unwilling to back Yugoslavian territorial claims against Austria and Italy. Domestically, the Yugoslavs were very angry to discover Soviet secret police operating within their borders. At the economic level, they complained that the U.S.S.R. was taking advantage of them through the operation of two joint stock companies, that the terms of commodity trade were unfair, and that the Soviets were not giving them sufficient aid.

Yugoslavia in 1948 was extremely vulnerable to economic warfare. The nation had suffered grievously from World War II, was attempting to rebuild as well as to industrialize rapidly, was dependent upon other Soviet bloc nations for more than half of her trade (which included all of her coal and coke needs, 85 percent of fertilizer, and 60 percent of oil), was receiving considerable aid and technical assistance of which almost 100 percent was from the U.S.S.R., and was not on friendly terms with the West.[20]

In December 1947 Stalin began applying economic pressure against Yugoslavia by delaying trade negotiations which were essential to Yugoslavia's Five Year Plan. In February 1948 the Yugoslavs were informed that talks would not be resumed until at least the end of 1948. On March 18 and 19 all military and economic advisors were withdrawn by the U.S.S.R. on the grounds that they were being treated inhospitably. All these measures were extremely serious to the Yugoslav economy. Apparently, they were used by Stalin in an unsuccessful effort to split the Yugoslav Communist party and deliver it into the hands of the pro-Stalin faction. In August, tourism from other Eastern countries ended; in September and October other Eastern nations delayed shipments of crucial goods to Yugoslavia and refused requests for trade negotiations. In February 1949 the U.S.S.R. canceled its long-term capital-aid agreement with Yugoslavia and refused its request to join CMEA; in June 1949 various Eastern nations canceled their trade agreements with Yugoslavia; finally, in July 1949, Stalin instituted a total blockade of Yugoslavia, ending trade and other economic relations between the nations for four and a half years.

Tito was not passive over this period and took many steps to offset these serious blows to the Yugoslav economy. The economy and its trade were reoriented toward the West, the level of domestic consumption was curtailed, a successful attempt was made to persuade the United States to unfreeze Yugoslavian gold it was holding, trade agreements were signed with Western nations, substantial aid was obtained from the West, and so forth. All these measures alleviated the situation in which Yugoslavia found herself, but did not compensate fully for the losses due to severed relationships with the Soviet bloc.

Soviet policy toward Yugoslavia in the 1948-1953 period was one of what Freedman calls "gradual escalation" toward blockade. Clearly, the blockade would have been much more successful if it had been instituted at once. Apparently it was applied gradually in the mistaken belief that tightening the noose another notch would bring Tito to heel. The blockade never had its desired political effect, although it hurt the Yugoslav economy. Western assistance reduced the damage. Maintaining the embargo after it had failed in its purpose, like the U.S. embargoes of Cuba and China, was more indicative of political pique or inertia than of serious intent. Although Tito's survival was partly due to the extraordinary internal strength of the regime and its willingness to fight for independence and ideology, the incident certainly must have demonstrated to the U.S.S.R. the limits to achieving serious political objectives through economic warfare.

The Early Years of the Khrushchev Era: Economic Relationships Reflect the Decline in Soviet Political Power

When Stalin died in 1953, he left a nation which had known no other ruler for almost three decades. His power was more absolute, both within the U.S.S.R. and in relations with the Soviet bloc nations, than any possible successor could hope for.

After Stalin's death the reduction in political control over Eastern Europe was dramatized by events in East Germany, Poland, and Hungary. Political and economic unrest in East Germany led to demonstrations in East Berlin almost immediately after Stalin died. A climax was reached on June 17, 1953, when tanks of the Russian occupying army were used to quell a riot in East Berlin. As noted above, the Russians relieved tensions generated by their military intervention by substantially reducing the burden of the East German war settlement and, in addition, extending the East Germans a credit of more than $100 million, of which about one-third was in convertible currency.

Difficulties in Poland began with workers' riots over economic conditions in Poznan in June 1956. The unrest finally culminated in Wladyslaw Gomulka taking power in October. The political situation was extremely tense, Russian troops in Poland were reported on the alert, and the top Soviet leaders flew to Warsaw for consultations, In the end, as with East Germany, the U.S.S.R. made economic concessions in the form of loans, compensation for the low price which had been paid for coal over a number of years, and so forth.

The most dramatic uprising was the so-called Hungarian Revolution, which occurred just a few days later and may have been sparked by the "Polish October." In Hungary, events appear to have been more purely political and less economic than in Poland and East Germany. In the face of a government which had explicitly rejected Soviet domination,

Soviet troops moved into Budapest and suppressed resistance. The Russians then again acted to alleviate the situation by extending a series of loans to the Hungarians; several other East European nations also extended credits to Hungary. The Russians also relinquished their interest in the remaining U.S.S.R.-Hungarian joint stock companies to the Hungarians.

While these visible upheavals indicate an unrest in Eastern Europe after Stalin's death, they also show that the situation was not beyond the control of Soviet leaders. It is also quite clear that while the U.S.S.R. was still willing to (and did) wield the "stick" if necessary, the "carrot" had become an important supplementary policy instrument. In addition to the instances just cited, Khrushchev wooed Tito with loans in 1955, thereby reversing Stalin's policies toward Yugoslavia. Generally speaking, Khrushchev eliminated the cruder forms of Stalinist economic exploitation of Eastern Europe within a few years after taking power. This was, in fact, an international counterpart of the domestic "deStalinization" policies highlighted by his long speech attacking Stalin and his methods at the Twentieth Party Congress in 1956 and by the large-scale amnesty of political prisoners in that same year. To sum up: Khrushchev's new approach to intrabloc relationships was due to a number of factors, including the rising political costs of Stalinist-type methods, reduced Soviet political power, a more liberal and flexible personality, and the rapidly growing strength of the Soviet economy, which made economic exploitation of other CMEA nations less necessary or attractive.

Stalin had controlled the Soviet bloc nations through an informal system of political ties which was unique to him. With his death, his successors had to seek more formal techniques of accomplishing the same objectives. The Warsaw Pact of May 1955, which established the Warsaw Treaty Organization (WTO), was the most important step taken in this period. It was also, in effect, an answer to NATO which, much to the distress of the Russians, had just brought West Germany into its fold. The Warsaw Pact has both military and political features. It effectively legalized the stationing of Soviet troops in the other Eastern nations by providing for joint command by a Soviet officer of WTO troops for purposes of mutual defense. WTO members were forbidden to participate in other alliances. Both these measures substantially infringed upon the political sovereignty of member nations. There was a degree of mutual self-interest in the pact, however, since it was partly directed at West Germany, whose possible military revival was feared by all the Eastern nations.[21]

At roughly the same time, an attempt was made to reactivate CMEA as a device to substitute for Stalinist control in the economic sphere. Until the mid-1950s, CMEA served no real function. The normal trade which took place resulted from bilateral agreements between each pair of nations. The abnormal economic transactions described above were the result of power politics. Power politics applied to intrabloc economic relations were losing their efficacy and, after the political events of 1956, were never the same. In fact, as we saw above, reparations had been largely canceled, amends made for the low price of Polish coal, and so forth. In addition, the U.S.S.R. extended loans, some in convertible currencies, to many of the nations of Eastern Europe.[22] In some respects, the shoe was on the other foot, and the U.S.S.R. was making economic concessions in order to curry political favor, or positive influence, as designated in Chart 3.1-I.B.1.a.

Despite the clear intention to mobilize CMEA and make it more effective, progress was slow indeed. Many decisions and administrative arrangements were made, but these were insufficient to steer a group of eight nations—each attempting to industrialize rapidly, each planning its own development without serious consideration to altering its path in order to coordinate with the others—into meaningful integration. The decision to coordinate national five year plans was made as early as 1954. However, for the quinquennia 1956-1960 and 1961-1965, "coordination consisted mainly of bilateral consultations between national planning organizations to review mutual requirements for goods deliveries,"[23] no tribute to the importance of CMEA.[24]

Various ad hoc committees were formed in 1955 and twelve standing commissions were established in 1956 to discuss technical issues concerning major industries (e.g., agriculture, chemicals, coal, power). Certainly these commissions were needed to provide know-how, expertise, and exchange of information necessary for rational decisions or integration. However, without a willingness to coordinate plans, these committees and commissions amounted to no more than forums in which ideas and information were exchanged.

An attempt was also made in 1957 to deal with the bilateralism and inconvertibility that were clogging trade channels. Each nation was to deposit its bilateral surpluses and deficits in the Soviet State Bank, where they could be offset against each other, with the hope of reducing the rigid bilateralism. This and later attempts failed, for reasons discussed below.

Clearly the upgrading of CMEA had little if any effect on trade during Khrushchev's early years. Intrabloc trade increased, as it was bound to, simply because the nations were all growing. But intrabloc trade, since 1953, was growing hardly faster than GNPs—an indication that integration was not increasing—and not as fast as East-West or East-LDC trade were growing. The slowness with which CMEA was moving in this period is highlighted by the fact that it was not until 1960 that a uniform classification system for foreign trade data was adopted, one which was different, unfortunately, from that used by all other members of the United Nations.

Perhaps the major innovations in the late 1950s were the first joint investment and joint enterprise agreements. The G.D.R. helped finance the building of new mines in Poland, taking repayment and interest in the form of coal deliveries rather than currency. And in 1959 Poland and Hungary jointly financed and now own the plant of the Haldex Corporation which processes coal slack. Many other joint investment projects were entered into at this time; Hungary and the G.D.R. helped finance chemical projects in Rumania; Czechoslovakia helped finance copper mines in Bulgaria and Poland. But no other joint enterprises were undertaken for a number of years. None of the joint investment projects involved the U.S.S.R., undoubtedly because of the bad experience the other nations had had with Soviet joint stock companies. All agreements were bilateral or trilateral and were negotiated without substantive assistance from CMEA agencies.

Two major multilateral projects involving the U.S.S.R. were begun in the late 1950s, namely, the giant electricity grid which was to unify the transmission of power throughout the bloc and the "Friendship Pipeline" for transporting Soviet oil originating in the Urals to refineries throughout the Soviet bloc. In both instances, each nation financed that part of the total investment which was made on its own territory. These projects represent good examples of what integration should mean for CMEA. Unfortunately, the ability of the CMEA nations to negotiate these two major projects cannot be taken to imply that the road to integration had been found and that henceforth progress would be rapid. The electricity grid and oil pipelines were projects which benefited all members of the bloc, and in which conflicts of interest were minimal. These were instances of economies of scale and cost reduction for all nations in the Soviet bloc, and of the U.S.S.R. helping meet the urgent and obvious raw-material needs of other bloc members. The other side of the coin was, of course, that as Soviet electricity and petroleum began to flow to the other Eastern nations, their economic and, therefore, political dependence on the U.S.S.R. increased.

We have seen that commodity trade remained the major form of contact among the Soviet bloc nations during Khrushchev's early years. The question which must be asked is whether or not the U.S.S.R. took advantage of its dominant economic and political position within the bloc to exploit the other Eastern nations in this trade by imposing unfavorable or discriminatory prices on them. We know this happened in the cases of Polish coal and Rumanian oil before 1956. We do not know whether unfavorable terms of trade were imposed in the early 1950s in the case of other imports or exports, however. Nor can we be absolutely sure that better terms prevailed after 1956. However, the view was widespread in the West in the late 1950s and early 1960s that Soviet exploitation extended to commodity trade in general and that it did not cease after the Polish and Hungarian events of 1956. This view was greatly strengthened by an important set of studies by an American scholar, Horst Mendershausen, which appeared in 1959 and 1960 and were based on the first Soviet trade returns published since before World War II. These returns included the quantities and values of goods exported to and imported from each of the U.S.S.R.'s trading partners. By dividing quantities into values, it is possible to derive average unit values (AUV) which, in the case of a homogeneous commodity, are equivalent to prices. The technique used by Mendershausen was to compare the prices (AUVs) at which the Russians traded in Eastern European markets with their prices in Western European markets, the latter providing the standard by which the former was judged. The results for the years 1955-1959 are schematized roughly in Table 3.3A.

That is to say, on the average, the Russians charged the East Europeans about 15 percent more than the West Europeans and paid East Europe about 15 percent less than Western Europe in each case for similar products. In terms of numbers of commodities, Eastern Europe paid more for and sold for less to the U.S.S.R. about three out of every

TABLE 3.3
Intrabloc and East-West Trade
(hypothetical prices)

A. SOVIET TRADE			B. BULGARIAN TRADE			C. WEST EUROPEAN TRADE		
PART-NER	EX-PORTS	IM-PORTS	PART-NER	EX-PORTS	IM-PORTS	PART-NER	EX-PORTS	IM-PORTS
East Europe	100	100	U.S.S.R.	100	100	U.S.S.R.	115	185
West Europe	85	115	West Europe	75	125	Other West Europe	100	100
			East Europe	100	100			

four products for which comparisons were possible. These data appeared to substantiate the popular belief that the Soviet Union was exploiting the nations of Eastern Europe. The U.S.S.R. was, the author argued, simply exercising its monopoly power in its economic relations with the nations of Eastern Europe. In light of this apparent discrimination, questions were raised as to whether Eastern Europe gained at all from trade with the U.S.S.R.

Serious reservations were soon raised concerning the methodology employed in these calculations. It was asked why, in judging intrabloc trade, Soviet-West trade prices should be taken as a standard of fairness. It was well known that the Soviet bloc nations had difficulty trading with Western nations. They often had to sell exports below Western prices in order to break into and hold markets, simply because Western firms preferred to deal with each other, either for political reasons or because of the extra red tape and uncertainties involved in dealing with nations behind the iron curtain. Prices also had to be discounted because, in many Western nations, exporters from the Soviet bloc were not granted MFN treatment and had to face discriminatory tariffs. With the exception of discriminatory tariffs, the same factors explain why Soviet bloc importers had to pay higher prices in the West than Western importers did. This set of facts suggests an alternative explanation to the Soviet discrimination hypothesis. The argument is that the U.S.S.R. does not discriminate against the Eastern bloc, but the West discriminates against the U.S.S.R. Interestingly, this assumption also explains the data in Table 3.3A. That is to say, the U.S.S.R. exports to

Western Europe at a lower price than to Eastern Europe because it is forced to if it wishes to make a sale; similarly, it has to pay a higher price for imports in order to get Western firms to deal with it. On the face of it, these two hypotheses would appear to have equal power in explaining the facts. Additional data are required if one is to choose between them. Most of all, one needs the trade data of some other Eastern bloc nation; further confirmation could be provided by Western trade data.

The initial tests were made with Bulgarian data for 1955-1959. The first test is to repeat the procedure used with Soviet data in Table 3.3A and compare Bulgarian exports and imports from the U.S.S.R. and Eastern Europe with those from Western Europe. If the Western discrimination hypothesis is correct, the results should be similar to those in Table 3.3A. If the Soviet discrimination hypothesis is correct, then the results should be reversed. In fact, the results were consistent with Western discrimination. Bulgaria exported to the U.S.S.R. and other Eastern bloc nations at even higher (by 25 percent) prices and imported from the U.S.S.R. at lower prices than from Western Europe (Table 3.3B). Obviously, if one believed in Soviet exploitation on the basis of Soviet trade data, one would be forced by the same logic to believe in Bulgarian exploitation on the basis of Bulgarian data. Polish data, later analyzed, yielded results similar to the Bulgarian.[25] The Western discrimination hypothesis reconciles these apparently contradictory results.

Western discrimination can also be tested directly by using Western European trade data and comparing the prices at which these nations trade with other Western European nations and with the Soviet bloc countries, respectively. This test was performed using British and Belgian trade returns. The results again indicated Western discrimination: the United Kingdom and Belgium charged Soviet bloc nations more and paid them less than other Western European nations for comparable commodities. These results are represented in Table 3.3C and are, in a sense, a mirror image of those in Table 3.3A.

A more direct test of Soviet discrimination was possible using the Bulgarian and Polish data. With these data one could compare the trade of these two countries with their trade with other Eastern bloc nations, thereby eliminating the distorting effects of Western discrimination. If there is discrimination, the Bulgarians (or Poles) would export at lower prices to and import at higher prices from the U.S.S.R. than from the other Eastern nations. The data for 1955-1960 suggested that no significant discrimination was evident.

These studies show no strong evidence in the trade returns of Soviet use of either monopolistic economic power or political power for economic gain in the normal intrabloc commodity trade of 1955-1960. This evidence cannot be taken as conclusive, however. Most important, calculations of the sort just described can only be made for relatively homogeneous commodities and thus include only a small part of the total trade. For example, trade in machinery and equipment cannot be included, although such products loom large in the trade of all nations. It is possible that exploitation, if it exists, occurs in categories of commodities like machinery and equipment, which are not standardized, which do not have a "world price," and in which the price finally set is arrived at through hard bargaining.

It is also worth keeping in mind that, as can be seen from Chart 3.1, there are trade-offs between economic and political objectives. Particularly after 1956, one would have expected the Soviets to attempt to deal on relatively "equal" terms in their trade with the other Eastern bloc countries. Recall also that the very existence of an intrabloc trading group implies a loss for all of the nations concerned (relative to East-West trade), losses of the smaller nations in this case not showing up as an economic, but rather as a political, gain to the U.S.S.R. (Chart 3.1-II.B.2). The subtle losses to the smaller Eastern nations of having to adapt to intrabloc trade are difficult to identify but are undoubtedly considerable.

Finally, as we shall show below, evidence for the past decade suggests that the U.S.S.R. not only has not exploited the other nations but may in fact have experienced losses from intrabloc trade.

The Later Years of the Khrushchev Era

The Soviet interest in upgrading CMEA continued and was strengthened in the second half of the Khrushchev era. As we have seen, very little progress toward integration had been made in the late 1950s. Soviet interest was further stimulated by several new developments. The first was the formation in 1958 of the European Economic Community (EEC), a political and economic union like CMEA, and of the European Free Trade Association (EFTA) in 1960. The EEC in particular appeared to the U.S.S.R. as a potential political and an immediate economic threat. The immediacy of the economic threat stemmed from the fact that the EEC, like all customs unions, maintained stricter barriers against outside exports than among partners at a time when the CMEA nations were trying to expand their trade with the West. Protection by EEC against agricultural products was particularly strong, and it was on these products in particular that the CMEA nations were relying to earn hard currency. (CMEA relations with the EEC are discussed in more detail in the next chapter.) Second, aside from the EEC, relations with the West were undergoing deterioration in other areas. Among other things, the U-2 crisis, the Berlin crisis, which led to the erection of the Wall in 1961, and the Cuban missile crisis in 1962 all contributed to a worsening of East-West relations and, consequently, an incentive to improve intrabloc relations.

Other events which led Khrushchev to search for greater integration with CMEA were the Sino-Soviet dispute and the break with Albania. Further economic integration was viewed as one device for encouraging unity with CMEA at a time of severe internecine strife within the Communist world. Finally, CMEA seems to have appeared to Khrushchev as a steppingstone toward an eventual world Communist state in which there would no longer be national borders or border guards, and in which the economic systems of all the socialist nations would be consolidated. This utopian vision appeared in an article in *Pravda* in 1959[26] and, while it may have been mostly rhetoric, it is not unlikely that Khrushchev hoped to take at least a few steps toward its realization.

ECONOMIC WARFARE AGAINST ALBANIA AND CHINA

At the same time that attempts were being made to improve CMEA integration (see below), the Soviet Union was faced with a rapidly deteriorating situation in its relationships with Albania and China.[27] These conflicts were mostly political and ideological and continue to defy resolution. Among other things, the Russians tried to convince both nations to change their views by resorting to economic "persuasion."

Albania

In the early period after World War II, Albania was very much a pawn in the Soviet-Yugoslav dispute. After the Germans withdrew, Albania was dominated by Yugoslavia and might well have been annexed, had it not been for the break between Yugoslavia and the U.S.S.R. By siding with the U.S.S.R. against Yugoslavia, the Hoxha faction gained control of the Albanian government and assured Albanian independence from Yugoslavia. The U.S.S.R. immediately took over the trade and aid obligations to Albania which Yugoslavia had once assumed. Relations between Albania and the U.S.S.R. were excellent until Khrushchev's rapprochement with Tito in the mid-1950s. The situation improved again after Tito's attack on the U.S.S.R. after the Hungarian Revolution. In 1957, Albania began to develop relations with China, probably as a consequence of China's attacks on Tito as a revisionist. Relations with China continued to develop, and despite fairly generous aid from the U.S.S.R., relations with the latter continued to deteriorate. The open break came at a conference in Bucharest in June 1960, when Albania sided with China on all important issues.

The Albanians were fairly dependent on the CMEA nations, particularly the U.S.S.R., which was Albania's major trade partner, larger than all other nations combined. The nations of CMEA accounted for over 90 percent of Albania's trade. Furthermore, the U.S.S.R. granted considerable aid to Albania, with the result that Albanian imports from the U.S.S.R. were typically double or triple her exports. Half these imports were machinery and equipment. There was also considerable technical assistance in installing and running enterprises and training students. All this was essential to Albania's ambitious industrialization plans. On the other hand, Albanian trade constituted less than 1 percent of Soviet trade and the U.S.S.R. imported almost nothing of importance from Albania.

Khrushchev's approach to Albanian dissidence, like Stalin's to Yugoslavia, was one of "gradual escalation." First, in March 1960, the U.S.S.R. revoked a 1952 scholarship agreement under which Albanian students in the U.S.S.R. were granted about 60 percent of their tuition and upkeep costs. Then, during the Albanian drought of 1960, Khrushchev reacted slowly to an urgent request for grain and, according to one report, requested payment in gold rather than extending credit as had been done in the past. Subsequently, the U.S.S.R. threatened to end all credits to Albania. The trade agreement signed in January 1961 was for one rather than five years and, for the first time, included no credits. Later that month, Soviet oil specialists were withdrawn despite Albanian protests.

None of these measures had any impact on Albanian policies. In April 1961 a Sino-Albanian trade agreement was announced under which Albania was to receive a very large credit, assistance in industrialization, and grain. Five days later, Soviet aid was formally canceled. At this time it was also apparent that the Russians were in the process of terminating trade relations. On December 3, 1961, diplomatic relations between the two countries were broken off; at about the same time trade relations with the U.S.S.R. were severed and Albania was excluded from CMEA.

In contrast with their break with Yugoslavia between 1948 and 1953, the other Eastern European nations maintained trade relations with Albania despite a temporary decline in 1962. Perhaps Khrushchev hoped to make it easy for the Albanians to return to the CMEA camp while making it painful for them to stay outside; perhaps he did not want to use up political capital by demanding a CMEA-wide embargo. In any event, the situation was indeed painful for the Albanians, since the Chinese were unable to substitute satisfactorily for the Russians in quality and quantity of aid. The language barrier alone was a formidable obstacle to closer Sino-Albanian relations—for how many in each country knew the other's language? Attempts at rapprochement have been made by the Russians at regular intervals, but with no success.

China

The Sino-Soviet dispute has been the single greatest setback to the international Communist movement, especially from the Soviet point of view. In Brzezinski's words: "it has been a tragic disaster, comparable in some respects to the split in Christianity several centuries ago."[28] The dispute between the U.S.S.R. and China is extremely complex, with many currents and countercurrents which cannot be dealt with here. In summarizing the dispute, Brzezinski divides the issues into three major categories: ideological (mostly "party"), foreign policy, and national. These three categories include no less than eighteen important issues on which the two nations have polemicized against each other. In this situation, the U.S.S.R. has employed economic warfare but certainly to a much smaller extent than would have been possible. While it is not possible to compare the importance of political and military pressure (e.g., stationing of troops on the border) with economic warfare, the latter appears to have been subordinated in this instance. Possibly, the U.S.S.R. realized by 1960 the relative impotence of economic warfare to win political battles, particularly against a large nation like China, and this explains its limited use.

The Chinese were never happy with the assistance they received from the U.S.S.R. While they probably appreciated the hundreds of complete factories installed by the Russians (they actually wanted more), the loan of thousands of technicians, gifts of thousands of blueprints, willingness of the Russians to take low-priority Chinese exports in exchange for machinery and equipment, and so forth, at the same time they had many complaints even in the early years of collaboration. For one thing, Soviet credits were far smaller than the Chinese had requested and felt they needed; they also resented Soviet insistence on payment for military materiel shipped during the Korean War; Soviet-Chinese joint enterprises in China were another source of friction; there were many other economic and political sources of irritation. In light of these dissatisfactions it is difficult to pinpoint the date of a "turning point" after which relations deteriorated. In 1955-1956, the Soviets were already making it clear that little or no more aid was to be forthcoming, that technical advisors might be withdrawn, that Soviet exports of machinery and equipment could not go on forever in such large amounts, and that China needed to rely more heavily on her own strength. Despite these hints, Soviet exports to China, particularly of machinery and equipment, continued to rise. Exports of Soviet machinery and equipment to China from 1955 to 1962 were as follows (in millions of rubles valued at $1.11 a ruble): 207, 274, 286, 538, 453, 97, 26.[29] However, Chinese exports to pay for the machinery and repay Soviet loans had to rise even faster; this put a severe strain on the Chinese economy. The aid issue was further exacerbated by the fact that the U.S.S.R., at the same time that it refused China further credits and demanded repayment of old credits, offered a very large loan to India in September 1959, only a few days after the Chinese-Indian border clash. Then, later in 1960, the U.S.S.R. withdrew all Soviet technicians almost without warning, with serious consequences to the Chinese economy. The Russians claimed that the technicians were withdrawn because the Chinese authorities were insulting them and trying to brainwash them. Four years later these consequences were spelled out by the Chinese in no uncertain terms. "Your perfidious action disrupted China's original national economic plan and inflicted enormous losses upon China's socialist construction."[30] The withdrawal of technicians occurred, it should be noted, during an economic crisis generated by the "Great Leap Forward" and a famine crop. Trade between the two nations, which had constituted 20 percent of Soviet trade and 50 percent of Chinese trade in 1959, continued to drop; by the mid-1960s it reached a small fraction of its former level, making up less than 1 percent of Soviet trade.

Not all Soviet economic actions in this period were negative. For example, the Soviets agreed to a five-year moratorium on repayment of one of the two large loans of the early 1950s. Also, the U.S.S.R. did not exploit China's dependency on it for refined oil. In 1962 and 1963, Khrushchev made conciliatory offers of increased aid, trade, and technical help to the Chinese. They rejected these offers and remained adamant on the many political and ideological issues dividing the two nations. By 1963-1964, they were over the economic hump anyway, having recovered from the disasters of the previous few years and having, by this time, opened channels of trade with Western nations. Trade with Eastern Europe, which had fallen off in the early 1960s, also recovered somewhat, probably with tacit Soviet acquiescence. Unlike the U.S.S.R., the Eastern European nations had been hurt by the shrinking of trade with China and were anxious to resume economic ties. India partially replaced China as a major buyer of machinery and equipment from the U.S.S.R.

Trade between the U.S.S.R. and China revived somewhat after the fall of Khrushchev. Political relations remained cold, however, and trade eventually fell to even lower levels than before. The Soviets attempted to achieve some political rapprochement and used offers of improved economic relations as a carrot. The cultural revolution, which eliminated any residue of pro-Soviet sentiment in the Chinese hierarchy, doomed these attempts to failure.

To sum up the China picture: the Russians failed again in their attempts to use economic pressure for political objectives. Their failure to use a total embargo (as in the case of Yugoslavia between 1948 and

1953) probably stemmed from several factors, including the realization that such an embargo would again fail, the desire to keep relations with China open to facilitate a rapprochement, the desire to avoid pushing China into the Western camp, and possibly the Soviet need for such commodities as tin, which China exported. In fact, it may well be that the Soviet Union reduced trade with China simply to indicate its displeasure and to say, in effect, "We are just not going to have any more than necessary to do with an unpleasant nation like you."

The U.S.S.R. may have learned the lesson that economic warfare is not a very strong weapon with which to achieve political goals. This is suggested by the facts that economic warfare has never been employed (at least on a significant scale) against often-dissident Rumania and that military, not economic, force was employed against Czechoslovakia in 1968.

THE CMEA CHARTER AND BASIC PRINCIPLES

The upgrading of CMEA around 1960, referred to above, was embodied in two formal documents, its Charter and an important statement on goals and methods entitled "Basic Principles of International Socialist Division of Labor." The Charter was ratified in 1959 and went into effect in 1960, more than a full decade—it is worth noting—after CMEA was formed. The Basic Principles were adopted in 1962. The two documents are quite similar and almost everything important is contained in both.[31] The documents stressed the desirability of coordination and cooperation in the economic, technical, and scientific spheres; the importance of improving division of labor by multilateral coordination of the separate national economic plans; the desirability of achieving high rates of industrialization and development, especially for the less-developed nations; and the eventual elimination of differences in levels of development among nations so that all can enter communism together.

Most important, the documents also stressed, as did the original statement of principles at CMEA's birth, that all nations were to be equal within CMEA, each was to have full independence and sovereignty and was not to be bound by the others' decisions on matters with which it disagreed. In other words, CMEA was to remain an organization in which action required "unanimity" rather than "majority" rule. CMEA was not endowed with supranational power. Clearly, since there were strong differences of opinion within CMEA over many possible courses of action relating to integration, CMEA's progress would undoubtedly be slowed as a result.

In order to enable progress with CMEA even without unanimity, Article IV of the 1960 Charter provides for the adoption of recommendations and decisions on matters with the consent of interested members only, such adoption not applying to other members. This is known as the "interested-party principle." As it turns out, the interested-party principle did not work, at least in the early and mid-1960s, because of the intensity of the debate over supranationality and fears, particularly on the part of the Rumanians, that they would be taken advantage of. In fact, they vetoed projects in which they were not interested, thereby preventing the "interested parties" from working together under the aegis of CMEA. Thus, the joint programming of Soviet bloc iron and steel production, which encompassed all CMEA members except Rumania and Outer Mongolia, was operated by Intermetall, an independent agency established in 1964 with head-quarters in Budapest. Similar independent agencies are the Common Wagon Pool, lacking only Mongolia's participation, and the Organization for Cooperation in Ball Bearings Industry, lacking only Rumania.

SUPRANATIONAL POWER VS. NATIONAL SOVEREIGNTY, 1962-1964

Despite the fact that the Charter and Basic Principles had supported national sovereignty against supranational power for CMEA, Khrushchev attempted to upgrade it in 1962 by calling for measures which implied a supranational power. These measures had to do mostly with coordination of planning and the nature of specialization, and before discussing the debate over supranational power, we digress briefly to explore these issues.

Coordination of Plans

So far coordination of plans had not been very "deep." Long-run *ex ante* coordination of plans could be implemented at several different levels. First, arrangements could be made for nations to increase or decrease output of specific commodities already being produced in the light of the changing requirements of its trading partners. Second, arrangements could be made for two or more nations to split up the production of multiproduct enterprises (for example, one nation producing five-ton trucks, the other two-and-one-half ton trucks, instead of each producing both kinds of trucks). This is called intraproduct specialization. Third, at a more profound level of division of labor, nations would stop producing entire ranges of products or industries and concentrate more heavily on others. This so-called interproduct specialization is harder to achieve, not only because of natural resistance to loss of an industry, but also because it is much harder to calculate comparative advantage when dealing with entirely different products than in intraproduct cases. Fourth, integration could proceed by joint financing of production, i.e., by capital flows as well as commodity flows. Fifth, two or more nations could jointly manage an enterprise, thereby joining capital and management. All these forms of coordination can be either bilateral or multilateral.

The coordination which has taken place so far in the Eastern bloc has been, with minor exceptions, mostly at the first and second levels and not on a very large scale. In the early 1950s, coordination took no more profound a form than the bilateral trading of surpluses which happened to develop. In 1954, the decision was made to coordinate national five-year plans. In the decade ending in 1965, implementation of this decision had been mostly on an *ex post* rather than *ex ante* basis, with national planning authorities doing little more than bilaterally reviewing mutual requirements *after* rather than *before* establishing their plans. Multilateral efforts were confined to the relatively trivial level of compiling material balances for a small number of commodities. Progress on specialization in the 1960s is summed up by Heiss:

> In practice, most specialization agreements have consisted of an allocation of production responsibility by type or size among countries already producing the items involved, permitting some economies of scale. Although several thousand products—concentrated in the engineering, chemical, and ferrous metals industries—are covered, the share of total output affected, even within these industries, is small (e.g., 6 to 7 percent of CMEA's machinery output).[32]

These figures are biased downward somewhat by the fact that the U.S.S.R. has such a small trade/GNP participation ratio. That is to say, the U.S.S.R. only trades about 3 percent of its GNP and one could not expect its specialization agreements to exceed this amount by much in specific industries. On some other issues Kaser says that: "In 1963 a Hungarian writer calculated that only 3-5 percent of total engineering output corresponded to the specialization agreements of Comecon";

that "no production lines seem to have been curtailed as a result of inter-product specialization"; and that "by 1961, the proportion of imported equipment in Comecon-member consumption was only 6.4 percent, against an estimate of 24 percent in the EEC."[33] As for multilateralization, a recent Soviet source says, "Until recently, multilateral treaties on production specialization and cooperation have not been practiced within the CMEA framework."[34] From this brief survey, one can only conclude that coordinated planning, specialization, and multilateralization made very little headway in the 1960s. Without supranational power invested in CMEA, this might have been expected. Some of the problems which developed are revealed in the following discussion on specialization.

Specialization

The problem of getting nations to agree to supranational planning and coordination of plans is highlighted by the history of the debates over specialization. As already noted, disagreements over specialization occur because no nation is willing to jettison an existing enterprise or industry. In the words of a Polish economist, "every socialist country accepts the wisdom of specialization," but "the difficulties appear when it comes to making actual specialization agreements . . . all socialist countries select, as a rule, the same or similar directions of specialization."[35] Among other things, this issue caused battle lines to be drawn between the more and less industrially developed nations in the Eastern bloc.

In the early stages of CMEA, it was more or less assumed that every nation would concentrate on industrializing as rapidly as possible, like the U.S.S.R. in the 1930s. By 1954, these policies had led to the development of a raw material shortage in the Eastern bloc. Industrialization had increased every nation's demand for raw materials and these demands had outstripped the development of supplies. While the U.S.S.R. reluctantly assumed responsibility for filling the gap (temporarily) and the CMEA members also began to import raw materials from non-Communist LDCs, the advanced nations of the bloc began to put pressure on the less advanced, especially Rumania and Bulgaria, to concentrate more on agriculture and extraction and less on industry. They felt that industrialization as a goal should be accomplished on a bloc-wide basis with comparative advantage dictating the directions of specialization of each nation. The CMEA LDCs, it was argued, were trying "to build up all the branches of industries; the existence of a socialist world system was not sufficiently taken into consideration in practice."[36] The LDCs, on the other hand, felt that each nation in the Eastern bloc was entitled to and should industrialize rapidly. One problem, already noted, was that the advanced nations did not want to give up the production of anything to the LDCs. As Montias points out, the LDCs should be encouraged to produce the simpler equipment (e.g., tractors, lathes, combines) as the advanced nations take over the production of more complex equipment in the metallurgical, chemical, and other industries. The simpler products generate large economies of scale and would be profitable to the LDCs—so profitable, unfortunately, that the advanced countries are unwilling to give them up.

Another battleground on which the specialization question was fought was in connection with the foreign-trade-profitability indexes used by the various Soviet bloc nations to determine, in the absence of rational prices, the composition of exports and imports (see Chapter 2). The LDC nations were opposed to uncritical use of the indexes on "classical infant industry grounds"—that comparative advantage must be viewed dynamically and not statically. As a Rumanian economist pointed out in 1957, "It is evident that if the profitability coefficient were decisive, a country with a weakly developed industry would find that the importation of finished products was more advantageous than their production. Such a conclusion would be tantamount to forsaking industrialization."[37] The Rumanians also pointed out that one should "take into account, along with calculations of economic effectiveness, the necessity of ensuring full employment, the preservation of equilibrium in the balance of payments, the role of a given good in raising labor productivity in the entire economy, the leveling of differences in economic development, and the consolidation of the country's defense capability."[38]

Much of the debate between the advanced and LDC nations centered on the issue of efficiency versus equalization, implied above. From an efficiency standpoint it makes sense to concentrate investments in new industry in the advanced nations, since they have the know-how, the skilled labor force, and the infrastructure to do the job most efficiently. On the other hand, the LDCs argue that the goal of efficiency should be subordinate to CMEA's avowed aim of equalizing development levels in all socialist nations. A Rumanian professor argued that specialization according to comparative advantage must be rejected, even if it leads to greater output for all nations, if it also increases the disparities in development levels between the richer and poorer nations.[39] In other words, equality is more important than efficiency. This is an argument that the advanced nations find hard to accept.

These, then, were some of the issues in the background as the debate over supranational power opened in 1962. Stalin had not cared about supranational economic power in the late 1940s and early 1950s because he could accomplish almost all of his objectives through the use of political power. Khrushchev wanted CMEA to have more power in order to substitute for the reduced political power which he personally was able to wield. He was, however, unwilling to jeopardize ratification of the Charter and Basic Principles by insisting on it before 1962. Many of the nations of Eastern Europe were hesitant about accepting supranationalism because of their bad experiences with the U.S.S.R. before 1956 and fears that the U.S.S.R. would dominate them through CMEA. Even if Soviet behavior before 1956 had been exemplary, the Eastern European nations might have been loath to give up sovereignty. A major difference, it should be recognized, between CMEA and the EEC and EFTA is that the former contains one nation which is much larger and more powerful than the rest and therefore more threatening, in contrast with the latter two organizations whose members are nations of more equal size and power.

The Debate

Khrushchev's proposal was first enunciated in August 1962 in an article in *Kommunist*, official journal of the Communist party, and then in a speech on November 19 to the Central Committee of the Communist Party of the Soviet Union.[40] He called for the establishment in Comecon of "a unified planning organ, empowered to compile common plans and to decide organizational matters."[41] The proposal involved coordination of long-term plans, including cooperative planning of investment projects and increased capital lending in the Soviet bloc. This was truly a proposal for the establishment of a supranational authority which could make planning decisions adverse to the interests of some nations, but nevertheless obligatory. As Khrushchev put it in his article in *Kommunist*:

International specialization is advantageous not only to small countries, but also to such large states as the Soviet Union. . . . The Soviet

Union is even prepared to reduce its output of some kinds of manufactures if it proves more expedient to produce them in other CMEA countries.[42]

This is the first major attempted break with the principle of national sovereignty which had been reiterated many times and had recently been codified in the Charter and Basic Principles. Actually, the U.S.S.R. had previously refused to enter into any specialization agreement involving a reduction in its production of specific goods.

The Rumanians, above all, fought this basic change in approach. They were reported to have threatened to leave CMEA if Khrushchev's proposals prevailed. In April 1964 they said:

> Our Party has very clearly expressed its point of view, declaring that, since the essence of the suggested measures lies in shifting some functions of economic management from the competence of the respective state to the attribution of super-state bodies or organs, these measures are not in keeping with the principles which underlie the relations between socialist countries. The idea of a single planning body for CMEA has the most serious economic and political implications . . . undoubtedly, if some socialist countries deem it fit to adopt in the direct relations between them forms of cooperation different from those unanimously agreed upon within CMEA, that is a question which exclusively concerns these countries.[43]

Other nations in the Eastern bloc sprang to the support of the Soviet position, while the Chinese supported the Rumanians. The Chinese accused the Soviets of using supranationality as a device for exploiting other members of Comecon, just as the "monopoly capitalists" were using the Common Market.

The polemics alluded to above had their material basis in some down-to-earth issues, the most important being the Galati Steel Works. In 1960, the Russians had agreed to supply Rumania with about half a billion dollars' worth of machinery and equipment for the expansion of these steel works.[44] These supplies never came. The proposal was strongly attacked. It was deemed unwise by other Soviet bloc members for Rumania to expand her steel output because: (1) the U.S.S.R. was expanding sufficiently to meet the needs of the bloc; (2) Rumania's contention that part of her increase in output would go to the West was criticized as inadequate grounds for going ahead with the investment; (3) the expansion was based on increased imports of iron ore and

CMEA policy was to establish "integrated iron and steel centres . . . preferably . . . in countries that are fully, or nearly fully, provided with ore and processed fuel, or at least possess one of the two."[45] From this incident, the Rumanians must have seen clearly the direction that international division of labor would take if their plans were subordinated to CMEA domination.

The debate raged for three years, with the Rumanians holding their ground. They managed to remain in CMEA despite their opposition to Khrushchev, who was unwilling to impose unanimity on the Rumanians at this point. For one thing, he wanted as much support as he could get in his dispute with the Chinese. For another, while he clearly desired greater intrabloc integration, both for political and economic reasons, there is some question as to how high a value he placed on it. Finally, it is important to stress that throughout this whole period, even though Rumania fought the U.S.S.R. to preserve what it viewed as its national self-interest, it remained internally a tightly controlled Communist state using orthodox central planning techniques. There was never any threat of Rumanian defection from the "system," such as Hungary posed in 1956 and Czechoslovakia in 1968.

The debate on supranationality was resumed later in the 1960s. Before returning to it, we will examine some other economic issues, some of which involved political or economic conflict.

OTHER INTEGRATION ISSUES

The major integration issue was supranationality versus national sovereignty. In the absence of either the grant of supranational power to CMEA or the exercise of raw political-military power by the U.S.S.R., integration had to proceed by other mechanisms. Some of these had the character of a zero-sum game, that is, a gain to one country involved an equivalent loss to another. Such is the case of determining the structure of relative prices to be used in intra-CMEA trade. Under these circumstances, of course, any resolution of the economic problem is affected by the political power and strategy of the nations involved. Solutions to other problems are more of the nature of positive-sum games, that is, everyone gains although some may gain more than others. So, for example, all the nations of CMEA stood to gain from a solution to the trading impasse created by inconvertibility and rigid bilateralism.

A CMEA Pricing System

Earlier in this chapter, the question of whether or not the U.S.S.R. uses its power to affect prices in intrabloc trade was discussed. This discussion assumed that the general framework of relative intrabloc prices were based, to a first approximation, on world prices, for reasons discussed in the preceding chapter. World prices have provided an uneasy compromise solution to the pricing problem for the past twenty-five years. It is an uneasy compromise because the particular pattern of price relationships which exists in world markets tends to favor some Eastern bloc nations over others. Thus it turns out that the year-to-year bilateral bargaining sessions over prices, as discussed above, are superimposed upon more fundamental world-price relationships which yield larger profits to some nations than to others.

The use of world prices actually began in the late 1940s, when the Soviet bloc nations found themselves without a price system of their own on which to base intrabloc trade. In 1950, because of the speculative rise in world prices of raw materials which resulted from the Korean War, it was decided to fix world prices at the levels which had existed just as inflation began (so-called 1950 "stop prices") for use in intrabloc trade. These prices were held for some three or four years and then began to be adjusted on an ad hoc basis for disparities with the new world prices. The raw material suppliers in the Soviet bloc must have been behind these changes since the "stop prices" deprived them of large profits. In 1958, it was agreed that prices in the near future would be based on 1957 average world prices, thereby formalizing the change from the 1950 "stop prices." Primary product prices were still high in 1957 and the raw material suppliers were content with this arrangement. Despite constant debate and recrimination over the equity of these prices, they were changed only on an ad hoc basis until it was agreed to use average world prices for 1960-1964 as a basis for prices in the 1966-1970 period.[46] As noted above, this last change hurt the raw material suppliers (U.S.S.R., Rumania, Bulgaria, and Poland), since the terms of trade of primary commodities relative to manufacturers had fallen about 10 percent from 1957 to 1960-1964. In fact, the U.S.S.R. was hurt so badly by this price change that, according to Kaser, this was one reason why the other bloc countries agreed in December 1966 to invest in the development of Soviet raw materials.[47] These prices apparently have remained the basis for CMEA trade in the 1971-1975 period, although subject to piecemeal ad hoc changes, such as the rise in the price of oil in 1975. Because of worldwide inflation, beginning in 1976 prices will be changed every year using as a standard the average of Western prices over the previous five years.

The use of historic world prices in CMEA has, among other things, resulted in the creation of a rigidity of trading relationships going beyond plain bilateralism. Because prices of raw materials have tended to be below what supply and demand would dictate in intrabloc trade, the raw material suppliers have attempted to segment their trade so that they exchange raw materials for other raw materials on the one hand and manufactured goods for other manufactured goods on the other. This is one way of avoiding unfair terms of trade when raw materials are exchanged for manufactured goods. This kind of barter, of course, reduces the possible gains from trade.

The practical debate over pricing had its theoretical counterpart. As noted, one goal of CMEA has been to develop its "own" independent pricing system based on socialist world market conditions. Such prices would be "fair" prices; in Marxist terminology, these prices would reflect "equivalent exchange." Those nations which have received poorer terms of trade under the world prices in use by the Soviet bloc have always argued that such world prices reflect "nonequivalent exchange." Their position is similar to that held by Prebisch and the Latin Americans that exchange between the advanced Western industrial nations and the nonsocialist LDCs is at prices or terms of trade which are unfair to the latter. While the Marxists argue that capitalist world prices are "nonequivalent" and socialist world prices "equivalent," the fact is that when it comes down to deciding a basis upon which to determine an "own" socialist world price system, differences of opinion are evident, each nation favoring that system which yields it the best terms of trade. The Bulgarians, for example, have struck for "man-hours" as the basis of their "own" system. Since the Bulgarians have the lowest labor productivity in the Soviet bloc, exporting labor-intensive and importing capital-intensive commodities, such a price basis would mean high prices for their exports and low prices for their imports. The advanced nations have opposed this standard and have argued for prices based on the costs of all factors of production; some want the inclusion of demand factors, and others still want world prices as the basis for prices in the Soviet bloc. There are almost as many formulas as there are countries and economists.

Who benefits most from the pricing arrangements which have prevailed in intra-CMEA trade? We pointed out earlier that many Western observers believe that the U.S.S.R. exploits the other CMEA nations through price discrimination. Despite the evidence presented above that this is not the case, this view has persisted, largely, no doubt, because it provides a kind of support for the views of those who feel strongly about Soviet political domination in the bloc. In contrast, over the past fifteen years (at least until the price increases of 1974), the U.S.S.R. has viewed itself as an economic loser rather than gainer in intrabloc trade. There is no reason to doubt the sincerity of Soviet views on this matter. It has been quite clear, as noted above, that raw materials are underpriced relative to machinery and equipment in intrabloc trade, and the U.S.S.R. is basically a raw material exporter and a much greater importer than exporter of machinery and equipment.

Two studies supporting Soviet complaints have recently been completed.[48] Subject to the limitations of the data, these studies prove not only that the Soviet Union does not gain much from trade but that it actually loses and would be better off not trading. Since most Soviet trade is with CMEA, the conclusion applies largely to intrabloc trade. The technique applied is to use a U.S.S.R. input-output table to calculate first how much in basic factors of production (capital, labor, natural resources) is required to produce, say, $1 million worth of exports. Then an estimate is made of how much of the same factors would be required if the U.S.S.R. were to produce $1 million worth of the products it actually imports. If a nation were benefiting from trade, presumably it would cost less in factors of production to produce the exports than to produce the imports. McMillan found the unbelievable: that a given value of exports cost the U.S.S.R. 15 percent more capital, 16 percent more labor, and 20 percent more natural resources than did the same value of import replacements. (His results were supported by Hewett's study.) Analyzing by country, Soviet losses were found to be concentrated in the trade with the more developed CMEA nations, especially East Germany and Czechoslovakia, but also Poland and Hungary. Since these nations all export machinery to and import raw materials from the U.S.S.R., Soviet complaints that they are not getting a fair deal in intrabloc trade are justified. Thus, if raw material prices were raised sufficiently, fewer raw materials would be needed to pay for a given amount of machinery and equipment and McMillan's findings would be reversed. This may soon occur, if it has not already, with the rise in prices of oil and gas in 1975.

All these years, the U.S.S.R. was clearly suffering, though not without complaint, very unfavorable intrabloc pricing arrangements. The economic and political power to enforce pricing arrangements which were much more to her advantage were there. Instead, she chose to trade off profits for "popularity," economics for politics.

Capital Flows: Aid and Investment

There are at least three justifications or explanations for capital flows among the nations of CMEA: one economic, one ideological, and one political.* Economically speaking, capital should flow from nations which have surplus capital and relatively low rates of return on investment to those which are capital short and stand to realize high rates of return. Efficiency and profitability are, of course, the major motives of private capital flows in the West. Ideologically, a major goal of CMEA, as stated in the Charter, is the equalization of levels of economic development among the CMEA nations so that they can all enter "full Communism" together. One method of achieving this goal is for the advanced nations to assist the LDCs through credits and other assistance. As usual, of course, those two goals may conflict—as in the Rumanian debate of the early 1960s about efficiency vs. equity. Finally, capital may be expected to achieve political goals. Obviously, political motivation is involved in "ideological" capital flow. But politics encompasses still more, and capital may flow wherever necessary to win friends and influence people regardless of whether it is efficiently or equitably used. This is particularly true of "aid," that is, credit extended on "concessionary" (below market price) terms.

Unfortunately, it is difficult to get data on intrabloc aid and investment. The extent of capital flows involved in various joint-investment projects are, with occasional exceptions, unknown. The best available data on Soviet loan commitments are presented in Table 3.4; unfortunately, this table is incomplete. Furthermore, there are few data available on loans by other CMEA nations and on the extent to which loans have been drawn down or repaid.

---

*This classification does not include the extraordinary capital flows to the U.S.S.R. through reparations, etc.

TABLE 3.4
Soviet Economic Aid to Communist Countries[1]
Million U.S. $

	1954-67	1968	1969	1970	1971	1972	1973	1974	1968-74	1954-74
Total	7,478	765	1,050	231	1,620	1,171	493	283	5,613	13,091
Eastern Europe	2,957	333	556	Negl.	1,111	–	–	–	2,000	4,957
Bulgaria	1,104	333	556	–	–	–	–	–	889	1,993
Czechoslovakia	14	–	–	–	–	–	–	–	–	14
East Germany	990	–	–	–	–	–	–	–	–	990
Hungary	348	–	–	–	–	–	–	–	–	348
Poland	378	–	–	–	1,111	–	–	–	1,111	1,489
Romania	123	–	–	Negl.	–	–	–	–	Negl.	123
Far East	1,067	–	–	–	–	–	–	–	–	1,067
China	495	–	–	–	–	–	–	–	–	495
North Korea	118	–	–	–	–	–	–	–	–	118
North Vietnam	454	–	–	–	–	–	–	–	–	454
Other	3,454	432	494	231	509	1,171	493	283	3,613	7,067
Albania	65	–	–	–	–	–	–	–	–	65
Cuba	1,472	432	494	231	509	631	493	283	3,073	4,545
Mongolia	1,609	–	–	–	–	–	–	–	–	1,609
Yugoslavia	308	–	–	–	–	540	–	–	540	848

[1] Excluding data for Eastern Europe prior to 1956 because war reparations and other assets and privileged arrangements obtained by the U.S.S.R. from these countries created a heavy net flow of capital toward the U.S.S.R. during these years; data are unavailable for North Korea and North Vietnam after 1965 and for Mongolia after 1967; the data exclude Soviet sugar subsidy payments to Cuba.

SOURCE: *Handbook of Economic Statistics, 1975* (Washington, D.C.: Central Intelligence Agency, August 1975), p. 70.

Economic motivations were clearly dominant in the joint investment and joint enterprise projects described above, the most important of which were the Friendship Oil Pipeline and the Peace Electricity Grid. This is true integration. But according to all reports, it has not occurred so far on a very large scale. Furthermore, with exceptions like the two just mentioned, most projects have been bilateral rather than multilateral. This is almost inevitable, given inconvertibility and rigid bilateralism and, until 1971, no all-CMEA investment bank. While economic motivations have been dominant, it should nevertheless be noted that the interdependencies which these projects create, especially those with the U.S.S.R., have an obviously important political dimension.

According to Janos Horvath, the total of loan commitments among all socialist nations from 1945 to 1969 was only $10.8 billion, of which $9.7 billion was drawn down. The Soviet Union was responsible for $8.8 billion, or all but $2 billion of this total. U.S. government estimates put the Soviet aid effort somewhat higher—at $9,293 million from 1954 to 1969 and at $13,091 million by 1974, as a result of a big increase in commitments in 1971 and 1972 (see Table 3.4).[49] The largest recipient of capital flows has been Cuba, which received approximately $4 1/2 billion in aid from the U.S.S.R. alone. Bulgaria, Mongolia, and Poland rank poor seconds. According to Horvath, China, possibly the poorest nation in the Communist bloc, ranked as second largest lender, with an $800 million total as of 1969. The only other net lender in the Communist bloc appears to have been Czechoslovakia.[50]

The small scale of these flows—probably less than one-sixth of one percent per year of donor GNPs, with the exception of 1971 and 1972—is self-evident. In comparison, official governmental aid granted by the major Western nations has probably averaged from one-half to two-thirds of one percent of GNPs, official plus private capital flows close to 1 percent.[51]

It seems fairly clear that the major motivation for most of the credits granted has been political. How else can one explain loans to other nations by China, the nation with the lowest per capita income in the Communist bloc? Would Cuba have received more than one-third of the credits extended by the U.S.S.R. if it were not the only Communist nation in the Western hemisphere? The credit extended to North Vietnam was motivated by obvious military and strategic considerations. Soviet loans to East Germany in 1953 (not shown in Table 3.4) and to Hungary and Poland in 1956 followed the uprisings in those nations, and the loan to Poland in February 1971 followed the food riots in Gdansk and other coastal cities in December 1970. Bulgaria may have been the major exception to the rule.

It is hard to explain the small scale of Soviet bloc credits in political terms. It might be argued that the total of some $13 billion in credits advanced since World War II was all that was required to mend fences and maintain stability in the bloc, particularly when political-military tools were available and used to achieve some of the same objectives. It could also be argued that while the motivation behind aid was primarily political rather than economic, economic factors nevertheless operated as a major constraining factor on the scale of the aid. First, as already noted, the very low interest rates—around 2 percent—which prevailed in the Soviet bloc on such loans provided a strong economic disincentive to donors who get much higher rates of return investing the same resources domestically. Second, as demonstrated in Chapter 2, given the over-full employment which characterizes these nations, aid to or investment in another nation always results in foregoing domestic use of such resources. Third, the Soviet bloc countries are all poor in comparison with the advanced Western nations and cannot be expected either to invest in or grant aid to other nations on the scale with which this is done by the advanced capitalist nations. In fact, in the Western scheme of things, China would be exclusively a recipient rather than a donor of aid. Finally, there are the other institutional and economic inhibitions mentioned already in connection with trade which are an obstacle to capital flows as well: irrational prices, inconvertibility, and bilateralism.

Labor Flows

Intercountry labor mobility has been marked largely by its absence among CMEA nations.[52] This has been true despite the existence of positive economic incentives, namely, higher wage levels in some nations than in others and surplus labor in some countries (mainly the LDCs) along with acute shortages in others. It is worth noting that both sets of incentives work in the same direction, that is, to encourage a flow from the less- to the more-advanced nations. In theory, this is a positive-sum game, and all nations should benefit from labor migration. In recent years some labor flows have occurred in CMEA: 3,000

Bulgarian lumberjacks to Siberia for which Bulgaria will receive payments in lumber; several thousand Hungarian workers to the G.D.R.; and a few thousand Polish workers to the G.D.R. There is, nevertheless, strong opposition, on principle, to such labor flows, in particular as a solution to employment problems; they are viewed as "capitalist." Perhaps even more fundamental is the fact that no satisfactory method has been found to the problem of determining the amount of compensation, if any, the donor nations should receive. The Communist nations feel they should be reimbursed for the training they have invested in their workers. This view is also presented by Soviet authorities as the basis of their recent exit tax on emigrants.

Labor flows do not look like a promising road to integration. Certainly not in comparison with the EEC and its more than 10 million immigrant workers!

Scientific-Technical Cooperation

One area in which it was generally believed that real progress would be made in CMEA was scientific-technical cooperation. It had often been argued that capitalism is held back by the private control of patents, preventing widespread exploitation of new ideas. This apparent barrier was removed from CMEA at the very beginning in 1949, when it was provided that there would be free exchange of documents relating to inventions and technological processes, as well as large-scale exchanges of scientists and specialists. Most of the Soviet bloc literature on technical exchanges is very positive and the figures presented, like those on the number of commodities under specialization agreements, give an impression of large-scale exchange of ideas and information. For example, one Soviet official said that the U.S.S.R. "has provided to other CMEA countries 75,000 sets of technical documents, standards and models and received 22,000."[53] These figures sound impressive and they may well be. On the other hand, another CMEA spokesman, not untypically, has complained that technical coperation "lags behind our needs and possibilities as well as behind the progress that has been achieved in this regard by the advanced industrial countries."[54]

It is difficult to evaluate the validity of this complaint. Several factors appear to have been responsible. First, while free dissemination of technology certainly has some advantages, it also has disadvantages. The major disadvantage is that the donors, usually the advanced nations, have no economic incentive to share with others the fruits of their research which are costly to them. Conversely, the recipients have little incentive to devote resources to research when they can obtain its results free of charge. This problem has become more important since the recent economic reforms with their increased emphasis on decentralized economic incentives. As a G.D.R. representative has argued, "scientific-technological findings represent merchandise whose exchange requires stimulation by economic means."[55] This principle now seems to have been accepted in CMEA. So far, however, it has not facilitated technical exchanges but has simply pushed the problem back to another level, namely, that of the appropriate payment. The difficulty in determining appropriate payment is partly a difficulty which is inherent in how to determine a charge for technological information and research and has also been a problem in the West; in the East, however, it is compounded by the usual difficulties relating to irrational prices and exchange rates.[56] This is the second set of factors slowing technical cooperation in CMEA. Third, and this may be the major deterrent, the CMEA nations have recently become aware of their own technological backwardness vis-à-vis the West, and their interest in importing technology from each other, particularly if they have to pay for it, is dwindling as they cast their eyes and their foreign exchange westward. Reasons behind this trend are discussed in detail in Chapter 4.

Inconvertibility, Bilateralism, and the International Bank for Economic Cooperation (IBEC)

Inconvertibility and the need to balance trade bilaterally between each pair of nations remains a serious problem for CMEA, substantially reducing the possible gains from intrabloc trade. A multilateral clearing agency was established in 1957 in an unsuccessful attempt to deal with the problem. In 1963, IBEC was created with the major purpose of multilateralizing intrabloc trade. All CMEA trade had to be transacted through the Bank and the balances recorded there (paid for) in newly created so-called transferable (*perevodnye*) rubles. These rubles were called transferable because in theory a surplus of transferable rubles in trade with one CMEA nation could be used to pay off a deficit with another. But simply declaring that a transferable ruble exists does not make it transferable or, for that matter, convertible. The objective conditions which result in "commodity inconvertibility" still exist. It does not matter whether a nation which has a trade surplus earns zlotys, leis, levs, or transferable rubles—the currency cannot be spent freely on unplanned imports from the other Soviet bloc nations. The final result of these attempts has been dismal failure. IBEC compensations never exceeded more than a few percent of total consumption.

That the IBEC transferable ruble technique could not succeed was foreseen by more than one Eastern economist. It was proposed as an alternative, especially by Poland, that IBEC develop a large fund of convertible currency and gold and that this be used instead of transferable rubles to settle CMEA trade imbalances. Thus, for example, while East Germany might be unwilling to run a surplus with Poland settled in zlotys or transferable rubles, it obviously would be willing to do so for convertible currency. There is considerable question, however, as to whether this would work, since Poland obviously would be loath to let a deficit develop with East Germany which had to be settled in convertible currency when this could also be used to settle a deficit with a Western nation. In fact, this raises the fundamental problem of how to keep the CMEA fund of hard currencies from flowing to the West.

Aside from this objection regarding its workability, two other factors may have militated against the use of hard currency reserves to settle intra-CMEA debts. First, it would have been politically difficult for the U.S.S.R. to permit Western convertible currency to replace transferable rubles as the means of payment in CMEA trade. Second, and this is more important, the burden of financing the scheme would have had to fall on the U.S.S.R. A convertible currency plus a gold fund adequate to multilateralize intra-CMEA trade would have to be in the billions of dollars, and the U.S.S.R. has been the only CMEA nation with reserves of such magnitude. In fact, until the recent rise in gold and petroleum prices, sufficient reserves may not have even been available.

Failure to solve the problems of inconvertibility and bilateralism is unfortunate, since all members of CMEA stand to gain from a solution. But the problem cannot be made to disappear by decree or by the use of administrative (IBEC) rather than economic measures. Only radical economic reforms which decentralize markets and price-setting and lead to much freer trade can solve the problem. Ultimately, therefore, convertibility and multilateralism can be viewed as largely political casualties—victims of the political forces which militate against the introduction of radical economic reforms in the CMEA nations. The obstacles to these reforms are discussed further in Chapter 6.

Developments Since Khrushchev

While individual steps toward integration of the CMEA nations continued to be taken after Brezhnev and Kosygin seized power in 1964, at a more profound level forces opposed to integration were developing. As we have seen, advocates of national sovereignty had won out over those favoring supranational power for CMEA. Capital, labor, and technical know-how flowed at an embarrassingly slow pace across CMEA borders, and ways of eliminating the obstacles to these flows which were acceptable to all nations were not immediately apparent. No headway had been made toward solving the problems of inconvertibility and bilateralism, which were stifling commodity trade, despite the establishment of the much-heralded IBEC. While Rumania participated in a number of joint investment projects in CMEA, including a chemical complex with the G.D.R. and Hungary and a paper-making mill with Czechoslovakia, she simultaneously continued her rapid drift toward the West. The percentage of Rumania's trade with the Western industrialized nations increased from 16 percent in 1958 to 45 percent in 1968. To the East, the Sino-Soviet conflict appeared no nearer resolution than before and remained the single most divisive issue in the Communist world. The estrangement of Rumania and China were responsible, in part, for the gradual decline in the 1960s of the percentage of intrabloc to total trade of the Communist nations, betokening, perhaps, reduced "integration." In contrast, intratrade increased much faster than total trade between 1960 and 1970 in both the EEC and EFTA in conformity with integration plans.[57]

Another major disruptive factor was the internal economic difficulties that all of the CMEA nations were experiencing. These difficulties were objectively recorded in the form of slower economic growth rates throughout the bloc. On the whole, GNP had grown extremely rapidly in every Eastern nation throughout the 1950s, but growth rates fell in the 1960s by an average of two percentage points. This deceleration, furthermore, stood in stark contrast to the continued successes of the nations of the European Economic Community and the increase in U.S. growth rates in that period. The reasons for the decline in CMEA growth rates are discussed in the next chapter. In short, these were related to the facts that the opportunities for "extensive" growth were declining and that the shift to "intensive" growth was particularly handicapped by the relative inability of centrally planned economies to develop, introduce, and diffuse new technology (discussed in Chapter 4). This fact, and its recognition, had two important consequences which adversely affected intrabloc integration.

First, internal economic reforms were introduced by each CMEA nation. The reforms were, of course, part of the Khrushchev heritage. His sanctioning of discussions of the well-known Liberman Reform proposals, as well as some initial experimentation along these lines, removed the taint of heresy from other Eastern European reform movements. The reforms which were introduced into the various nations, including the U.S.S.R.'s so-called Kosygin reform, differed from each other in timing, nature, and extent. As noted earlier, the Hungarian and Czech reforms were the most profound and allowed a substantial degree of decentralization of decision making to the level of the enterprise. Both reforms practically eliminated central planning by direct controls. On the other hand, central planning was maintained by most of the other nations in much the same detail as before. However, an attempt was made to improve planning by rationalizing pricing, consolidating enterprises into industrial associations, reducing the number of planning targets, and the like. Furthermore, some of the enterprises and industrial associations in some countries were allowed limited authority to trade in foreign markets without having to deal through the foreign trade combines. Implementation of these various reforms forced a rethinking of the whole question of cooperation and integration within CMEA, since they involved not only changes in economic mechanisms but changes which varied from country to country. Thus, for example, if—as was the case in Hungary—many enterprises were freed by the reform from central-planning directives and allowed to make decisions based on market criteria, it would be inconsistent to require these same enterprises to fulfill a planned role in CMEA. Furthermore, it became clear that such enterprises would find it more natural to transact business with other decentralized enterprises—capitalist or socialist—than with, say, a Bulgarian or Soviet foreign trade organization operating under state directives.

Second, the economic slowdown, with its difficulties in the area of technology, created a strong incentive in all of the Eastern nations to look westward for help. True, as noted above, there was a considerable transfer of technology within the Eastern bloc and a very substantial trade in machinery, equipment, and other manufactured products. However, it was no secret that many of the products being traded between CMEA nations were of relatively low quality and that in most areas, Eastern technology lagged behind Western.

Despite the difficulties CMEA was experiencing and despite the pull that potential East-West trade created—or perhaps because of it—Soviet interest in making CMEA integration more successful was renewed in the 1966-1968 period. There was a revival of attacks on Rumania on the issue of supranationality and, as usual, the Rumanians responded vigorously. By this time, no more than half of Rumania's trade was with CMEA nations, and she was the one nation in the group not dependent on the U.S.S.R. for oil. Her interest in further CMEA integration had ebbed to a low point. At this time, Rumania was supported in her opposition to supranational planning by Czechoslovakia and Hungary. The latter nations were not necessarily opposed to greater integration in CMEA; in fact they were for it. Their support for Rumania was based first on the fact that, despite the developing internal reforms, implementation of integration seemed destined to be grounded in "centralist" techniques rather than market mechanisms because of the very limited nature of the reforms in most of the other CMEA nations, and especially in the U.S.S.R. Second, both nations wanted very much to expand their East-West trade and feared that integration might take place at the expense of such an expansion. In terms of our customs union model, they were afraid that integration would be trade-diverting rather than trade-creating.

The conservative leaders, Gomulka (Poland) and Ulbricht (G.D.R.), wanted integration for political reasons. Much like the Russians, they believed that integration would make the Eastern bloc more monolithic. The Poles were also motivated economically to push for more integration. As a still relatively backward nation they stood to benefit a great deal from increased cooperation with the two most advanced nations in the bloc, Czechoslovakia and East Germany. However, they did feel that integration could not be implemented by purely administrative measures; greater use of market instruments and financial measures were necessary as a supplement to long-term planning coordination. While East Germany was interested in strengthening Comecon for political reasons, it was less interested in it as an economic institution. East Germany's major trading partners were the U.S.S.R. and West Germany, and it was able to deal with these two nations satisfactorily on a bilateral bargaining basis. As the most advanced nation in the Eastern bloc, East Germany needed little from the other Eastern European nations.

THE BREZHNEV DOCTRINE–CZECHOSLOVAKIA, AUGUST 1968

Before August 1968 it was not at all clear how far the Czech and Hungarian reforms might develop in the direction of market socialism. The situation appeared fairly open. On the one hand, even without drastic reforms, the Rumanians had been defying the U.S.S.R. on supranationality, had diverted their trade significantly to the West, and were engaging in an increasing number of industrial cooperation agreements and joint ventures with Western nations. In the latter activities, they had plenty of company among other CMEA nations. On the other hand, while Hungarian and Czech trade had not shifted sharply to the West, their reforms were fairly significant and did promise to evolve further into true market socialism à la Yugoslavia. Furthermore, these two reforms did give promise of facilitating East-West trade and leading Czechoslovakia and Hungary away from CMEA.

The Czech reform, however, did embody another set of dimensions which in 1968 was not present (as yet) in the Hungarian reform, at least to the same degree, and certainly not in Rumania or in any other CMEA nations. We refer to the fact that decentralization of economic power and activity was accompanied by an analogous liberalization in the political and intellectual spheres. In fact, there was an unprecedented development of freedom of speech and press in 1968, genuine elections appeared to be in the offing, and it was clearly just a matter of time before workers' councils assumed control of state enterprises.

In August 1968 Soviet-led Warsaw Treaty Organization troops marched into Czechoslovakia; shortly afterwards, the Dubcek regime was deposed. It seems clear that the Czech reform had gone, in the Soviet view, beyond tolerable limits just as the Hungarian political situation had gotten out of hand and threatened the stability of Soviet hegemony in Eastern Europe in 1956. In a speech in Warsaw November 12, 1968, Brezhnev enunciated the Moscow or Brezhnev Doctrine, as it is now called:

When the internal and external forces inimical to Socialism seek to influence the development of a Socialist country with the aim of restoring the capitalist system, when the threat to Socialism in this country becomes a threat to the security of the entire Socialist community, then this ceases to be a national problem. It becomes a general problem which must be the concern of all Socialist countries.[58]

The invasion of Czechoslovakia and subsequent enunciation of this doctrine meant, in effect, that the U.S.S.R. was openly assuming supranational political powers. The assumption of these powers was in defiance of previous understandings by Warsaw Pact members that each nation possessed political sovereignty on internal matters and that its territory was inviolate.[59]

To the extent that the attempts to confer supranational economic powers on CMEA were politically rather than economically motivated, these attempts were no longer so necessary. In fact, despite Khrushchev's brave words in 1962, the U.S.S.R. had never been very enthusiastic about economic integration for its own sake. As a large, self-sufficient nation, its potential gains from trade were never on such a scale that the U.S.S.R. would have been willing to subordinate its domestic planning to overall CMEA direction or control. The result was that in the immediate aftermath of the Czech invasion, pressures to confer supranational economic power on CMEA subsided for the moment. The events of August 1968 did, however, have two important effects on the future of CMEA nations. First, as suggested above, it was quite clear that the "economic" reforms had to be just that—spillover into politics was to be avoided at all costs. Immediately following the Czech invasion, the Czech and Yugoslavian reforms were subjected to a barrage of criticism. At first there was some feeling that this presaged a return to strictly centralist planning. This was not the case, however. The Russians were not strongly opposed to reforms per se but simply to reforms which threatened the monolithic political structure. Nevertheless, it is probably true that aside from internal political opposition to reform in each Eastern nation, the Czech experience bears some responsibility for the fact that conservative rather than radical reforms continue to dominate the Eastern European scene. It is a minor miracle and tribute to their "dexterity" that the Hungarians have succeeded in maintaining their radical reform relatively intact. They have managed to keep economics and politics fairly well separated, a case of skating on very thin ice. They have also consistently supported the U.S.S.R. in its foreign policies.

The second major consequence of the events of August 1968 was that the incipient disintegration of CMEA, for the various reasons mentioned earlier, was effectively halted for the time begin. As one observer put it, even Rumania then began to attend CMEA meetings regularly.[60] While East-West relations were not forbidden or even seriously discouraged, they certainly could no longer be flaunted as Rumania had been wont to do. It was also clear that serious attempts to reduce obstacles to CMEA integration would continue to be made.

POLAND, DECEMBER 1970

The above conclusions regarding the implications of the Brezhnev Doctrine are not inconsistent with the events surrounding the Polish riots in December 1970. These events, like the invasion of Czechoslovakia, were quite revealing of the attitudes and concerns of the Soviet leaders.

The Polish riots in Gdansk and Szczecin were triggered by Chairman Gomulka's decision to increase the prices of food and other necessities by some 15-20 percent in mid-December of 1970. The strikes and worker demonstrations spread to other cities, including Lodz. The rise in prices, while obviously badly timed just before Christmas, probably would not have generated such a reaction had it been an isolated setback to the standard of living. In fact, the Polish economy at the time was probably mismanaged as badly as that of any CMEA nation since Czechoslovakia in the early 1960s. Gomulka had introduced bits of reform here and there, but they were poorly coordinated and the result had been virtual stagnation for several years, particularly in the standard of living. It was not only that there was little increase in the quantity of consumers' goods available; in addition, the warehouses were full of goods which no one would buy because they were of poor quality or generally not in demand. In addition, inept agricultural policies and poor weather had sharply reduced the supply of meat, and industrial reforms had led to rising unemployment.

Within a few days after the initial riots, the Gomulka government fell and Edward Gierek took power. The U.S.S.R. made no move to interfere and, in fact, extended Poland credits in February 1971 to help Gierek put the nation back on its feet.

Why did the Russians not intervene as they had done in Czechoslovakia two years earlier? Basically because Czechoslovakia represented to the U.S.S.R. a case of potential political disaffection, albeit potential economic success, whereas Poland was a case of economic failure but with no immediate threat of political disaffection. In Czechoslovakia, intellectuals and liberals were in the vanguard of change; in Poland, the working class was demanding an improved standard of living. A rising standard of living is a goal that, in recent years, Communist governments not only pay lip service to but are prepared to guarantee, if possible; political freedom is not. "Consumerism" has become a fact of life in CMEA. The U.S.S.R. is clearly concerned with the long-term political instability which may result from the economic slowdowns which the CMEA nations have been experiencing, and this is a major reason for continued experimentation with reforms and for increased East-West trade. Poland represented to the U.S.S.R. a situation in which a reliable but incompetent leader was replaced by a reliable and—it was hoped—more competent one.

THE COMPREHENSIVE PROGRAM AND AFTER

Even as the Czech reform was being partially dismantled and the Rumanians were being scolded for their economic drift to the West, discussions were proceeding on how to achieve better CMEA integration. The debates which took place before the Comprehensive Program was adopted have been admirably chronicled by Schaeffer (1972). The interests, desires, and fears of each country on virtually all issues are discussed. In truth, the Comprehensive Program which was finally adopted in July 1971 does represent a compromise among many diverse interests.[61]

Just what is the Comprehensive Program? Basically, it is a long-term (fifteen to twenty years) set of proposals which cover an enormous range of economic and scientific activity. On the economic level, planning includes coordination of programs aimed at increasing division of labor, foreign trade flows, and joint investment projects. The amount of coordination activity envisaged is truly enormous and will, if implemented, occupy the energies of thousands and thousands of persons. There is to be joint planning of individual branches of the economy by interested nations. Capital investment is to be coordinated in areas of mutual interest. Planning is to be bilateral and multilateral. Joint research is to be conducted in a long list of scientific and technical areas.[62] A full forty pages are required to list the sectors and kinds of "industrial collaboration" which are to take place.[63] Direct ties between agencies and organizations of Comecon are to be expanded. New international economic associations are to be created to facilitate collaboration, and so forth. Clearly, everything imaginable is included.

The Comprehensive Program represents an attempt to grapple with some very difficult problems, but it is not at all clear that the solutions and mechanisms adopted are adequate to the tasks. Greater integration appears to be hoped for, as demonstrated by the fact that over the period 1971-1975 intra-CMEA trade is expected to grow considerably faster than total trade—according to the individual plans of each of the CMEA nations.[64] If fulfilled, this would represent a significant reversal of the secular trend since 1955 in which the percentage of intra-CMEA to total trade declined in favor of East-West and East-LDC trade. Since it had been agreed during the earlier discussions that the Comprehensive Program would not interfere with East-West relations, and it was clear that expansion of East-West relations was held in high priority in practically all of the CMEA nations, the validity of these plans must be called into question. Much increased East-West and intra-CMEA trade would have been possible simultaneously, of course, if the total trade of the CMEA nations had been expected to expand more rapidly than before. In fact, the rate of increase in total CMEA trade is expected to decline. It seems clear, therefore, that this represents a case in which conflicting goals have not been reconciled successfully, a fact which is reflected in inconsistent plans.

Fears that the U.S.S.R., which was primarily responsible for initiating the Comprehensive Program, would insist on supranational power for CMEA were much on the minds of the smaller nations, but these fears were essentially unfounded. The Comprehensive Program assures that socialist economic integration is to be carried out:

... on an entirely voluntary basis and is not accompanied by the creation of supranational organs, nor does it affect matters pertaining to internal planning. . . .

... on the basis of respect for national sovereignty, independence, and national interests, of nonintervention in the internal affairs of nations, and of total equality, mutual advantage, and comradely reciprocal aid . . . .[65]

Basically, the Brezhnev-Kosygin formula for integration through the Comprehensive Program is, by a multiplication of administratively determined projects, to interlock the CMEA economies with each other on a much larger scale than before. Among other things, this would include investment on a much larger scale by Eastern Europe in the development of Soviet raw materials. Over the long run, if such a process were successful, integration would occur without the need for supranational power. One may, of course, question whether large-scale integration will develop via such a mechanism; and whether integration so motivated is likely to be economically efficient; and what political pressures, if any, have been required to get some of the projects on the drawing boards.

On planning techniques and criteria for improving division of labor, the Comprehensive Program has almost nothing to say. There is one vague statement on planning:

Comecon member nations proceed from the fact that the system of economic and scientific-technical collaboration of COMECON member nations is based on common patterns of socialist construction, on the fundamental principles of socialist economic management, and on the organic combination of the coordination of plans as the basic method of organizing collaboration with the more extensive employment of commodity-monetary relations.[66]

By referring to "organic . . . coordination," this statement clearly envisages some degree of *ex ante* coordination rather than the *ex post* coordination which has characterized the past, and also a kind of coordination which presumably is based on rational economic calculations. Nowhere is there any clue as to how, precisely, this is to be done. Reference to "collaboration . . . based on fundamental principles of socialist economic management" further confuses the issue, since these "principles" differ considerably from country to country as a result of the different timing and character of various economic reforms. This interpretation is supported by the admission that there will be "more extensive employment of commodity-monetary relations." But until central planning by direct controls is given up by the U.S.S.R. and the other nations which have not adopted liberal reforms, rational organic coordination will not be implemented and commodity-monetary relations will not be substantially expanded. Elsewhere it is stated that expansion of trade ties "will continue to be based on government monopolies of foreign trade."[67] This does not suggest such liberalization or expansion of commodity-monetary relations.

The program refers to "joint planning of individual branches of industry" as a "new form of collaboration in planning."[68] It is not clear just what is new about it, particularly in view of the fact that it also states, "The autonomous nature of internal planning is preserved under joint planning. Under joint planning, national ownership of corresponding production facilities and resources is retained."[69]

The part of the Comprehensive Program dealing with convertibility and multilateralism digs no deeper, in my opinion, than does the section on plan coordination. The Comprehensive Program refers to the development of unplanned trade, to the development of a "collective currency" which will eventually (by 1980) be convertible into national currencies, and to further study of foreign trade pricing.[70] As already indicated above, convertibility and multilateralism require as necessary (though not sufficient in themselves) conditions that planning be accomplished by market mechanisms and prices be rationalized, and that national currencies then be linked to each other by effective exchange rates. This requires radical internal reforms, but there is nothing in the program to suggest that such reforms will materialize. Only the Hungarians have been unambiguously in favor of such reforms; the U.S.S.R. and East Germany remain steadfastly opposed to them, as do the Rumanians and Bulgarians. The goals of unplanned trade and convertible currencies remain just goals, with no hints as to how they are to be achieved. In fact, the introduction of the term "collective currency" along with the "transferable ruble" suggests some sort of compromise over issues which could only be resolved to the depth of inventing a new term. It may well be the case, as noted earlier, that the U.S.S.R. is hopeful that the Comprehensive Program will lead to successful integration simply through its multiplication of administrative measures, thereby ending the need for radical reforms. Given enough integration by administrative measures, of course, little would remain to be done by market mechanisms, since all trade flows would be predetermined. How efficient such integration would be is another question, of course.

The most positive financial measures may be a proposed increase in activity by IBEC and, especially, the use of the new International Investment Bank (IIB), which began business in January 1971, before the Comprehensive Program was adopted. It is promised that IBEC will use credit and interest more actively and more flexibly to promote trade turnover, and that the question of increasing the bank's capital with convertible currency will be studied. A high interest charge on intrabloc debts would have the beneficial effect of encouraging some genuine multilateralism in intrabloc trade, at the same time that it encourages chronic debtors to settle their accounts. The effects are likely to be minor, however, if, as is likely, the interest charges are not differentiated by country and do not reflect market conditions for each currency flexibly and accurately.

The International Investment Bank was established with a capital of 1 billion rubles, of which 300 million is in convertible currency or gold. It is designed to grant medium and long-term credits to finance projects in CMEA of mutual interest. It can lend from its own capital but it is also authorized to raise funds in third countries. Interest rates on loans within the CMEA bloc vary from 4 to 6 percent; on convertible currency loans for purchases in the West, rates are governed by conditions in world financial markets. The IIB, by its creation of what might be called a formal bloc-capital market, cannot help but multilateralize, somewhat, bloc-capital flows. Whether or not these flows will also be expanded, and by how much, will depend on the loan policies of the Bank as they unfold, and also on the extent to which the Bank is able to expand CMEA bloc investment operations through loans from the West. The prospects for either multilateralization or expansion of CMEA bloc capital flows through the IIB do not appear, to me, to be very great at this point. It must be remembered that intrabloc capital transfers are implemented by intrabloc commodity transfers (imports of capital equipment, etc.) when the loans are drawn upon, and exports of other commodities when the repayments are made. So long as there is inconvertibility and bilateralism and the internal economic conditions which make these distortions necessary, the capital transfer process will be as inhibited as the trade process is.

The IIB, incidentally, represents a break with the principle of unanimity in CMEA affairs. First, it was agreed that the IIB would be a CMEA organization even if one or more CMEA members refused to join, and the Rumanians did not join initially. Second, it was agreed that IIB decisions could be implemented if three-fourths of the members were in favor of them; unanimity was not required. When this latter decision was made, it was not clear what its implications were. In the course of discussions, its impact was weakened and it was interpreted, finally, to apply only to minor issues, major issues still requiring unanimity.[71]

The IIB can be used, in principle, to facilitate one or both of two of CMEA's goals: the equalization of levels of development and per capita incomes and the facilitation of planned integration through the financing of joint investment projects. The equalization goal is always presented as one of the major goals of CMEA, and in this the Comprehensive Program is no exception. Actually, the per capita incomes of the CMEA nations have been substantially equalized over the past two decades, as Table 3.5 indicates.

TABLE 3.5
National Per Capita Income in CMEA Countries

	BUL-GARIA	HUNGARY	GDR	POLAND	RUMANIA	U.S.S.R.	CZECHO-SLOVAKIA
1950	0.6	1.2	1.3	1.1	0.5	1.0	1.6
1970	0.8	0.9	1.3	0.8	0.8	1.0	1.2

SOURCE: *Foreign Trade*, April 1972, p. 7 (published in U.S.S.R.).

Equalization has taken place, however, not primarily as a result of CMEA integration and capital flows, as the Eastern literature would have us believe, but primarily because growth of GNP among capitalist and socialist nations alike appears to be related to rates of investment, levels of development, and other such factors.[72] It appears unlikely that intrabloc capital flows are much used for the specific purpose of equalizing levels of development or, if so used, can have a significant impact.

An attempt will certainly be made, however, to use the resources of the IIB to facilitate that part of the planned integration which involves joint investment projects. Many of these projects, as we have noted, foresee the development of future CMEA raw material supplies. Since the U.S.S.R. contains the bulk of the undeveloped raw material reserves in CMEA, it may be that a good share of the IIB credits will be extended to the U.S.S.R. Even before the IIB, capital flows from Eastern Europe to the U.S.S.R. for this purpose had been increasing. If the IIB is used predominantly for this purpose, the enthusiasm of the smaller CMEA nations for this new institution may be dampened. In the past, of course, the smaller CMEA nations have done well on raw materials imported from the U.S.S.R. The high degree of economic interdependence between the U.S.S.R. and these nations which has resulted has been part of the U.S.S.R.'s payoff, not always an adequate one to judge from the frequent Soviet complaints about terms of trade. The future of this relationship may contain new stresses and strains. New raw material developments are for the most part farther (into Siberia) from Eastern Europe and require huge overland transport costs as well as greater capital investments. Western prices of raw materials are rising, especially of fuels, and the U.S.S.R. is interested in better terms of trade with CMEA as well as in earning more hard currency. The price of Soviet petroleum to Eastern Europe was doubled beginning January 1975, even though the old price had been contracted for through December 1975. Because prices were not raised sooner, that is, in October 1973 when OPEC prices went up, and are still considerably below the price the U.S.S.R. can get in the West, the rise in price which occurred reflects the ambivalence of the Soviet position. On the one hand, they do not want to give up too much in economic gains for Eastern bloc solidarity; on the other hand, they are willing to subsidize their "empire" within certain limits.

Concluding Remarks

The major economic goal of the CMEA countries has been rapid economic growth. A major political goal of the Soviet leaders and also of some of the leaders of other socialist nations has been to maintain the political integrity of CMEA as well as domestic political control in their own nations. These goals were, by and large, achieved fairly successfully in the 1950s.

Over the past fifteen years, Soviet bloc economic performance has deteriorated, with growth rates declining significantly and other economic difficulties appearing. The solution to these economic problems would appear to be radical reforms that involve substantial decentralization of economic activity and a recrudescence of market relations. Such reforms, however, would change the internal power structure in each nation, substantially reducing the control exercised by the existing political elite; they would also inevitably lead to a weakening of the economic ties among CMEA nations.

Thus, the Soviet bloc leaders are faced with the dilemma that they cannot simultaneously sustain the existing levels of economic growth and political control. Attempts to resolve this dilemma have led to reforms which do not threaten political control, but which also do not go to the root of the economic problems. The political impediments to more radical reforms are discussed in Chapter 6. The dilemma has also led the Communist nations to look to the West for help and has been a factor in their interest in détente. East-West relations are the subject of Chapter 4.

Chapter 4

East-West Economic Relations

This chapter is concerned with the economic relations between the socialist nations, primarily of Europe, and the advanced Western industrial nations. Many of the factors, both political and economic, which were discussed in the preceding chapter on intrabloc relations, affect East-West relations as well, but in the opposite direction. That is to say, since intra-CMEA and East-West trade comprise most of the subject with which we are here concerned (East-LDC trade, considered in Chapter 5, is much smaller than the other two), political and economic forces which encourage or discourage intra-CMEA or East-West trade are apt to have the reverse effect on the other. Those factors already dealt with in Chapter 3 can, therefore, be presented more briefly here. The chapter begins with a brief overview of some of the major political and economic forces, followed by some data on the magnitude of East-West trade and a short discourse on how East-West trade is conducted. After this introductory material, the main arguments of the chapter are set forth.

An Overview

Intrabloc relations were studied above with the aid of models of economic and political power, economic integration, and economic warfare. The first and third of these models is relevant to East-West trade relations. In particular, the economic warfare model has considerable applicability to the first fifteen years after World War II, for, as everyone knows, until recently the postwar period was most accurately characterized as the period of the Cold War. The Cold War basically described a political situation in which a large part of the industrial world was divided into two camps, capitalist and socialist, and these nations opposed each other in the diplomatic arena. The tools of economic warfare formed part of the arsenal of weapons.

As leader of the Western bloc, the United States' economic objective was to slow up the economic and military development of the socialist nations (see Chart 3.1-I.B.2). This was to be accomplished primarily by depriving these nations of strategic goods, that is, commodities which give military end-products and are important to the production of military end-products or to the economic growth and health of the socialist economies. Ancillary to this, they were to be denied credits and loans, most-favored-nation status, and so forth. In order for these measures to be effective, the United States had to secure or "induce" the cooperation of other major Western industrial powers in applying these various sanctions (Chart 3.1-I.B.2).

As leader of the Eastern bloc, Soviet objectives were somewhat different. First, since the Eastern bloc was and is the economically weaker of the two, the U.S.S.R. was in the position not of primarily trying to "hurt" the United States and its allies—since this was hardly feasible—but rather of making itself as invulnerable as possible to Western economic warfare and in general building itself up economically and militarily as rapidly as possible. Second, unlike the United States, which was in the position of trying to secure cooperation from allies of long standing, the U.S.S.R. was in effect "making" socialist allies out of nations which had previously been capitalist and, in many instances, had also had hostile governments. The stern political and military measures required to accomplish this objective were matched initially, as we discussed in Chapter 3, by dramatic economic measures (Chart 3.1-I.B.2 and II.B.2). In effect, the Soviet objective was to interlock the economies of the Eastern world, making them as dependent upon each other and particularly upon the U.S.S.R. as possible and to isolate them economically from the West. In this effort, they were strongly assisted by Western trade controls.

From an economic standpoint, neither the smaller Western nor the smaller Eastern nations were as enthusiastic as the two great powers about the enforced disruption of trade patterns. The United States, as the richest nation in the world, with a trade dependency ratio of no more than 5 percent, historically had very little trade with the U.S.S.R. and Eastern Europe and stood to lose little from these policies. The U.S.S.R. also depends little on trade and, at the time, actually stood to gain from these policies once she was cut off from the West by the strategic embargo. For, in fact, she actually acquired a trading bloc, albeit a small one, by the measures which were taken. The smaller nations, in either case, were not happy about the enforced isolation. With trade-dependency ratios ranging from 10 to 50 percent, they could not accept trade diversion on such a scale without feeling the losses involved. This was particularly true of the Eastern European nations, which were mostly poorer than the nations of Western Europe and had been more dependent than Western Europe on East-West trade (see below). In addition, the nations of Eastern Europe were anxious to reduce their economic dependency on the U.S.S.R. as one way of reducing their political dependency on their powerful neighbor.

While economic warfare never ceases to be relevant to an understanding of East-West trade, particularly to that between the U.S. and the U.S.S.R., its importance has eroded steadily until the present, when its role is minor. By the mid-1950s, the power of both the United States and the U.S.S.R. to prevent East-West trade between the smaller nations was diminishing. The dependency of Western Europe on the United States declined as Marshall Plan aid came to an end in the early 1950s and as European economic recovery went into high gear; the changes described in Chapter 3 that accompanied the end of the Stalin era and beginning of the Khrushchev era had a similar impact. Given reduced political control over their economic activities, Eastern and Western Europe moved to "recreate" the trade which had been diverted after World War II. As the years passed, the Cold War between the United States and U.S.S.R. also diminished in intensity. For one thing, Soviet acquisition of an atomic arsenal and the resulting balance of terror provided a slightly more stable framework within which the two major powers could peaceably interact. The Russians were clearly more interested than the Americans in East-West trade for the very fundamental reason that they had and still have more to gain from it. The economic difficulties which the U.S.S.R. and the other CMEA nations encountered in the 1960s provided an additional impulse to the opening up of trade channels. Political obstacles relating to the Cuban Missile Crisis, the German problem, and the Vietnam War delayed détente. As these problems faded, pressures for détente increased and achieved a measure of success. The character of the détente has been affected by the asymmetry of interest with which the two major nations view mutual trade and investment. Because it is less interested in mutual trade than the U.S.S.R., the United States has attempted to use increased trade to extract political concessions (Chart 3.1-I.B.1.a). The U.S.S.R., on the other hand, has shown itself willing to make some concessions for increased trade and investment. This so-called "linkage politics" has characterized the negotiations of the post-1970 period. Increased economic interaction between the two nations has raised in each nation questions concerning how much interdependence is strategically wise. That is, neither nation wishes to place itself in a position of being so dependent upon the other that it can be subjected to economic pressures or warfare (Chart 3.1-I.B.2).

Dimensions of Trade

The trends in intrabloc trade presented in the previous chapter are practically reversed in East-West trade. When East-West trade has declined, it has been because intrabloc trade has been growing; similarly, expansion of East-West trade has usually been at the expense of intrabloc trade. From a global standpoint, East-West trade is not very important quantitatively and would be overlooked if it were not for its political implications. Socialist trade amounts to a little less than one-eighth of world trade; East-West trade is about 25 percent of CMEA trade, and in 1972, for example, amounted to about $8 billion (each way), or less than 2½ percent of world trade in that year. In 1938, it was much greater: 74 percent of the present socialist nations, trade and 6½ percent of world trade (see Tables 4.1 and 4.2).

East-West trade is a much smaller part of Western than of Eastern trade: 9.5 percent in 1938 and around 3 percent in 1975. This is as should be expected since all but two of the Eastern nations (U.S.S.R. and China) are small, and these two nations have been relatively autarkic. If one compares the almost 30 percent of socialist trade that is

TABLE 4.1

East-West Trade As a Percentage of
Regional and World Trade: 1938-1972

	WORLD	DEVELOPED WEST	EAST
1938	6.4	9.5	73.8
1948	2.6	4.1	41.6
1953	1.3	2.1	14.0
1955	1.6	2.5	16.7
1960	2.5	3.5	19.2
1965	2.6	3.8	22.4
1967A	2.8	4.1	25.2
1967B	2.4	3.4	28.3
1970	2.1	3.0	29.1
1973	2.1	3.0	29.0

SOURCES: 1938-1967A from Josef Wilczynski, *The Economics and Politics of East-West Trade* (London: Macmillan; New York: Praeger, 1969), pp. 52, 54. West is calculated to include Western Europe, Canada, United States, Japan, South Africa, Australia, and New Zealand, thereby excluding Latin America, most of Africa, and much of Asia. Eastern nations include the eight in Europe (not Yugoslavia), Mainland China, Mongolia, North Korea, and North Vietnam; 1967B-1973: Eastern countries here are only European CMEA countries and this accounts for its smaller percentage of World and West and larger percentage of East (since CMEA engages in more East-West trade than do other Communist nations). Figures estimated from U.S. Department of Commerce, *Selected U.S.S.R. and Eastern European Trade and Economic Data* (Washington, D.C.: Government Printing Office, May 1975); data for the Developed West and World taken from the International Monetary Fund's *Direction of Trade* (various issues) and the *International Economic Report of the President* (Washington, D.C.: Government Printing Office, March 1975).

NOTE: The percentage of total Communist bloc trade to world trade may be calculated by dividing the world percentage by the East percentage and multiplying by 100.

East-West trade today with the less than 3 percent that East-West trade constitutes of the trade of advanced capitalist nations, it is immediately obvious that East-West trade is more important to the East than to the West.

In the past 10 years, a substantial capital flow started from West to East in the form of joint-investment projects and also, separately, arrangements for transfer of technology. These are discussed in a later section.

TABLE 4.2
East-West Trade by Country, Selected Years
(percent of total)

	1952	1958	1967	1973
Bulgaria	9.4	10.5	16.4	14.6
Czechoslovakia	19.9	17.0	19.1	23.6
East Germany	23.3	19.1	19.8	27.9
Hungary	21.2	22.8	25.0	28.2
Poland	30.7	32.1	28.7	39.8
Rumania	11.7[a]	18.4	31.8[b]	41.7
U.S.S.R.	13.8	16.3	20.0	26.6

SOURCES: 1952, 1958, 1967: calculated from: Paul Marer, *Soviet and East European Foreign Trade, 1946-1969* (Bloomington: University of Indiana Press, 1972); 1973: *Statisticheskii Ezhegodnik Stran-Chlenov Soveta Ekonomicheskoi Vzaimopomoshchi*, Moscow 1974, p. 333. It is not clear that the 1973 data are exactly comparable to those of the preceding years.

[a]This figure includes Rumanian trade with Western LDCs, which may have amounted to as much as 25 percent of the total (i.e., 3 percent).

[b]This estimate varies sharply from a U.S. government estimate of 38.1 percent. Joint Economic Committee, U.S. Congress, *Economic Developments in Countries of Eastern Europe* (Washington, D.C.: Government Printing Office, 1970), pp. 545-550. In general, the estimates of this source coincide very closely with the estimates made form Marer.

Conduct of Trade

As noted earlier, the socialist nations have nationalized international trade, and trade between each pair of nations is largely planned in advance as a total package with prices and quantities fixed and exports and imports roughly balanced. In each case, the foreign trade sector is integrated with the national economic plan, or develops from that plan. Within this framework, trade negotiations and operations are conducted by the respective ministries of foreign trade and their subordinate foreign trade combines. With minor exceptions in some of the Eastern European countries, producing (export) and consuming (import) enterprises have no contact with each other.

East-West trade does not follow a fixed stereotype but varies from country to country and often from transaction to transaction. At one extreme, the trade of the U.S.S.R. and East Europe with the United States has been, until recently, on a purely ad hoc basis, with individual American buyers and sellers each making their separate deals with one or another socialist foreign trade combine. Quantities bought or sold and prices settled upon in different transactions have been negotiated on the market in complete independence of each other and on the surface appear no different from transactions between private business-men of different capitalist nations. Appearances are somewhat deceiv-ing, however, since many Western nations require or have required their exporters and importers to submit proposed transactions to a govern-ment agency for approval and licensing. Such procedures are expensive, time-consuming, increase the risk element in trade, and act, therefore, as a trade deterrent.

Because of the special nature of trade with Communist countries, the businessmen in many Western countries have formed associations, consortia, and so forth to facilitate their dealings with Soviet bloc nations. The Japanese, for example, have one association for trading with China and another for the U.S.S.R. and Eastern Europe. The British have a similar arrangement. An individual enterprise can, of course, trade with the Communist nations on an individual basis if it so desires. Quite often the trade associations operate with government support and are, in fact, an important cog in the machinery of implementing trade agreements between East and West. Many Western commentators feel that associations or consortia are necessary to shore up the bargaining position of private enterprises, which are at a great disadvantage when dealing with a huge state monopoly. While some enterprises may secure better trading terms because they are members of an association, the fear of being taken advantage of appears to be largely illusory. The socialist foreign trade monopolies occupy a very minor position in the world market and are usually not in a position to exercise monopoly powers. They are monopolists within their own borders but not much different from the average substantial capitalist enterprise on the world market. The proof is in the material presented in the preceding chapter, which showed that the socialist monopolies typically had to buy at higher and sell at lower than world prices in Western markets.

Finally, it should be mentioned that a not insubstantial part of East-West trade is pure state-trading between governments. Examples are exports of grain by Canada and Australia and imports of various materials for government stockpiles (manganese, magnesium, uranium) by U.S. agencies.

A large number of Western nations have trade agreements with the Eastern nations in order to facilitate East-West trade. As of 1968, there were approximately 150 such bilateral agreements.[1] They usually set a target value for the overall level of trade as well as specifying lists of potential commodity exports and imports. In addition, the agreement may contain provisions concerning arbitration of trade disputes, methods of transport, method of payment, exchange of trade missions, tariff questions, credit arrangements, and so forth.

These provisions demonstrate the value of trade agreements to both East and West. Nevertheless, the prime purpose of such agreements is to meet the needs of the centrally planned economies to integrate the foreign trade sector into the overall plan, as discussed in Chapter 2. This purpose is served less successfully in East-West than in intrabloc trade simply because by the very nature of the situation capitalist governments are limited to "facilitating" purchases and sales by their traders but cannot be held legally responsible, as can a Communist nation, should the projected trade fail to materialize.* Nevertheless, the agreement does provide a means of partially bridging the institutional gap between the systems and increasing the level of trade. From this standpoint it is also advantageous to the Western nations, which use these agreements to their own special advantage. For example, many Western nations have insisted on balanced trade agreements with the Communist nations in order to avoid a loss of convertible currency. Others have used the agreements to gain competitive advantages in Eastern markets for their traders over other Western traders.

It is worth noting that the word *facilitate* used above means, among other things, that the Western nation agrees to remove such discriminatory obstacles to transactions with Eastern nations as quotas, licenses, and exchange controls. Since these controls are largely a product of the Cold War, one might expect that as (and if) the détente develops, trade agreements will become less important on this account, at least. Should the Eastern economic reforms ever lead to decen-

---

*This should not be taken to imply that the Communist nations have always fulfilled their obligations 100 percent under trade agreements; they have not.

tralized planning, then part of the remaining rationale for East-West trade agreements will have disappeared.

An important problem stems from the relative insulation of Eastern bloc domestic markets, namely, the absence of information on potential exports and imports and price trends in each. Western enterprises are accustomed to basing their activities on "market research." In the centrally planned economies, research of this sort is not possible: it is difficult to gain physical access to many areas and enterprises; domestic prices provide almost no clue regarding the price at which an Eastern nation might be willing to buy or sell a product; there is almost no information as to whether potential exports or importables will be allowed in the plan—or, if allowed one year, whether they will be allowed the next, or what future production and requirements are likely to be. Since it is relatively difficult in any case to do business with an Eastern nation, inability to project trends raises the risks and uncertainty that much higher.

In this section, so far, we have not mentioned a novel and burgeoning form of economic intercourse between East and West, namely, the many different types of cooperative ventures undertaken jointly by Western and Eastern enterprises and organizations. They represent a significant institutional adaptation to the requirements of East-West trade, particularly on the part of the Eastern nations.

The Cold War: 1945 to the Mid-1950s

Immediately after World War II, it looked very much as though, with the exception of the United States, East and West would resume their prewar trade ties. Trade between Western and Eastern Europe (excluding the U.S.S.R. and East Germany) reached 1938 levels (in real terms) by 1948 despite the fact that Eastern agricultural output and Western industrial output had not reached prewar levels. Projections by the OEEC (Organization for European Economic Cooperation) in planning for the Marshall Plan in 1947 foresaw East-West trade levels at twice the volumes actually achieved.[2] The Swedish government had made a loan to the Russians, and the United Kingdom and the U.S.S.R. had already concluded a trade agreement which foresaw expanding trade. On the other hand, the political stands taken by the United States and the U.S.S.R. were each viewed by the other as extremely hostile, and this was eventually reflected in the economic field.

Which nation started the Cold War is still a matter of debate which will not be judged here. Clearly, both the U.S. and the U.S.S.R. adopted policies which were viewed as hostile by the other. Some scholars date the beginning of the Cold War as V.E. day in May 1945, when ships carrying Lend-Lease supplies to Murmansk were ordered to turn back. Others view this incident as what one might expect in light of Soviet political strategy already revealed by their aggressive activities in Rumania, Bulgaria, and Poland. In 1946, the U.S. granted the British a $3¾ billion long-term recovery loan. A Soviet request in 1946 for a long-term loan of $1 billion was, for a long period of time, "lost in the files" and eventually allowed to die. The lines were drawn still more firmly in 1947: Winston Churchill's hard-line speech in Fulton, Missouri; the Truman Doctrine on aid to Greece and Turkey; the four-power clash as to whether reparations should come out of current German production; and finally the Marshall Plan.

The Marshall Plan gave promise of breaking the trend of steadily increasing East-West tensions. Originally conceived in a speech by the U.S. Secretary of State, General George Marshall, on June 5, 1947, the plan offered U.S. financial assistance for the reconstruction of Europe. The U.S.S.R. was (apparently reluctantly) included in the offer. In the words of George Kennan, then a member of the State Department planning staff, "If anyone was to divide the European Continent, it should be the Russians, with their response, not we with our offer."[3] The Czechs, not yet Communist, officially accepted the invitation, and Poland expressed great interest. France and Britain extended an invitation to the U.S.S.R. to join them in preliminary discussion on procedures in Paris later that month. The Soviets accepted, and Molotov arrived in Paris with a large staff of experts, apparently prepared for serious business. The conference failed and the Russians packed off for home. They argued that the only acceptable form of aid would be outright gifts to be used by the recipients as they saw fit. For the United States to dictate how the aid was to be used would lead to the subjugation of Eastern Europe, as well as Western Europe. Clearly, they feared a loss of their own influence in Eastern Europe. The United States, on the other hand, wanted to exert some control over the uses to which the aid was to be put. They were afraid, particularly in the case of Eastern Europe, that uncontrolled aid would be used to strengthen Communist governments through Soviet influence. The Russians also objected to the inclusion of Germany in the plan, fearing its eventual restoration as a great power. When they withdrew from the Marshall Plan, they forced the Czechs to withdraw their acceptance and prevented the other Eastern European nations from participating.

Failure of the Paris Conference was an important factor in making the split of Europe temporarily irreversible. The Cominform was formed in September 1947 and CMEA in January 1949; the Communist coup in Prague took place in February 1948, and a few months later the Russians sealed off Berlin, leading to the Berlin Air Lift. The United States began constructing its economic warfare apparatus against the Communist nations in 1948, at the same time that the Marshall Plan to rebuild non-Communist Western Europe went into full operation, and at the political level, NATO was formed in 1949. Hostilities in Korea broke out in June 1950, leading to the complete embargo on trade with China.

The net effect of these various political and politically inspired economic events was a sharp drop in East-West trade. As a percentage of total Eastern trade, it declined from 74 percent in 1938 to 42 percent in 1948 to a nadir of 14 percent in 1953 (see Table 4.1). It also declined sharply in importance relative to world and Western trade. It is worth inquiring how such a sharp shift in patterns was originally implemented and subsequently maintained. The answer is: largely through trade controls of various sorts, although other factors were also at work. Among the latter, at least two come immediately to mind. First, like other World War II belligerents, the socialist nations were busy reconstructing, were in difficult economic straits, and had severe balance of payments problems which forced them to reduce trade with the West and to compensate by expanding trade with each other on a bilaterally balanced basis. Second, the Marshall Plan naturally fostered trade among the West European nations and with the United States and away from the East. Third, the Communist nations found themselves largely cut off from Western capital markets and trade credits. This was true in the case of governmental loans because of the Cold War and exclusion from the Marshall Plan, and, in the case of private credits, because the shift to Communism increased risks too much in the eyes of the Western business community. As far as private foreign investment was concerned, of course, this was forbidden anyway in the socialist states.

Since they are implicit, it is impossible to document the existence of trade controls among the socialist nations which could have played a role in changing the structure of trade after World War II. But it seems clear that to a certain extent the Eastern nations deliberately redirected trade among themselves as they assumed similar political and ideological identities, not to mention adopting similar techniques of central planning by direct controls. Clearly, the redirection resulted, first, from decisions made and embodied in the central plans as to what was to be produced domestically and what was to be traded, and, second, from the long-term bilateral trade agreements that each CMEA country had with every other and the annual negotiations over the specifics of trade conducted under these agreements. There were, of course, links between the domestic plan and the trade negotiations since the latter must have been dovetailed with the former if either were to be implemented successfully. The Soviet Union clearly played a dominant role in the redirection process (which, it should be noted, may have been in part a reaction to Western controls), as evidenced by the fact that the shifts to trade with the U.S.S.R. were much more dramatic than those between the individual Eastern nations (see Table 3.1).

The American trade-control system has been borne by the Export Control Act of 1949, originally designed to substitute for various ad hoc export-control measures for strategic goods and products in short supply after World War II. In theory, the Act applied to exports to all nations; in practice, licenses were granted readily to all nations but those in the Communist bloc. When the Export Control Act was first passed, practically every commodity which might be deemed to have military or strategic value was on the Department of Commerce Commodity Control List and required a validated license for export to Eastern Europe and the U.S.S.R. The Act was, if anything, tightened still further during the Korean War and not liberalized until around 1956. The embargoes on China and North Korea, incidentally, were implemented under the Trading with the Enemy Act, originally passed in 1917. This Act covered not only exports but imports and all other commercial and financial arrangements.

Most of the nations of Western Europe exercised controls over trade after World War II, partly as a war legacy and partly because balance of payments difficulties demanded it. These nations were not, however, as interested as the United States in controlling exports of strategic materials to the Eastern bloc. The British, for example, sold fifty-five jet engines to the U.S.S.R. in 1947. Largely at the behest of the United States, discussions on a common embargo policy between the United States and seven nations of Western Europe were begun in 1948 and led in 1949 to the so-called Consultative Group. This group formed a Coordinating Committee, since called COCOM, which met regularly though informally to discuss the list of goods which should not be exported to the East. Membership in this group has expanded to fifteen nations, including Japan. In 1951, the United States formalized its relationship with COCOM in the Mutual Defense Assistance Act, known as the Battle Act. Under this Act, the President was empowered to terminate all military, economic, and financial aid to any COCOM nation that shipped strategic products on the so-called COCOM lists to the East. Since this was the time of Marshall Plan aid, the penalty was potentially severe. Penalties were rarely, if ever, applied, despite frequent breaches of the Act. In 1952, a China Coordinating Committee (CHINCOM) group, applying similar but stronger controls over trade with China, was also set up.

While the export controls of the Western European nations were less severe than ours, their quantitative import controls (qrs, or import quotas) were broader and more stringent. This was probably due more to the chronic balance of payments difficulties with which they were beset after World War II than to any inclination to discriminate against the East. Nevertheless, it is true that their quotas on imports from the East have been more extensive and maintained longer than those against the West.

Discriminatory use of quotas against the Communist nations by the United States has been restricted largely to a few commodities alleged to have been produced by forced labor. Our major effort to discriminate against Soviet bloc imports to us was by denial of MFN status to all nations but Yugoslavia, under the Trade Agreement Extension Act of 1951. This meant that products imported from the Communist nations were subject to the very high rates of the Smoot-Hawley Tariff Act of 1930. Because the United States has, since 1923, automatically granted MFN status to its trade partners, imports from all other nations have benefited from the many tariff reductions negotiated after 1930. There is some question as to whether denial of MFN had much effect right after World War II, particularly on the U.S.S.R. On the one hand, most Soviet exports to the West were raw materials, subject either to small tariffs or none at all; on the other hand, as is still the case, the quality, not the price, of manufactured goods appears to be the major deterrent to increased sales of these products in the West. For the most part, the Western European nations have extended MFN to the socialist nations.

As can be seen from this discussion, it is impossible to assign the blame categorically for the relatively reduced level of East-West trade.* The one piece of evidence is the fact that while U.S. and COCOM exports to the U.S.S.R. drop sharply in this period, those of the European neutrals and of Finland rose at least until 1952.[4] This suggests that Western controls may have been, at this early stage, more stringent than Eastern. If this is the case, it is undoubtedly partly due to the fact that in this economic confrontation, the Western nations were the "haves" and the Eastern nations the "have-nots." It is easier and more natural for the "haves" than for the "have-nots" to conduct economic warfare. To a considerable extent, Western economic warfare was offensive, Eastern defensive. In fact, it is interesting to note that, throughout the period, the U.S.S.R. shipped scarce and strategic materials like chrome and manganese ore to the United States. This should not be taken to mean that the U.S.S.R. was not engaged in economic warfare with the United States but simply that other considerations, like need for hard currency, had to be weighed in the balance, and economic warfare was more "defensive" and aimed more at improving the U.S.S.R. position (including securing the "allegiance" of Eastern Europe) than at hurting the United States and its allies. It is also interesting to note that throughout this period the smaller nations on both sides did their best to moderate the situation and, according to some sources, the volume of illegal East-West trade was substantial.[5]

The stagnation and relative decline of East-West trade ended in 1953-1954. Many factors were responsible. To the Eastern nations, as

*Actually, in absolute values, East-West trade remained fairly constant or declined only slightly. The relative drop was due to the fact that all other trade was increasing very rapidly due to the recovery from the war.

we have indicated, the separation of trading blocs was probably more stringent than they had expected or wished. The U.S.S.R. undoubtedly did want to break up established trade patterns between East and West and substitute for them an interdependency between East Europe and the U.S.S.R. The success of Western trade controls, however, may have resulted in an overfulfillment of Stalin's plans. Separation of East and West had probably reached, for the U.S.S.R., a point of diminishing returns. As early as April 1952, the U.S.S.R. held a conference in Moscow to which Western businessmen were invited. Large purchase orders were dangled before their eyes as the Soviet Union apparently tried to increase at least its own trade with the West. Because of Western controls, however, the conference was a failure. There was very little of value which the U.S.S.R. could import from the West, and it was difficult to earn hard currency through exports to the West because of the network of quotas and discriminatory tariffs, not to mention the "dollar shortage" which Europe was experiencing at the time. The Marshall Plan was still in full operation, and there was little possibility of enticing Western Europe into increased trade.

In 1953 and 1954 there was some easing of political tensions in both camps. Stalin's death in March 1953 was certainly a watershed. Even before Stalin's death, there were good reasons for some relaxation of controls by the U.S.S.R. It was clear that Eastern Europe was under control and the U.S.S.R. no longer faced enemies on all its European borders. To the east lay the now-friendly behemoth, China. Since 1949, the Russians had had the atomic bomb, and the military picture had become one of stalemate with little immediate danger of war. Yet it seems unlikely that Stalin was either capable of changing his approach to the West or was under the same kind of pressures to do so as his successors because of the absoluteness of his power both domestically and in Eastern Europe. Stalin's successor, Georgi Malenkov, on the other hand, was much less sure of himself. Shortly after taking power he had had to contend with riots in East Germany, and domestically, he felt sufficiently insecure to institute a "new course" which involved a better deal for the consumer. He even ordered large imports of consumers' goods to keep the lid on the discontent at home. Moreover, two major political events contributed to relaxation of tensions at the time: the end of the Korean War in 1953 and the Indochina Armistice in 1954.

The COCOM nations were also ready for some relaxation of controls on trade with the East, not only for political reasons, but for economic reasons. The Marshall Plan period had ended, and although American aid continued to flow to Western Europe, the flood had turned into a trickle. This took the possible sting out of Battle Act sanctions designed to keep the Western European nations in line, that is, loss of American assistance was no longer a serious threat. Secondly, Western Europe was still suffering hard-currency balance of payments problems which could be alleviated by a resumption of trade with the socialist nations. Finally, of course, it had become clear that whatever effects the embargo was having, it was certainly not changing the military-strategic balance. The U.S.S.R. had, after all, now built its own hydrogen bomb.

As a result of the various political and economic factors mentioned above, the Western European embargo lists against Eastern Europe and the U.S.S.R. were substantially shortened in 1954 and 1955. The United States objected unsuccessfully to these changes and maintained its own list intact, but was successful in preventing Western Europe from eliminating the so-called China differential—the amount by which the CHINCOM list exceeded the COCOM. Political tensions continued to dissipate and the atmosphere was pervaded in 1955 and 1956 by a "Geneva spirit," the result of the relatively amicable four-power conference in Geneva in 1955. The United States, in 1956, finally also cut its export control list for the first time. In 1957, the British government announced unilaterally that it was abolishing the China differential. This was strongly opposed by the United States but greeted approvingly by the nations of Western Europe. The result was the end of the CHINCOM group, with China now placed on the same footing as the European socialist nations and the United States continuing to maintain its complete embargo.

The Early Years of the Khrushchev Era

East-West trade improved under Malenkov and was further encouraged after Khrushchev (and Bulganin) came to power in 1955. Much of the increase in trade which developed resulted, of course, from the gradual decline in Western controls. Since Western controls were probably even more restrictive than Eastern, relaxation of the former would naturally have led to more trade. Furthermore, the Western controls were more often than not on commodities which were noncompetitive with those in intrabloc trade and which were high on the Eastern purchase lists. At the margins, the CMEA nations stood ready to buy many additional commodities as they became available.

Khrushchev himself was certainly partly responsible for the reduction in Western trade controls as well as the resulting increase in East-West trade. Within a few months of taking power, he and Bulganin launched their "offensive of international amicability."[6] The succession of trips all over the world by Bulganin and Khrushchev, as well as the so-called "Geneva spirit," lasted for several years and represented a period of somewhat reduced tensions between the Soviet bloc and Western Europe. Relationships with the United States remained fairly tense, however, and the United States was extremely suspicious of Soviet motives. The U.S.S.R. did its best to drive a wedge between the United States on the one hand and Great Britain and France on the other, trying to capitalize on the split that developed out of the Suez Crisis in 1956. These efforts came to naught as Western fences were mended in 1957 with NATO forces being placed, for the first time, under a unified command. In addition, it was agreed that NATO forces would be equipped with nuclear weapons and that Intermediate Range Ballistic Missile (IRBM) bases would be situated on NATO territory.

Even as Khrushchev's diplomatic dealings with the West were both positive and negative, so were his efforts toward East-West economic cooperation. Following the Geneva summit, he met with West Germany's Adenauer and then Great Britain's McMillan; both meetings are reported to have dealt at length with possibilities of increased trade. In June 1958 Khrushchev proposed a comprehensive trade agreement for a large expansion of trade in "peaceful" goods with the United States. President Eisenhower turned the cold shoulder to this bid by replying:

> As you know, the United States export and import trade is carried on by individual firms and not under governmental auspices. There is no need, therefore, to formalize relations between United States firms and Soviet trade organizations. Soviet trade organizations are free right now, without any need for special action by the United States Government, to develop a larger volume of trade with firms in this country. . . .[7]

The proposal was reiterated in 1959 by both Khrushchev and Mikoyan on their respective visits to the United States, but with no greater success.

While Khrushchev was actively seeking to augment Soviet trade with the West, his interest in greater East-West trade for Eastern Europe may not have been as enthusiastic. The events in 1956 in Poland and Hungary may well have made Khrushchev desirous of insulating Eastern Europe from Western influence and temptation. When, in the aftermath of the 1956 riots, Poland was allowed by the United States to buy surplus agricultural commodities under Public Law 480 and was then extended a twenty-year credit of $30 million, Soviet leaders condemned the Polish leaders for accepting such favors. (Yugoslavia was attacked at the same time on similar grounds.) The only weapons used, however, were words.

Khrushchev's moves to increase East-West trade were undoubtedly also motivated by economic and other factors, some related to his innovative and flexible personality. This was exemplified in 1957 when he instigated a large-scale reorganization of the Soviet economy, moving away from its traditional ministerial or industrial structure to one based on regions. This was the first major change in Soviet economic organization since planning began in the late 1920s. At the same time, the Sixth Five Year Plan was discontinued midway and a new Seven Year Plan (1958-1965) was instituted. In 1962, Khrushchev gave his blessing to the Liberman economic reform discussions and actually allowed some proposals to be tried out on an experimental basis.

While these examples are cited to suggest that dramatic economic initiatives were not foreign to Khrushchev's personality, they have further implications. The changes in internal economic policies suggest that domestic economic problems may even then have motivated Khrushchev to seek additional East-West trade, much as Brezhnev and Kosygin have been so motivated more recently. Another factor which may have worsened the Soviet economic picture at that time was the virtual end of its more obvious raw exploitation of, and concomitant need to extend substantial credit to, the other CMEA nations after the Polish and Hungarian uprisings in 1956.

While the socialist nations (wth the exception of Poland) clearly had little opportunity to expand trade with the United States, they were very hopeful, for both political and economic reasons, of increased trade with Western Europe. These hopes were threatened by the formation in the late 1950s of the European Economic Community and (to a lesser extent) the European Free Trade Association. The formation of the EEC, in particular, had both political and economic dimensions, even though the organization was fundamentally an economic association of nations.

There are several reasons for this. First, while the EEC is basically economic, it developed from initiatives which were originally also political. In fact, one of its abortive predecessors, the European Defense Community, was essentially an attempt at political unification. The supranational powers required for success were unacceptable to several nations, particularly France, and negotiations collapsed in 1954. Even the European Coal and Steel Community (ECSC), another and active predecessor to the EEC, had power to make decisions in this limited but important area of production which were binding (hence supranational) on the participating nations. Second, the Eastern nations worried that the very substantial degree of economic integration envisaged by the EEC would have political spinoffs, as well it might have. Third, the EEC was in its fetal stage in 1956 and 1957, a time when the United States was busily attempting to strengthen NATO. In that context, the EEC was irrationally viewed as an economic arm of NATO. Finally, of course, the EEC was comprised of some of CMEA's closest and most powerful neighbors, including West Germany. The CMEA nations were apparently genuinely worried around 1963 that inclusion of West Germany in an organization like the EEC might lead to its military regeneration, particularly its acquisition of nuclear weapons.

The economic consequences of the EEC were taken as a serious threat to CMEA interest in expanding East-West trade. The EEC members represented their largest trading partners in the West and it was clear that East-West trade would suffer as intra-EEC trade barriers were reduced. The CMEA members were particularly worried about the special protective measures taken by the EEC with regard to agricultural products, since these comprised a substantial part of Eastern exports to the EEC. The EEC was subjected to abusive attacks, and CMEA refused to recognize it officially even though it was the market equivalent of CMEA and, in fact, had some supranational powers which CMEA did not. The formation of the EEC certainly was one of the factors which spurred the attempts at that time to make CMEA a more effective organization.

The Early 1960s: Intensification of Economic Interest in East-West Trade

In this section, an attempt will be made to sketch some major economic developments in the internal affairs of the CMEA nations in the 1960s which sharply intensified their interest in East-West trade. It should be stressed, however, that the smaller nations of Eastern Europe were strongly motivated at the same time to seek more East-West trade not only for its own sake but for political reasons—to reduce their great dependence on the U.S.S.R. In this sense, the smaller Eastern nations have always wanted détente as much for political as for economic reasons. Also for political reasons, the U.S.S.R. has not been anxious to see economic ties develop between the West and Eastern Europe.

Before turning to the economics of the 1960s, let us first review briefly the economic factors motivating the Eastern nations to open trade channels with the West in the 1950s. The enormous shrinkage in relative importance of East-West trade and the concomitant rise in intrabloc trade after World War II were largely the result of political forces and occurred at the expense of what had been natural and profitable trading relationships between the nations of Eastern and Western Europe. In effect, the CMEA nations constituted a trade-diverting customs union whose members traded primarily with each other despite the existence of many more profitable opportunities for trade with their former Western partners. As part of a small and relatively high-cost trading enclave, the members of CMEA must always have had a desire to enter the world "bargain basement," with its lower prices and greater variety of available products.

All of the other factors discussed earlier that reduce the relative desirability of intrabloc trade would also serve as incentives for more East-West trade. Certainly the rigid inconvertibility and bilateralism, major weaknesses of CMEA trade, must have impelled the Eastern nations to turn outward. In their trade with the West, which has always been conducted entirely in convertible currency, multilateralism was possible and practiced. Earnings from exports to one market could be and often were spent on imports from another. This was an attraction which could not be ignored.

Another attraction of the Western market was the higher quality and attractiveness of most machinery and equipment and manufactured goods. Low quality is to be expected under central planning by direct controls, particularly under pre-reform planning. Managers of enterprises have little incentive to produce high-quality products or to adapt themselves to the needs of their customers. Their targets are quantity, not quality. They do not sell their products to customers—their products are distributed by the plan to the customers. Even if their customers are dissatisfied with the quality of the product, they would be loath to complain since, with over-full employment planning, shortages are perennial and buyers are prepared to put up with what they can get and be grateful. All these weaknesses carry over into intra-Comecon trade. Trade flows are planned; producers and consumers never see each other. Needless to say, an entirely different ethos prevails in the highly competitive world market, with the result that products are usually of much higher quality.

All these disadvantages of the CMEA markets must have caused Eastern nations to glance enviously at the world market in the 1950s. Yet, it seems fairly clear that, in this period, Eastern interest in East-West trade was much less intense than it has been since, say, the early 1960s. Relative dissatisfaction with intrabloc trade in the earlier years was probably muted by the considerable domestic economic successes (as viewed by the authorities) which were recorded, not to mention political controls. The major economic objectives of this period were industrialization and, through industrialization, the prior goal of rapid economic growth. These objectives were successfully achieved in the 1950s. By Western calculations, the GNPs of the CMEA nations as a group grew by about 6 percent;[8] by Eastern calculations, growth was closer to 8½-9 percent.[9] These growth rates are creditable by any standards.

The 1960s tell a different story. Economic difficulties beset the CMEA nations, accompanied by a sharp slowing of growth rates. While different nations experienced different degrees of slowdown, the nations as a group averaged, by their own official calculations, a rate of growth 2 percent lower in the 1960s than in the 1950s.[10] Economists explain the slowdown by pointing out that the CMEA strategy of development has been "extensive" rather than "intensive" and that while this was appropriate for the 1950s, "intensive" development is now called for. Basically, growth through extensive development means increasing the employment of and reallocating the factors of production, whereas intensive development refers to growth via an increase in the productivity of the factors of production in the existing structure of the economy. During the 1950s, central planners equipped with unprecedented economic powers put unemployed workers to work, transferred underemployed peasants from fields to factories, moved women into the labor force, and generated very high rates of investment by refusing to let consumption standards rise proportionately with the GNP, as would have occurred under free market conditions. This generated rapid growth. But most of these sources of growth provide one-time gains, and once achieved they provide little scope for further growth. Exhaustion of large-scale gains from extensive growth is undoubtedly largely responsible for the slowdown of the 1960s.

There is considerable evidence that intensive growth did not take over in the 1960s. Growth in labor productivity has been much slower in Eastern Europe than in Western Europe and Japan, and capital productivity actually declined.[11] It has been estimated that the rate of growth of Soviet total factor productivity, that is, the increases in GNP per unit of new inputs of labor and capital, which was moderately respectable at 1.7 percent a year from 1950 to 1958, declined to .7 percent from 1958 to 1967[12] and is estimated to have been actually negative,* −.7 percent, from 1967 to 1973.[13] Clearly, the U.S.S.R. and Eastern Europe have not grown "intensively," that is, they have not been very successful at raising productivity levels. The reason appears to be that while they were quite good at massing factors of production and at restructuring their economies, central planning with direct

---

*A negative total productivity means that the percentage increase in GNP generated over a period was actually less than the increase in factors of production (labor and capital here) employed. Typically, GNP increases are greater than increases in quantities of factors of production because the measured factors of production are not all of the factors which have gone into increasing output. For example, in a measurement like this, no account is taken of improvements in technology, of skills of workers, of economies of scale, and so forth.

controls is not a technique designed to achieve efficiency in most of the diverse forms in which it expresses itself. Realization of these facts has been responsible for the various attempts in each of these countries to reform their economic systems, as indicated in Chapter 1.

The most significant set of "inefficiencies" of central planning from the viewpoints of understanding both the slowdown in economic growth and recent developments in East-West trade are those relating to new technology—its invention, development, and diffusion. While it has always been known that changing technology is important for economic growth, its importance was typically understated, the central role in growth having been assigned to the rate of investment. A careful econometric study by Robert M. Solow of MIT[14] demonstrated that roughly four-fifths of that part of U.S. economic growth, from 1900 to 1950, which was attributable to capital investment, was due to changes in the quality of the capital—that is, to changes in technology—whereas only one-fifth was due to the increase in the quantity of capital—that is, the rate of investment. This may be difficult to understand; perhaps a simple example will illustrate the point. In 1950, television sets, of extremely low quality by today's standards, sold for between $400 and $500 (at least $750 at the 1973 price level). They were very large, used lots of material, but had tiny low-quality screens. Today, a vastly superior set containing considerably less material is sold for between $100 and $150. In effect, to provide the same amount of satisfaction from TV today with 1950 technology would require a minimum of five or six times more resources. To put it another way, most of the growth in the television industry is attributable to improvements in technology, not just to quantity of investment. Recent changes in the hand- and desk-calculator field have been an even more dramatic example of the importance of technology for growth.

Thus, technology is extremely important for intensive growth. It is one of the major variables responsible for increasing labor and capital productivity. Organizationally, the pre-reform centrally planned economies have not been well adapted to innovating, developing, and diffusing technology. At the level of enterprise, pay-and-bonus systems have provided little incentive to change technology. Bonuses have been tied to the achievement of output or sales targets, not to the quality of product. The fact that new technology might increase the quantity of output which a factory produces adds little incentive because targets have usually been raised commensurately under such circumstances, leaving the manager no better off than before. Moreover, the introduction of new technology itself often involved transitional losses and risks, such as losses of bonuses during the installation and learning periods, as well as possible losses, in some instances, if new technology required changes in the excessively rigid supply system. The development and application of technology has also been impeded by organizational factors. Unlike the situation under capitalism, where there is constant feedback between research and development and producing units in large Western enterprises, these units have been effectively separated from each other in socialist countries. The R & D technicians often do not know the problems of the enterprises but work on whatever happens to interest them, and the enterprises bring few, if any, problems to R & D units with which they have little, if any, official connection. Major exceptions in the U.S.S.R. are the military and aerospace industries. This fact, the priorities given these industries in supplies, and the insistence of the authorities on "quality" explain their relative success and technologically advanced state.

The recent reforms have, of course, been directed at these technology-related problems as well as at many others. So far, however, the various measures which have been adopted have not made an appreciable difference. As noted in Chapter 1, except in Hungary the reforms have been very conservative and have concentrated on improving the system of planning under direct controls, rather than on introducing markets, prices, decentralization, and flexibility into the system. It remains to be seen whether further developments under conservative reforms can solve the technology problems, or whether technology and other economic problems will eventually drive the socialist nations into adopting more radical economic reforms.

Inability to solve successfully problems relating to the development of new technology without introducing major economic (and possibly political) reforms has provided the Eastern nations over the past ten years with a strong additional motive to engage in East-West trade. Some observers look upon the attempts of the Eastern nations to import technology on a large scale as a calculated substitute for, or way of avoiding, radical reform.

Renewed interest in imports from the West, especially in technology, has not been matched by an increased ability to finance these imports.

Importing technology, often involving foreign construction of turnkey plants* and, in the case of the U.S.S.R., very capital-expensive development of mineral resources, has led to serious hard-currency balance-of-payments problems. The foreign exchange gap has its counterpart in a domestic savings gap in the sense that being over-fully employed economies with no surplus resources available, the Eastern nations are never able to finance all desirable investment projects. Under circumstances like these, it has been natural for nations with lower per capita incomes to look to their better-off neighbors for capital. Thus in recent years, the Eastern nations have been interested not only in trade with, but in borrowing investment funds from, the advanced Western industrial nations.

These appear to be the major economic factors which have impelled the CMEA nations to seek more trade and investment with the West in recent years.

Political and Economic Developments in the Early and Mid-1960s

Impelled by the economic factors just outlined, all the CMEA nations pushed for greater East-West trade. There were considerable differences in strategy, however, among the various nations. In particular, the U.S.S.R. took a much more conservative approach than did Poland, Hungary, and Rumania, for example. The Western nations were also split in their strategies, with the United States continuing to remain much more aloof than the nations of Western Europe.

The push for greater East-West trade by the nations of Eastern Europe was hampered somewhat in the early 1960s by the economic slowdowns in all these nations, slowdowns which eventually led to the economic reform movement. This was in striking contrast to the late 1950s, when they were all experiencing investment booms causing them

---

*Turnkey plants are plants constructed entirely in the importing nation by foreign technicians. When completed, all that remains to be done, figuratively, is to give the purchaser the key with which to turn the plant on.

to look beyond Eastern Europe for supplies. At that time, the Western nations were experiencing recessions and were looking for markets, so the needs of the two groups of nations were complementary.[15]

Nevertheless, there were many facilitating factors. In particular, the nations of Western Europe broke sharply with the United States on issues of economic controls. The COCOM embargo lists were regularly revised downward and the gap between these and the U.S. lists increased greatly. The new European philosophy behind the COCOM lists was that they should contain only truly strategic commodities that were not available to the socialist nations; items which could only be justified on grounds of slowing Communist economic growth were to be excluded.

By the early 1960s, Western Europe's balance of payments problems had all but disappeared. This enabled the Western Europeans to treat trade with Eastern Europe much more liberally than before. Previously, they had often been reluctant to expend hard currency in trade with Eastern Europe or to allow full convertibility of surpluses that an Eastern European nation might earn in trade with them. This reluctance largely disappeared, facilitating multilateralism in East-West trade. Just as important, the Western European nations and Japan broke with U.S. credit policies toward the Soviet bloc. An original "gentlemen's agreement" to align credit policies had been drawn up in Berne, Switzerland, in 1934. In 1958, under pressure from Washington, members of the "Berne Union" agreed to limit commercial credits to the socialist nations to five years. This loose agreement was never seriously honored. Japan, not a member of the Berne Union, extended credits for more than five years; they were soon followed by state-owned Italian institutions. Competition for Eastern business in plant and equipment was much too brisk for the gentlemen's agreement, and in 1964, both French and British government instrumentalities guaranteed much longer-term credits.

In 1964 the United Kingdom granted a twelve-year credit to Czechoslovakia for the purchase of fertilizer plants, and a fifteen-year $300 million grant to the U.S.S.R. for chemical factories.[16] Other smaller credits were granted at the same time. France followed closely on Britain's footsteps, signing a commercial agreement on October 30, 1964, which provided for similar credit conditions. Other Western nations followed France and Britain's example. Since then, despite protests at first from the United States, it has been "every man for himself" with credit being granted almost exclusively on commercial grounds.[17]

What was true of exports and credits was also true of imports. The United Kingdom took the lead in 1964 in eliminating the severe import-quota system which had been in effect on imports from Eastern Europe since the end of World War II. Virtually all discriminatory controls were removed on the assurance that products would not be "dumped."[18] QRs remained primarily on commodities whose import might cause dislocations in the British economy.[19] France was the first of the original EEC nations to relax import controls. In 1964, about 90 percent of the goods imported from Eastern Europe was subject to QRs. These were reduced by half by 1966 and by more than 80 percent by 1968.[20] The example of the United Kingdom and France was soon followed by other Western European nations.

While many steps toward trade liberalization were undertaken unilaterally by the Western European nations, others were influenced by and undertaken in the context of one- and five-year bilateral trade agreements. These agreements went a long way toward regularizing East-West trade relationships. As noted earlier, by 1968 the socialist nations of Europe as a group had 149 trade agreements with advanced Western nations; seventeen involved the U.S.S.R. The only Western nations with no such bilateral agreements were Ireland and the United States.[21] In the early stages, most were trade agreements, pure and simple. By the mid-1960s, the proposed levels of cooperation went much further. In 1965, for example, the U.S.S.R. and France signed an agreement which involved scientific and technological as well as economic collaboration, establishing a permanent high-level commission and many joint working groups. This was followed by similar agreements with many other Western European nations.

It seems highly probable that had it not been for the course of external political events, American economic and political strategies toward the Soviet bloc, like the Western European strategies, might have become more friendly after 1960. The years from 1960 to 1962, however, were marked by many traumatic events, the most dramatic of which were the U-2 crisis in 1960, construction of the Berlin Wall in 1961, and the Cuban Missile Crisis in 1962. An economic casualty of these events was the end of grant and loan aid and MFN to Poland and

Yugoslavia, and the expansion of export controls to apply to all products affecting economic and military potential, rather than just the latter. Some relaxation of controls occurred again in 1963, particularly in connection with the large grain sales to the U.S.S.R. President Johnson made several additional attempts to foster East-West trade by trying to extend MFN, relax Export-Import Bank controls on credits to the Eastern nations, and relax export controls. He was defeated in all these efforts, however, by Congress, which felt that such relaxation was inappropriate vis-à-vis nations that were supporting our enemies in the Vietnam conflict. It was not until 1969 that a turning point was finally reached. The Export Control Act was superseded by an Export Administration Act with the stated purpose of encouraging peaceful East-West trade. This Act represented the beginning of the U.S.-U.S.S.R. economic détente.

Although the U.S.S.R. and the smaller nations of Eastern Europe benefited from liberalization of Western Europe's trade and credit controls and from the network of bilateral agreements, there were several respects in which some of the Eastern European nations went much beyond the efforts of the U.S.S.R. to further East-West relations. We refer here to attitudes toward the EEC and GATT, coproduction and comarketing agreements, joint ventures, and serious efforts to shift trade toward the West at the expense of trade with CMEA.

RUMANIA'S DISSIDENCE

To take these issues up in reverse order, the one nation to shift its trade sharply to the West was, of course, Rumania. Despite the considerable relaxation of trade controls and the proliferation of trade agreements, East-West trade as a percentage of total Eastern trade rose very slowly—with the exception of Rumania. Between 1959 and 1968, Rumania's trade with Western Europe as a percentage of total trade rose from 20 to 45 percent. The U.S.S.R. and Bulgaria rank next with 8 and 5 percentage point increases respectively over this period. In other words, CMEA's total exports to and imports from Western Europe rose by 230 and 280 percent respectively from 1959 to 1968, in comparison with increases by Rumania of 490 and 880 percent.[22] The explanations of Rumania's behavior were suggested in the previous chapter. Among the CMEA nations, Rumania was one of the most anxious to escape

Soviet political and economic domination. As the debates over supra-nationality of CMEA presented in Chapter 3 clearly show, the U.S.S.R. was interested in preventing Rumania from concentrating on industrial development at the expense of her agricultural and raw material base. In effect, Rumania considered herself put in the position of a colonial dependency. For this very reason, however, Rumania was—and still is—the country in European CMEA least dependent upon the U.S.S.R. for raw materials and therefore most free economically to break the bonds of CMEA trade. Furthermore, since Rumania is one of the relatively underdeveloped CMEA nations, she exports little of real value to the U.S.S.R. Finally, Rumania's very conservative domestic economic and political policies have provided a degree of immunity from Soviet interference that Czechoslovakia and Hungary, for example, apparently lacked.

JOINT VENTURES

Perhaps the most interesting development over the past fifteen years has been the burgeoning of long-term cooperation agreements between Western enterprises and industries in socialist nations. Rumania and Hungary and, of course, Yugoslavia have been more innovative along these lines than the other Eastern nations. While most people view these agreements as completely novel, there was an important precedent in the 1920s in the U.S.S.R. when, as part of the New Economic Policy, Western "concessionaires" were brought in to participate in a number of mining and manufacturing enterprises. Moreover, joint investment projects also exist between CMEA nations. Nevertheless, the new East-West variants have captured public attention because of the speed of their growth, the spectacular size of some of the recently projected U.S.-U.S.S.R. Siberian energy ventures, as well as their political and ideological implications. In fact, their numbers are not of great importance. By 1972, there had been roughly 200 ventures over a ten-year period, with a paid-in cumulative value of less than $2 billion, compared with the approximately $14 billion total for East-West exports and imports in 1972 alone.[23]

The new arrangements take many forms. The simplest are those in which the Western enterprise sells a license or package of technology to the Eastern nation. Somewhat more complicated is the case where the

Western firm provides equipment and supervises the construction of a so-called turnkey plant. Still more complicated are those open-ended arrangements in which the Western partner contributes material, management, transportation, marketing, and/or any other services in the production-distribution process on a continuing basis. The Eastern Europeans view the latter cases, in which cooperation extends over a period of time, as true joint ventures. Under the usual Western definitions of a joint venture, most of these would not qualify because the Western partner has no equity in the undertaking, that is, the plants are entirely owned by the Eastern European country. Exceptions to this are theoretically possible in Yugoslavia, Rumania, and Hungary, which, in the late 1960s and early 1970s, passed laws allowing Western firms to hold up to 49 percent of the equity in the ventures. It seems unlikely that a foreign investor would ever be allowed the controlling interest in a venture in a socialist nation; in fact, it is unlikely that in many of these ventures the foreign participants will even be allowed to hold equity, since this is usually forbidden even to private nationals of the socialist nations. Fortunately, most of the "rights" which inhere in the West in minority or majority stock ownership can be assured instead through various contractual arrangements. Among the most important of these are the rights of management, the right of profit-sharing or some other form of compensation, and the right to sell out.[24] As long as Western investors can get a "bundle of rights" which reasonably approximates ownership or the desired part of the "bundle," they can be expected to participate if the terms are otherwise satisfactory.

The motives behind the many different undertakings are manifold. To the Western enterprise, the venture may represent a way of getting cheap labor, assured, protected markets that are otherwise unavailable, large supplies of raw materials (especially in ventures with the U.S.S.R.), a chance to profit by marketing Eastern products in Western markets; recently, even the benefit of Eastern technology has been an inducement. In many respects, the motives here are similar to those of Western multinational firms which operate out of several countries at the same time. Eastern motives are somewhat different, running more in the direction of need for capital, acquisition of technology and production and management techniques, and assistance in marketing products in the West. That is to say, these agreements represent possible solutions to some of the major economic problems of the Eastern nations. (Some Eastern nations have joint ventures with the LDCs, in which their role and motives are similar to the usual Western role in East-West ventures.)

Despite the parallel between East-West joint ventures and Western multinational enterprises, there are many differences. The major one is, as noted, that of ownership and control. In contrast with the multinational, the East-West venture usually denies the Western partner ownership (and always denies it ultimate control) when the venture is physically located in the Eastern nation, as it usually is. Furthermore, with the exception of some of the projected U.S.-U.S.S.R. energy ventures, East-West ventures have been fairly small scale in comparison with the wide-ranging multibillion-dollar operations of many of the multinational operations. Also, in most (but not all) cases, Western collaborators receive payment in the form of part of the output of the project rather than in money. This reflects the inconvertibility of the Soviet bloc currencies and their severe balance of payments problems. This is a substantial handicap under ordinary conditions and certainly tends to reduce the opportunities for more ventures, but the disadvantage is currently minimized, if not completely offset, by the inflation which has beset most Western nations and the instability of the Western international currency system. One way of avoiding or reducing the risks of inflation and devaluation is to arrange for payment in kind.

The development of East-West ventures is interesting because it has involved, on both sides, considerable organizational adaptation to a new situation. On the one hand, one finds Western businessmen willing to invest money and resources without equity and without necessarily receiving management rights or a right to share in profits in the traditional sense. Furthermore, they have also demonstrated a willingness to deal in markets in which they have much less information and control than usual. That they are willing to make these changes must be attributed to the everlasting search of the "capitalist" for profit-making opportunities and strong disinterest in the military-political-strategic consequences of their activities. No special restraints on these investments have been applied by Western governments in addition to those already mentioned in connection with export and credit controls. On the other hand, the willingness of the socialist nations to collaborate is quite striking, since they are fully cognizant of the consequences of their activities. Most notable is the willingness, at least in theory, of Yugoslavia, Hungary, and Rumania to allow some foreign private ownership of industrial and service enterprises within their borders, contrary to fundamental Communist ideology. To be sure, the governments in question watch these ventures and control their operations and the nature of the profit-sharing. Nevertheless, that foreign private ownership is allowed at all in a Communist country is something this writer would never have dared to predict. Also important, though somewhat less fundamental, is the willingness of the Eastern nations to enter into various forms of industrial and technological cooperation agreements with Western enterprises. These agreements generally lead to a much closer relationship than simple commodity trade, especially as the latter is practiced by the socialist nations with, among other things, the necessity of often accepting foreign technicians and management specialists as quasi-permanent residents.

The willingness of the socialist nations to compromise and undertake these new forms of collaboration with the West represents an effort to solve some of the profound economic problems which beset their economies in the 1960s. These same problems are responsible for their efforts at domestic economic reform. While the problems of the U.S.S.R. have been as serious as those of the small nations, the U.S.S.R. has moved more slowly, both in regard to domestic reforms and to coproduction agreements with the West. This undoubtedly reflects, in part, a lesser dependence on foreign trade. It also reflects, however, the fact that the Soviet Union is "the keeper of the ideology" and is therefore undoubtedly more concerned than the other nations about the degree to which socialism may be corrupted and the adverse effects this might have on Soviet control over the Soviet bloc. Conversely, the smaller nations may be motivated to undertake these new forms of collaboration in part by their desire to weaken the control exercised by CMEA and the U.S.S.R. over their economic and political life.

EEC AND GATT

The formation of the EEC was greeted by CMEA with concern, hostility, and nonrecognition. From an economic standpoint, the EEC reduced CMEA sales in the West; politically, the EEC was feared as a possible instrument of NATO. These fears were exacerbated by the

French-West German treaty of January 1963, which raised a fear that the Germans might obtain nuclear weapons. The strength of Soviet feelings toward the EEC as an economic unit is suggested by the fact that the Soviets broke off trade talks with France in the early 1960s because France would not lower its trade barriers to Soviet exports to the levels accorded within the EEC. While the U.S.S.R. and CMEA as a group refused to recognize or deal with the EEC at this time, several CMEA members implicitly recognized the EEC by signing agreements which the EEC had signed and by negotiating agreements with an agency of the EEC on trade in specific agricultural commodities.[25] Economic self-interest dictated these moves. With declining growth rates and economic reforms, Eastern Europe was inclined to turn westward for more trade and investment. Poland led the way and, in 1964, had technical discussions with the EEC on its agricultural exports and level of tariffs and quantitative restrictions facing its exports in general. Rumania followed close behind.[26] The only Eastern European nation not anxious for closer relations with the EEC at that time was East Germany, which had its outlet to the West through West Germany and stood to lose its dominant position as machinery exporter to other Soviet bloc nations. The U.S.S.R. maintained its policy of nonrecognition until the early 1970s, when, as we shall see, the détente plus the EEC's assumption of power in representing member nations in economic negotiations forced the issue.

The U.S.S.R. has always opposed the General Agreement on Tariffs and Trade (GATT) and its predecessor, the abortive International Trade Organization (ITO). The major purposes of GATT, as noted in Chapter 2, have been to increase world trade by reducing trade barriers, particularly tariffs, and to encourage nondiscriminatory trade primarily through the mechanism of most-favored-nation agreements among members. GATT was formed largely as a reaction to the chaos and shrinkage of world trade which accompanied the Great Depression of the 1930s. GATT has certainly played a part in the greater stability and expansion of trade until the various financial crises of the 1970s. As nonmembers of GATT, the CMEA nations failed to benefit from the periodic reductions in tariffs and quotas which were received via MFN by all of the GATT members (numbering eighty-two nations by 1960, forty-five of them LDCs). The Soviet bloc nations were, of course, annoyed to be so discriminated against in Western markets, particularly in view of the fact that their products were not competitive in the West in any event.

The Soviet Union's basic strategy has been to try to obtain the benefits of GATT membership without joining the organization. In 1955, an attempt was made to get MFN on QRs from the European nations belonging to OEEC. This unsuccessful attempt was followed by several attempts to get UN agencies like the Economic Commission for Europe (ECE) and the Economic and Social Council (ECOSOC) to arrange trade-cooperation agreements. In 1960, to get better treatment on QRs, the U.S.S.R. tried unsuccessfully to join the OECD (which had just replaced OEEC). Still another strategy attempted by the U.S.S.R. and several of the smaller nations was the introduction of two- and three-column tariff systems, the highest of which applied to those Western nations which denied them MFN treatment. Given central planning, these tariffs could not function like Western tariffs, in the sense that lowering them did not open the planned economy to more trade, but simply redistributed existing trade. This was immediately clear to Western nations and the tactic produced no results.

All attempts to bypass GATT failed, but the U.S.S.R. and the other CMEA nations achieved some of their objectives during the 1960s via the network of bilateral trade agreements negotiated with the advanced nations of Europe. MFN on tariffs was usually extended and some relaxation of discrimination on QRs also took place.

As with the cooperation agreements and the EEC, some of the smaller nations have taken a less dogmatic view toward GATT than has the U.S.S.R. In the late 1940s and early 1950s, attacks by Poland on the ITO and GATT were matched in intensity only by the Soviet Union's attacks. Nevertheless, in 1957 Poland applied for GATT membership, apparently in fear of losing markets due to the forth-coming establishment of the EEC. Investigations were begun by GATT, and in 1959, the Polish government offered to negotiate global quotas in exchange for tariff concessions, since "reciprocation" appeared to be a major stumbling block. Poland was not extended MFN at this time, but she was allowed to participate in the work of GATT and to engage in exchange of information. As a result of closer relations with GATT members, Polish trade with the West appears to have increased some-what. Poland then asked to be allowed to participate in the Kennedy Round trade negotiations and proposed that adjustment in her annual plan would be made so that she could reciprocate tariff concessions. In March 1965, she was admitted to Kennedy Round negotiations and agreed to a global quota under which she would increase her imports from the other contracting parties by not less than 7 percent a year in exchange for MFN tariff treatment. The other GATT members were allowed to maintain QRs and other discriminatory import controls against Poland, at the same time committing themselves to progressive reduction and eventual elimination of any discriminatory element in these restrictions.

Since Poland's accession to GATT, Rumania and Hungary applied (in 1968 and 1969, respectively) and were admitted (in 1971 and 1973, respectively) to membership. Rumania did not like the Polish 7 percent formula and finally agreed to increase imports from GATT nations by the same percentage that its total imports increased. Hungary, after much debate, managed to convince GATT that because of its economic reform, its tariffs were "real" tariffs in the sense that lowering them opened the Hungarian domestic market to Western competition. Hence, Hungary's admission was on the same basis as that of a Western nation.* A promise was made by GATT to reduce Western QRs against Hungarian and Rumanian products gradually.**

GATT is basically an apolitical organization in the sense that nations are not prohibited from joining on political grounds. Political issues have arisen, of course, since some groups of nations (the advanced nations) appear to have fared better than others (the LDCs) under its rules and operations. Nevertheless, by its admission of Poland, Rumania, and Hungary and its willingness to adapt its rules and procedures to the special circumstances of "central planning" in the cases of the first two nations, the organization has, in a sense, proved that in principle it is not opposed to the inclusion of Communist nations. By joining GATT, all three Communist nations have also shown that economic interest can transcend ideology. That the

---

*Since Hungary's admission, many observers have expressed doubts that the Hungarian tariffs are sufficiently "real" to have warranted admission on terms different from Rumania and Poland.

**It is perhaps worth noting that Czechoslovakia was a charter member of GATT and remained a member even though the occupation by the Warsaw Treaty troops took place shortly afterward. Her participation in GATT activities has never been substantial.

158

U.S.S.R. has apparently not attempted to prevent other CMEA nations from joining GATT may be attributed partly to the nonpolitical character of GATT. Furthermore, membership in GATT poses virtually no threat to the dominance of CMEA trade among CMEA nations, certainly no more threat than does securing MFN treatment from Western nations on a nation-by-nation bilateral-agreement basis. Soviet failure to apply for GATT membership is probably a partial reflection of its success in achieving MFN status from many nations through bilateral agreements. It also may reflect the fact that it is less dependent on foreign trade than are the smaller nations. Finally, as leader of the Soviet bloc, it may feel some ideological inhibitions against joining what has been called "the rich man's club"—an organization dedicated to liberalizing and improving the functioning of the capitalist world market.

U.S.-Soviet Détente and the Commercial Agreement

The Export Administration Act of 1969 represented a turning point in trade relations between the United States and the CMEA nations. The passage of this Act was made possible by the beginning of a détente between the United States and the Soviet Union that developed for a number of reasons, mostly political and military, but partly economic. During the late 1960s, in comparison with the late 1950s and early 1960s, both nations had several reasons for wanting détente. The motives of the two nations differed in some respects, and this asymmetry of interests led to what has been called "linkage" politics, or the trading off of concessions in one area of interest for concessions in some other area of interest.

LINKAGE POLITICS

Perhaps the one area in which interests came closest to coinciding was the attempt to control the strategic arms race which still constitutes an enormous drain on the resources of each nation, without providing additional security to either. Another major U.S. interest was to keep the Russians from unduly complicating the course and final settlement of the Vietnam quagmire. The United States also hoped and is hoping for Soviet forbearance in a settlement of the Arab-Israeli conflict. The U.S.S.R. has a similar though possibly less important interest in this; the Russians are, however, at least motivated to avoid a superpower confrontation on the Middle East situation.

What Vietnam was to the United States, China is to the U.S.S.R. The U.S.S.R. has been strongly motivated to avoid any other major military involvements, especially since the Ussuri border incident with the Chinese in 1969. Just as Vietnam has immobilized a significant portion of American military resources over the past decade, so the U.S.S.R. has been forced to commit significant amounts of materiel and manpower to the Chinese border. The American reopening of relations with China has, of course, given both of these nations additional bargaining chips in their separate relations with the U.S.S.R.

Another area in which both nations had interests which détente might serve well was Western Europe. The United States has continued to have many problems with its NATO allies, some caused by its one-sided concern with the U.S.S.R., China, and the Middle East and the neglect of Western Europe and Japan in the early 1970s. On the other hand, because of the overwhelming importance to Europe of peaceful East-West relations, détente has also cemented U.S. relations with its allies. The U.S.S.R. was also very interested in seeking new and better political relationships with Western Europe to match CMEA's much improved economic situation. Once and for all, they wanted to stabilize the political boundaries and relationships, especially those between East and West Germany, and to reduce the military burden generated by political tensions. To this end, after many false starts, they initiated a wide-ranging Conference on Security and Cooperation in Europe (CSCE), which was finally concluded in Helsinki in the summer of 1975. They also initiated talks on mutual and balanced reduction of armed forces in Europe (MBFR) which are still in progress.

In all these areas, even those in which overall interests are mutual, agreements are not easily obtained because conflicts of interest exist on many of the details. In order to come to an agreement benefiting both parties, each has to make sacrifices and there is always the difficult question of weighing and comparing costs and benefits. In addition, the situation is complicated by the fact that overall gains and losses on any particular issue may differ substantially between the U.S. and the

U.S.S.R. As mentioned previously, existence of more than one set of issues under discussion at one time further complicates the picture and makes an evaluation of gains and losses still more speculative. However, through the so-called linkage process it also makes possible an agreement that would otherwise never occur. While the prior discussion may suggest that trading off agreement and concessions on one issue for agreement and concessions on another may be a mechanical matter, this impression is misleading. In fact, the achievement of agreements on several issues may result not from equivalent trade-offs but simply from the establishment of a "climate," which in this case is called "détente" and which facilitates agreement. As Henry Kissinger remarked in June 1972 when introducing the SALT accords on arms limitations: "We have . . . sought to move across a broad range of issues so that progress in one area would add momentum to the progress of other areas."[27]

While we have spoken here of one national interest (U.S.) versus another national interest (U.S.S.R.), we are of course referring to the interest as expressed by the dominant group in each country. In fact, in each country there may be sharp division of opinion on every issue. This creates some instability in the position taken by the nation, puts constraints on the flexibility with which a nation can approach negotiations, and opens up the possibility of a reversal of position.

SOME FURTHER ECONOMIC AND STRATEGIC CONSIDERATIONS

As we have suggested, while increased trade and investment with the U.S.S.R. were viewed as economically desirable by the U.S. government and by interested segments of the business community, its economic importance to the U.S. government was much less than its importance as a bargaining chip toward other goals such as Soviet cooperation with settlements in Vietnam and the Middle East, moderation in the arms race, and so forth. Soviet interests in economic cooperation were also undoubtedly linked to other goals, but obviously they placed somewhat greater weight on the economic benefits than the United States did, although it is easy to overstate their interest.

The interest the U.S.S.R. does have in trade and investment from the West stems largely from technological backwardness and relative shortage of capital, at least as viewed from the standpoint of planners trying to do more with their resources than is possible. The Ninth Five Year

Plan (1971-1975) projected large-scale modernization and technological change in the consumer sector of the Soviet economy.[28] Needless to say, R & D resources will continue to be poured as usual into heavy industry and the military and aerospace industries. Soviet need for modernization is incontrovertible. In Premier Kosygin's words in 1965: "The pattern of production of machinery and equipment being turned out by many branches [of Soviet industry] does not conform to modern standards."[29] An American scholar calculated that in 1962 Soviet technology overall lagged behind that of the United States by twenty-five years.[30] The shortcut to "catching up," of course, is to borrow technology. This is especially true in view of the Soviet failure to introduce effective reforms which would speed up and encourage endogenous technological change and diffusion. Soviet interest in expanding economic relations with capitalist countries for these purposes was stated explicitly in the Ninth Five Year Plan: "Consideration is being given to mutually beneficient cooperation with foreign firms and banks in working out a number of very important economic questions associated with the use of the Soviet Union's natural resources, construction of industrial enterprises, and exploration for new technical solutions."[31]

The question arises as to why the U.S.S.R. appears to be more interested in importing technology and capital from the United States than from other nations. There are several possible reasons. First, trade and investment with the United States has been depressed relative to East-West trade in general. Thus, U.S. trade with all the Eastern nations made up 15 percent of total U.S. trade in 1938, 31 percent in 1948, and 5 percent in 1970. It is only natural that with political tensions reduced this trade will rise to more normal levels. Second, the United States is by far the most technologically advanced nation in the world, as indicated by the measures of GNP per combined unit of labor and capital for different nations. Taking the United States as 100, Northwest Europe records only slightly more than 50, and Japan, Italy, and the U.S.S.R. about 40. Furthermore, the United States is the only industrial nation whose size and market potential are comparable to the Soviet Union's, and this is relevant in determining the type and scale of technology. Finally, the United States, for real or imaginary reasons, has always epitomized for the Russians the advanced capitalist industrial economy, the one upon which they would like to model themselves. This may be a carryover from the good experience in borrowing technology from the United States during the initial industrialization period of the late 1920s and early 1930s. Third, as noted, the U.S.S.R. wants not only to purchase technology but to borrow capital. Much of the capital they wish to borrow is related to the import of technology, but much of it is simply buying "time." This is particularly true of the enormous raw material developing projects in Siberia, especially in gas and oil. On favorable terms, the Soviets would be willing to borrow large amounts of capital. In fact, the only country which is rich enough to finance either many of the individual projects or a large proportion of the total is the United States. (Harold Scott, President of the U.S.-Soviet Economic Trade Council, reported in Fall 1973 on *The Advocates*, a TV program, that the Soviets had a list of $120 billion worth of projects for which they were seeking financing.)

Despite the fact that the U.S. Administration is pushing trade and investment with the U.S.S.R., there are many voices in the background expressing a variety of concerns. First, there are those who fear that exporting technology to the Russians will enable them to overtake and surpass the United States. This is not a rational fear. In the words of J. Irwin Miller, head of the well-known Presidential Committee: "In today's world, no nation can continue to rely heavily on the . . . importation of technology to improve its relative industrial position. To do so may appear to be cheap in the short run, but could turn out to be a sure way of perpetuating second-class industrial status."[32] Furthermore, as long as other nations' industrialists are prepared to supply technology to the Eastern nations, the only sufferers from a policy of denying export of our technology are American businessmen and the American balance of payments. Finally, those who fear that the U.S.S.R. will overtake the U.S. do not understand that exporting technology to the U.S.S.R. or to Eastern Europe is not like exporting it to Japan. Under the Japanese system, newly imported technology is improved on and diffused rapidly; the centrally planned systems, however, provide relatively infertile soil along these lines.

Another set of concerns relates to the large natural resource investment projects in the U.S.S.R. Many of these billion-dollar projects are planned for twenty-five or more years, envisioning long-term interdependence. Usually, the longer the duration of an investment project the greater the risks, and these projects are no exception. They are particularly risky, of course, not from the Soviet side but from the American side. For many years, Americans will pour money, technology, equipment, and management into the U.S.S.R. without any return and without any effective way of removing or recovering even the tangible part of the investment should political events make this desirable. When production finally does get underway, repayment begins in the form of deliveries of oil, gas, and so forth. This raises doubts in the minds of many observers as to the wisdom of allowing the development of dependence on the U.S.S.R. for such strategic products. Can the Soviets not blackmail the U.S. by threatening to withhold shipments of strategic products and to expropriate American capital? These concerns are not without foundation, but in my opinion they are exaggerated. From a political standpoint, it is the long-term interlocking of economies which, while perhaps somewhat risky, nevertheless adds an element of stability to détente and renders economic relations more of a bargaining chip in other areas than it would otherwise be. Economically, neither dependence on Soviet raw materials as currently projected nor capital investments on Soviet soil are likely to be large enough to force compromise of American political interests in the event of a breakdown in détente. There is still, however, a question as to whether our investments could not be more profitably directed at developing domestic sources of oil, gas, and so forth. This is an empirical question and, it would seem, one which should be confronted by the business community rather than by the government. In general, one must rely on the business community to make sound economic decisions regarding investments in the U.S.S.R. If these investments mean that the United States is going to get cheap raw materials from the U.S.S.R. over the next few decades and at the same time delay the exhaustion of our own reserves, this factor should be weighed in the balance against some of the risks mentioned above.

As we have noted, the U.S.S.R. runs fewer risks than the U.S. does from heightened economic interdependence. Nevertheless, from the Russian standpoint, there may also be risks. Recall the chaos in China when the U.S.S.R. withdrew its technicians and failed to finish many "turnkey" plants. Recall also that despite the hiatus in relations, China promptly repaid her debts to the U.S.S.R. There is no particular reason to suspect that the U.S.S.R. would, short of war, renege on its debts—it never has before. There are also risks, in the eyes of the Soviet leaders, in having hundreds of foreign technicians living on their soil, and risks in making many of the institutional adjustments which are required to facilitate the proposed projects.

U.S.-U.S.S.R. TRADE AGREEMENT

The first steps toward the U.S.-U.S.S.R. Trade Agreement were taken in November 1971 when then-Secretary of Commerce Maurice Stans went to Moscow for official talks.[33] This was followed by two Russian visits to Washington in 1972 and climaxed in May 1972 by the Moscow summit meeting between President Nixon and Secretary-General Brezhnev at which the "basic principles of relations between the United States and the Union of Soviet Socialist Republics" were agreed upon. The seventh Principle states that

the United States and the Soviet Union regard commercial and economic ties as an important and necessary element in the strengthening of their bilateral relations and thus will actively promote the growth of such ties. They will facilitate cooperation between the relevant organizations and enterprises of the two countries and the conclusion of appropriate agreements and contracts, including long-term ones.[34]

In October 1972 a set of commercial agreements was signed by the two countries. These agreements were part of a larger set of agreements between the two nations, including agreements on science and technology, space, medical science and public health, and environmental protection. Some provisions of the basic commercial agreements are briefly sketched below.

A major obstacle, settlement of the Soviet Lend-Lease debt, was overcome. This was important because the United States negotiators had insisted upon such a settlement as a prerequisite for the whole trade agreement. It probably would have been politically impossible in the United States to have gotten confirmation for a trade agreement without the Lend-Lease settlement. On the other hand, the Lend-Lease issue was the one on which the Russians were most emotional, according to Secretary of Commerce Peter Peterson.[35] The United States was asking the U.S.S.R. to pay for part of the estimated $2.6 billion (out of a total of $10.8 billion) worth of goods estimated to have remained in their hands at the end of World War II. The Soviets viewed Lend-Lease as part of a mutual war effort in which they had contributed more than 20 million lives and sustained enormous destruction. Efforts to settle this question had failed several times in the past, with the Americans refusing to take less than $800 million and the Soviets refusing to offer more than $300 million. The final settlement of October 1972 was for $722 million, including interest. This was to be paid in annual installments of approximately $24 million ending in the year 2001. Payments by the U.S.S.R. were tied to Congressional extension of MFN treatment to the U.S.S.R. and were to be suspended in 1975 if MFN were not forthcoming. Agreement by the U.S.S.R. to settle the Lend-Lease debt made it possible, of course, to eliminate the Johnson Act limitations on U.S. credits; apparently, after fifty-five years, the statute of limitations will finally take care of Russia's World War I debt to the United States.

Emotional factors aside, it made good economic sense for the Soviets to have agreed to this settlement, and they may have felt this too. First, to the extent that trade with the United States increases, the gains from trade can be weighed in the balance. Second, to the extent that they receive credits, the gains from these credits can also be weighed in the balance. Third, they may never actually have to tighten their belts to pay off the Lend-Lease debt, since the annual payments may always be more than offset by extensions of otherwise unavailable credit. That is, their debtor position vis-à-vis the United States will rise rather than fall as a result of the Lend-Lease debt payment. Finally, being accorded MFN treatment would have increased their profits on existing trade (by lowering tariffs) and increased their exports to the United States as well. Despite these economic advantages, it must have been extremely difficult for Secretary Brezhnev to tell his colleagues and the Russian people that he had agreed to a payment.

There is evidence that President Roosevelt was against requiring any repayment of Lend-Lease. In his letter of transmittal to the *Eleventh Report to Congress on Lend-Lease Operations* for the period ending July 31, 1943, he said:

The United Nations are growing stronger because each of them is contributing to the common struggle in full measure—whether in men, in weapons, or in materials. Each is contributing in accordance with its ability and its resources. Everything that all of us have is dedicated to victory over the Axis powers. The Congress in passing and extending the Lend-Lease Act made it plain that the United States wants no new war debts to jeopardize the coming peace. Victory and a secure peace are the only coin in which we can be repaid.

In 1924, Louis Marin expressed similar views in the French Chamber of Deputies: "While war still raged, statesmen in every country appealed to the common cause. Some gave their ships, some munitions, some the lives of their sons, some money, and today only those who gave money come saying to us: 'Give back what we loaned.' "[36]

It is not clear that the U.S.S.R. will reap large gains if it is accorded MFN. As indicated earlier, most Soviet exports to the United States are raw materials and primary products which are allowed to enter the United States duty free or with low tariffs, hardly different, if at all, from MFN rates. It is possible, of course, that being accorded MFN, the U.S.S.R. will be able to increase exports of some finished products on which high discriminatory tariffs must now be paid. The United States stands to gain little or nothing from being according MFN by the Russians for reasons analyzed in Chapter 2. This is of no concern, however, since a major Soviet interest in the trade agreement is to buy more American goods.

Fears of Soviet dumping or of a very large influx of Russian products if MFN is granted led to the inclusion of a market disruption clause in the Agreement, a fairly extreme form of protection of the U.S. domestic market. In effect, it prevents the U.S.S.R. from competing successfully with domestically produced American goods.

Settlement of the Lend-Lease debt made possible extensions of credit to the U.S.S.R. Under the credit agreement, the Export-Import Bank (Eximbank) can supply both direct credits and guarantees to Americans exporting to the U.S.S.R. via the Soviet Foreign Trade Bank (Vneshtorgbank) at terms granted elsewhere.

Among other items, the Agreement also provided for expanded government commercial facilities in each country, expanded private business facilities, and an agreement to favor third-nation arbitration in the case of trade disputes. In the case of disputes, most Western businessmen have in the past used, sometimes reluctantly, the Soviet Foreign Trade Arbitration Commission. While Soviet courts have had a reputation for fairness in these matters, Americans have traditionally preferred to have third-nation arbitrators. The two nations also signed a

Maritime Agreement which dealt with port access, freight rates, sharing of cargo, and so forth.

The Joint U.S.-U.S.S.R. Commercial Commission which was set up at the Moscow summit meeting to work out the details of the Trade Agreement is still in existence, working on a number of important problems relating to patents, licenses, copyrights, taxation, joint ventures, and general issues which may arise and impede normalization of trade relations.

This concludes our survey of the trade agreement between the United States and the U.S.S.R. This agreement can be taken as representative of the kind of agreement that the U.S.S.R. has signed with many Western nations, although it does contain special clauses (e.g., Lend-Lease).

SOVIET ANNULMENT OF THE TRADE AGREEMENT, 1975

The Trade Agreement, so laboriously put together over a period of a few years, was annulled by the U.S.S.R. in January 1975, shortly after being approved by Congress in its passage of the Trade Reform Act of 1974. The annulment occurred despite the fact that many of the other linkages in the détente had been negotiated. Examples include: the two SALT Agreements and the Vladivostok Accord on arms control; Soviet restraint in many ways with regard to our handling of the Vietnam peace agreement; possibly Soviet restraint in the Middle East crisis; binational cooperation in space and in many other scientific areas; U.S. restraint during the events in Czechoslovakia, August 1968, and Poland, December 1971; and Soviet relaxation on the Jewish emigration issue.

It is impossible to pinpoint precisely which of several factors was primarily responsible for Soviet rejection of the Agreement. It is, however, fairly easy to list the several factors which must have weighed in the final Soviet decision.

First, the value to the U.S.S.R. of the Trade Agreement was reduced after 1972 by two events: the rise in the price of gold which, it soon became clear, would be stabilized for some time in the neighborhood of $150 an ounce; in the fall of 1973, the quadrupling in price of oil as well as the rise in the price of gas and other raw materials exported by the Russians. These events gave the U.S.S.R. a windfall of roughly $3 billion a year which had not been expected when the Trade Agreement was being negotiated in 1971 and 1972. With $3 billion or so more in hard currency earnings every year, the Russians were not prepared to make as significant concessions as before in order to get the advantages of a trade agreement with the United States.

Second, in both the Trade Reform Act and in the renewal of the Export-Import Bank authority, clauses were included which limited Eximbank credits to the U.S.S.R. to $300 million over a four-year period in absence of further Congressional sanction. This so-called Stevenson Amendment detracted from the Trade Agreement in two respects. In the opinion of many knowledgeable observers, the U.S.S.R. was more interested in credits from the United States, especially Eximbank subsidized credits, than in a lowering of tariffs through extension of MFN. The Soviets had in mind large-scale projects and multibillion-dollar credits. This possibility initially was lost with the Stevenson Amendment. Also, in a broad sense, the Amendment was not consistent with MFN, because it denied "equal treatment" by putting a limit on the credits to which the U.S.S.R. was entitled at the same time that no formal limits were placed on the credits which could be extended to any other nation.

Finally, the Russians were clearly upset over the emigration issue which had been "linked" into the Congressional discussions on the Trade Agreement by Senators Jackson and Vanik, among others. Basically, pressures by the Jewish community and Congressmen representing their interests, along with a feeling that the U.S.S.R. would do almost anything to get more American credit and technology, led to the demand that the Soviets ease their restrictions on emigration, particularly of Jews, as part of the price for MFN. It was obvious that the Russians had made concessions on this issue, and emigration increased substantially between 1968 and 1974, but the concessions were the result of "quiet diplomacy" and informal agreement. When the Congress insisted on putting an amendment in the Trade Act which made the grant of MFN to the U.S.S.R. legally dependent on freer emigration, the affront to Soviet national sovereignty went beyond tolerable limits. Matters were certainly not helped by Senator Jackson's announcement to the world from the White House steps of the passage of the amendment.

These seem to be the three major factors behind cancellation of the Trade Agreement by the Russians. The first two factors cited robbed the Agreement of much of its potential economic value to the U.S.S.R.; the third required a demeaning political concession which strained the limits of "linkage" to its breaking point. It is not clear what will follow from here. The U.S.S.R., although incensed over the Trade Agreement amendments, has indicated quite clearly that détente is still on. Scarcely two months after the annulment, the Russians indicated that they considered a follow-up of the Vladivostok discussions of November 1974 on the limitation of offensive nuclear weapons a major objective for the coming year.[37] They also judiciously maintained a low profile on the situation in Cambodia and South Vietnam as it rapidly deteriorated. Trade and investment with the United States are also continuing, but undoubtedly, with the exception of grain imports, much will be diverted to Western Europe and Japan, which long ago granted MFN and in 1975 extended approximately $8 billion in new credits to the U.S.S.R.

For its part, the United States executive branch was also anxious to keep détente alive. President Ford, in his State of the Union speech to Congress on April 10, 1975, proposed rehabilitating the Trade Agreement. This resolve was shaken, in the context of election year politics, by Soviet military intervention in Angola. Despite apparently reliable reports that the United States had covertly intervened in Angola at least as early as the Russians, Secretary of State Kissinger nevertheless stated in January 1976 that the U.S. would not pursue the Trade Agreement in 1976 because of lack of "foreign policy restraint"[38] by the U.S.S.R. On the other hand, attempts to reach a new accord on strategic arms limitations continue (January 1976) despite Angola because of its very high priority among U.S. Administration objectives; and a proposed embargo on grain sales to the U.S.S.R. has been ruled out, according to *The New York Times*, because of its "political and economic effect . . . on the farm states."[39] These recent events indicate the complexities and limits of "linkage politics."

Other Recent Developments

Throughout the 1960s CMEA refused to recognize the EEC and in fact attempted to undercut it by calling for the establishment of a permanent regional organization for security and economic cooperation in Europe. The growing spirit of détente between East and West, as well as the U.S.-European squabbles that followed the Western international monetary crises beginning in 1971, tended to reduce the threat of EEC in the eyes of CMEA members. At the same time, the EEC forced the issue by representing the "community" in all trade agreements with other nations and by forbidding members to negotiate new trade agreements with the socialist nations on a bilateral basis.[40] The consequence of this combination of events was easy to predict. On March 20, 1972, in a speech to the Fifteenth Soviet Trade Union Congress, Brezhnev left no doubts about the Soviet willingness to deal with the EEC:

> The Soviet Union is far from ignoring the actual existing situation in Western Europe, including the existence of such an economic grouping of capitalist nations as the Common Market . . . . Our relations with the participants in this grouping, naturally, will depend on the extent to which they, on their part, recognize the socialist part of Europe—specifically the interests of the member countries of the Council for Economic Mutual Assistance. We are for equality in economic relations and against discrimination.[41]

Negotiations took place between the two groups of nations in June 1975. Both parties, of course, viewed interbloc economic cooperation as part of a larger package including issues relating to the political and military security of Europe and the ongoing conferences on these issues. Nevertheless, it is still not absolutely clear that economic bargaining between the two blocs will materialize, because of objections that have been recently raised to this type of EEC policy by some of its own members which would prefer more flexibility in their individual trade relationships with other nations.

Should economic relationships between the two blocs nevertheless be negotiated, the U.S.S.R. will undoubtedly play a greater role in CMEA-EEC relations than if relations were binational. Since the U.S.S.R. has typically been a more conservative force than Eastern Europe in East-West economic relations, the end result of such an arrangement might be to dampen the development of freer East-West economic ties.

While various CMEA nations have both negative and positive dealings with GATT and EEC since the late 1950s, the International Monetary

Fund (IMF) and the International Bank for Reconstruction and Development (IBRD) were almost completely ignored. This picture has been changed, finally, with the accession of Rumania to IMF membership in 1973. It is not hard to understand why the Communist nations ignored the IMF for so long. As nations with rigid commodity and currency inconvertibility, with exchange rates which are not real prices and serve no substantive function, and with an intrabloc trade conducted on a rigidly bilateral basis, the IMF would be the last kind of organization they might be expected to join. For, if the IMF stands for anything, it is convertibility, multilateralism, and equilibrium exchange rates which function as prices. Furthermore, membership in the organization cannot help these nations achieve IMF goals. As we have noted earlier, only radical economic reforms involving substantial decentralization of economic power could enable the socialist nations to move in the direction of convertibility and multilateralism.

Under these circumstances, it is surprising, at first, to find any CMEA nation suddenly joining the IMF and, in particular, that the first member should be Rumania, with a relatively orthodox centrally planned economy, and not Hungary, the one nation in the Eastern bloc that has made substantive moves toward decentralization in both internal and external economic relations. There appear to be both political and economic explanations of Rumania's behavior. On the political side, her application to the IMF undoubtedly is part of the overall pattern of edging away from (although not trying to leave) CMEA represented by her relatively large percentages of East-West trade, friendliness toward China, and so forth. The spirit of détente certainly assists these efforts. On the economic side, there are distinct advantages to membership in the IMF and IBRD. Members can draw upon the Fund for convertible currencies in time of need, they are eligible for development loans from the IBRD, and they are eligible to share in the newly created Special Drawing Rights (SDRs), the new international currency created by the Fund to supplement world monetary reserves.

Given the hard currency shortages which beset the CMEA nations, and given détente, it is reasonable to expect that others will shortly follow Rumania's lead and apply for IMF membership. What is more difficult to understand is why the IMF would be interested in membership by CMEA nations. As noted, there is nothing the IMF can do to help these nations move toward IMF goals. Furthermore, the financial situation of the Western world is in such a state of disarray that to bring into the IMF nations with entirely alien international financial arrangements can only confuse matters still further. On the other hand, the IMF authorities may have reasoned that many of its members, particularly some of the LDCs, have been in constant difficulty and have never moved significantly toward conforming with IMF goals either; so why not admit Rumania? Moreover, in an era of détente, the political pressures are all favorable to admission. To admit Rumania and other CMEA nations may add little or nothing toward the achievement of IMF goals. On the other hand, the costs are nothing more than a small amount of financial assistance, which many Western nations are making available on an individual basis anyway.

Chapter 5

Trade and Aid with the Non-Communist Developing Nations (LDCs)

The socialist nations of Europe began to have serious political and economic relations with the non-Communist LDCs around 1955. Trade with and aid to these nations have grown fairly rapidly over the past fifteen to twenty years, yet remain a quite small percentage of total world trade and aid. In 1973, Soviet and East European exports to the LDCs were $4 billion and $2½ billion, respectively; the corresponding import figures were $2½ and $2 billion. In round figures, then, this trade constituted only a little less than 1 percent of world trade, around 4 percent of total LDC trade, 7 percent of the trade of Eastern Europe, and 15 percent of the trade of the U.S.S.R. By the end of 1974, Soviet economic and military aid extended (but not all drawn) to the non-Communist LDCs since World War II totaled $9.6 and $11.8 billion, respectively. The comparable figures for Eastern Europe were $5.3 and $1.3 billion, respectively. In contrast, economic aid by the Western governments through 1973 totaled $123 billion and U.S. military aid alone reached above $25 billion.

The relatively limited economic relations between the Soviet bloc and the LDCs is not hard to understand. Between them, the two groups command no more than one-third of the world's GNP and little more than one-fourth of world trade. Furthermore, the Communist nations are much less qualified to give aid since their per capita incomes average well below those of the wealthier Western nations. In fact, Communist

China, with a lower per capita GNP than most LDCs, ranks second among the Communist nations as an extender of aid to the non-Communist LDCs. Many other factors could be cited, among which the many decades of head start that the Western industrial nations had with the LDCs is not the least.

Despite their relative smallness, Soviet bloc-LDC relations are nevertheless important: one reason is that the LDCs make up a large part of the arena in which East and West compete. The competition, of course, has economic, political, and military dimensions. The military arena, with its obvious political dimensions, has been the hottest; East and West were on opposite sides of the Vietnam and Middle Eastern wars. In addition, the major powers have used their nonmilitary trade and aid in their attempts to influence the character and gain the friendships of the many dozens of other, often volatile, LDC governments. Finally, the competition has had its more purely economic dimensions of fighting for markets and for access to raw material supplies. A second reason for the importance of Soviet bloc-LDC relations is the strategic placement and concentration of a good part of the socialist aid. India and the United Arab Republic, two key developing nations, have been the two major recipients of Soviet aid. For example, Soviet bloc aid "financed 33 percent of the UAR's 1960/61-1964/65 plan, 17 percent of public sector investment in industry and energy under India's third five-year plan (1961/62-1965/66), and 20 percent of all investment under Mali's 1961-1965 five-year plan."[1] Furthermore, the U.S.S.R. has often offered support in the context of Western refusal of support: the Cuban boycott by the United States; French withdrawal from Guinea; U.S. refusal to build the Aswan Dam or Bokharo steel mills. Third, some of the major projects sponsored by the socialist nations have had a dramatic character which has captured public imagination. Cases in point are the Aswan Dam in Egypt and the Bhilai and Bokharo steel plants in India, all built with substantial Soviet assistance.

It should be obvious from the preceding discussion that the economic and political power paradigm used as a framework for discussing intrabloc relationships has much less, if any, relevance in the present context. To begin with, the socialist nations do not have independent political power over the LDCs. The political power they may have in some specific instances derives largely from the exercise of economic power, and the degree of economic power the socialist nations can exercise is small and probably results largely from aid to, rather than the trade with, the LDCs. With a few exceptions, the trade of the socialist nations is too small (approximately 5 percent) a part of the trade of the LDCs for the former to be able to exert significant market power. To an overwhelming extent, trade is simply for trade's sake along comparative advantage lines. One minor exception is the ability of the U.S.S.R., because of its enormous relative size, to act as a "buyer of last resort" for raw material exporters who face softening markets. Over the years, the U.S.S.R. has engaged in such "distress" buying of Egyptian cotton, Burmese rice, Brazilian coffee, and other commodities. Of course, this amounts to aid rather than trade since the U.S.S.R. paid, in effect, more than the market price (would have been). That this form of aid has often been unwillingly granted has frequently been demonstrated later when the U.S.S.R. has turned around and reexported the imported product in competition with the original seller, thereby forgoing the goodwill previously earned. The more important source of economic power is economic and military aid, since the aid market, especially on the side of the donors (suppliers), is much smaller and more oligopolistic than the commodity trade market. However, unlike the U.S.S.R. in intrabloc relations, which felt that it could use its economic-political power for negative purposes (embargoes) as well as positive political ends, the power deriving from aid to the LDCs is much too weak. Such power can only be used to gain political favor, which, as we shall argue, is its main purpose. To try to use it negatively would not only be futile but would negate its purpose.

Some Economic Aspects of Trade and Aid

There is a strong economic basis for CMEA-LDC trade. While political developments were certainly favorable to the opening of intensive relations between the two groups of nations in the mid-1950s, it is important to note that economic conditions were equally favorable. As noted in Chapter 3, in the 1954-1956 period the CMEA nations suddenly found themselves confronting a raw material crisis. Following the Soviet pattern of the 1930s, each Eastern European nation had rushed pell-mell into industrialization after World War II, restructuring its economy as fast as it could away from the production of agricultural products and raw materials. In addition to the ideology of "industrialization," avoidance of the extractive industries can also be attributed to the shortage of capital that rapid industrialization generated, related to the fact that extractive industries, with the exception of housing, are the most capital-intensive of all—much more capital-intensive than manufacturing. As noted earlier, the U.S.S.R. agreed at the time to put its finger in the dike, a temporary solution which has taken on some permanence. In addition, the CMEA nations were motivated to turn to the raw material-exporting nations of the Third World, particularly since at this time political factors dictated a similar strategy.

The motivation to turn to the LDCs rather than to the West for raw materials was fortified by another important economic consideration, namely, that the raw materials could be purchased from the former by exports of machinery, equipment, and manufactured goods. CMEA exports of these latter products were largely unacceptable in the Western industrial nations, since they were usually of inferior quality and technology to those produced in the West.

Complementarity between the two groups of nations becomes evident when one considers the situation of the LDCs, particularly in the 1950s and 1960s. On the one hand, these nations were always looking for new and stable markets for their surplus output, and surpluses were common in this period. On the other hand, they were constantly short of foreign exchange to meet demands created by rising per capita incomes and with which to buy the machinery, equipment, and manufactured products needed for industrialization. Trade with the CMEA nations promised at least a partial solution to both problems. Table 5.1 shows the commodity trade pattern between the two groups of nations for a representative year, 1964, supporting statistically the high degree of classical complementarity between them: in 1964, more than four-fifths of CMEA imports from the LDCs were foods and raw materials and more than two-thirds of their exports were manufactured goods and machinery. Such complementarity does not exist, of course, in the China-LDC trade.

In a second major respect, the socialist nations and LDCs have found themselves mutually compatible in trade. As we have explained, nations

TABLE 5.1
CMEA Trade with LDCs by Commodity Groups, 1964
(in percent of total)

	IMPORTS		EXPORTS	
	U.S.S.R.	EASTERN EUROPE	U.S.S.R.	EASTERN EUROPE
Foods and beverages	38	37	5	13
Crude materials, inedible, except fuels	45	46	4	4
Mineral fuels	0	1	13	4
Manufactures	13	12	13	38
Machinery and Equipment	0	0	59	29
Other	4	5	6	12

SOURCE: Carole A. Sawyer, *Communist Trade With Developing Countries: 1955-1965* (New York: Praeger, 1970), Tables 16, 17, 20, 21.

which engage in central planning suffer currency and commodity inconvertibility and, in consequence, have a strong proclivity to bilaterally balanced trading relationships with other nations. Most of the LDCs have suffered fairly constantly since World War II from severe balance of payments problems and, as a result, have applied stringent controls to their trade, suffered from currency inconvertibility, and in many instances also conducted their trade with other nations so as to achieve bilateral balances. Thus, the desire of the nations in each group to control trade for balance of payments reasons, while constituting a barrier to their trade with many advanced Western nations, actually facilitated their trade with each other under existing conditions.

While comparative advantage and bilateralism have facilitated CMEA-LDC trade, trading relationships have not always followed a smooth path. Bilateralism, while often necessary under existing conditions, is always a sub-optimal rather than optimal way of conducting trading relationships. It does usually reduce the volume of trade to the amount that the "weaker" of the two partners can sell to the "stronger." Often, imbalances are planned for or develop unexpectedly. In many of these cases, the arrangement is for the deficit nation to pay the balance in convertible currency. The U.S.S.R. has typically run sizable deficits with Malaysia for rubber and with Rhodesia for copper and paid for these with £ sterling.[2] On the other hand, in many other

178

instances, LDCs have run up surpluses with socialist nations which are not payable in convertible currencies. Under these conditions, they are faced with the problem of "commodity inconvertibility," that is, it is unclear what they can buy to work off their surpluses, when they can buy it, and at what price. They are, in effect, at the mercy of the debtor nation (although there is no evidence of deliberate misuse of their position by socialist trade partners). Referring to the problems of the bilateral trading system, a Ghanian delegate to a United Nations Conference on Trade and Development (UNCTAD) meeting said that it results

... in the need for individual developing countries to balance their trade and payments with individual centrally planned economies with whom they had entered into bilateral agreements. The danger in that was that individual developing countries might sometimes be compelled to make unsuitable purchases of goods from their trade partners in the centrally planned group for the sole purpose of achieving that balance. The outcome was that the country concerned failed to make maximum use of its export earnings.[3]

The imbalance problem under bilateralism works both ways, of course, and there are also instances where the LDC runs a deficit which it cannot immediately pay off. Here it is not commodity inconvertibility, but rather the poverty and serious balance of payments situation that many LDCs find themselves in, that prevents settlement.

One of the goals that the socialist nations seek in their trade with each other is "stability" to facilitate their planning process. They advertise this trait as an advantage of trade under central planning.

The development of trade relations with socialist countries assures a guaranteed market for the export products of underdeveloped countries, and creates a stable market not subject to economic fluctuations. The planned character of the economy of socialist countries presupposes the conclusion of long-term trade agreements in which the conditions of delivery are firmly fixed: their volume, time period, prices, etc. ... This alone eliminates the tremendous instability which exists in the demand for the prices of export products of underdeveloped countries as a result of the cyclical character of the development of capitalist production.[4]

Instability has been one of the major problems of LDC trade because supply of agricultural products fluctuates sharply with weather and

179

demand; prices of both agricultural products and other raw materials fluctuate more sharply with business conditions than do those of manufactured products. Presumably, a major advantage offered the LDCs by the centrally planned economies is greater stability. No studies, to my knowledge, have been conducted to determine whether or not prices are more stable in CMEA-LDC than capitalist-LDC trade. The presumption is that they are. A few studies have been made, however, of the relative stability of trade value in the two sets of markets. These studies suggest that the quantities of primary commodities purchased from the LDCs by the leading Western industrial nations are actually more stable than those purchased by either the U.S.S.R. or the Comecon nations as a group.[5]

Economic motives rank much lower in the nonmilitary aid programs to the LDCs than in trade (although there is often a link between the two). Before discussing this assertion, it is important to clarify the sense in which the term *aid* is used. Economists use the term to mean any transfer made on "concessional" terms, i.e., the donor is not asking for payment (or repayment) or is not asking for full payment (the price including interest is below the market price). Pure aid, then, would be defined as the gift of a commodity or the granting of a credit which need not be repaid and on which there is no interest charge. Anything in between pure aid and a pure market-price transaction is "concessional." This characterizes most of the so-called aid of advanced nations. It is also true of most Communist aid to the LDCs. In fact, however, the preponderance of the aid arrangements between these groups of nations is more accurately described as exports or other assistance which are financed under a credit arrangement and which must be repaid with interest. The credit terms are usually concessional, however, and therefore qualify as "aid." We refer primarily to the fact that the interest on most credits had been 2½ to 3 percent, and on occasion as high as 4 percent. This low rate of interest undoubtedly stems in part from the ideological bias against the use of interest in Communist countries, which prevailed until the reforms of the mid-1960s. With the exception of grants made by some capitalist nations and some subsidized loans of national and international aid organizations, these rates are below the prevailing rates of interest on international loans. They are also far below the rate of interest which would prevail in the Communist nations if market forces could seek their equilibrium level.

To test the possibility of an economic motivation in the Soviet bloc aid programs, it is important to think of these programs in the context of over-fully employed economies in which the extension of aid, or credits, must automatically result in the sacrifice of an equivalent domestic investment program (as described in Chapter 2). Furthermore, with over-full employment planning, the socialist nations have found themselves chronically short of capital and constantly unable to complete scheduled projects. Under these circumstances, the economically rational procedure is to eliminate those projects that use the most capital, take the longest time to "pay off," have relatively low rates of return, and are least "essential" as this term is usually defined, that is, are not in defense or heavy industry. This description of a relatively undesirable investment project fits investment in foreign aid perfectly. That is to say, annual extension of credits have been relatively large (in comparison with individual domestic investment projects), with low rates of interest, usually repayable over a period of from eight to fifteen years after completion of the project (recently more quickly), and usually repayable in foodstuffs and raw materials which, while useful, are not of the highest priority to the planners. It is one thing to export machinery and equipment which has been produced specifically to pay for current imports of foodstuffs and raw materials. It is another to reduce the rate of investment in domestic industry in order to subsidize imports of food and raw materials in the distant future. The Soviet leadership, at least, is well aware of the costs to them of extending (subsidizing) aid to the LDCs. In 1958, Premier Khrushchev acknowledged that "our economic and technical assistance to developing countries is rather disadvantageous to us from the commercial point of view." In the same year, an editorial in *Pravda* complained that "it would be more advantageous for the Soviet Union to build new plants in [our] country with these funds and to export finished goods."[6]

The preceding discussion strongly suggests that much Soviet and East European aid to the LDCs is not economically motivated. The fact that China probably has a lower per capita income than many of the LDCs to which it has extended aid and that its aid is on more concessionary terms than that of the CMEA nations attests to an even greater lack of economic motivation. One is forced to conclude, then, that politics—or diplomacy—plays an important role in decisions regarding the Communist aid programs. This conclusion is supported when the geographical patterns of these programs are examined.

Soviet bloc military aid is obviously more political than either economic aid or trade. This is true of military aid in general, of course, but most Soviet bloc military aid has been extended in crisis (confrontation) situations during which major and abrupt shifts in the internal and external political status quo in which the payoffs may be immediate and dramatic may take place.

While politics rather than economics clearly dominates decisions regarding the direction and relative, if not absolute, amount of military aid, it may well be that the economic gains from military aid exceed those from a comparable value of economic aid. The reasoning behind this paradoxical statement is as follows: One reason why economic aid is not profitable is, as noted above, that it has what economists call a high opportunity cost, that is to say, the nation extending aid is deprived of the use of the resources embodied in that aid for high priority domestic purposes. The military industries operate according to different principles. First, military goods and services are not produced in peacetime for use but rather for potential use. Most military products probably never get used. Second, for leading military nations like the U.S.S.R. and U.S., their rate of technological change is very rapid and the need to maintain stockpiles of the most advanced weapons is viewed as urgent. This implies that such nations find themselves involuntarily accumulating even larger stockpiles of obsolete (to them) weapons. The cost of maintaining such inventories is not trivial. The accumulation of relatively worthless (to them) stockpiles and cost of inventories are part of the price of staying ahead in the arms race and are borne willingly for this reason by the major powers. Clearly, any price they can get for obsolete weapons reduces future maintenance costs, yields a surplus profit on sunk costs,* and, unlike economic aid, does not deprive the nations, particularly if it is fully employed, of the use of its resources for other purposes.

The extension of economic and military aid to LDCs has inevitably involved the socialist nations in the provision of technical assistance in

---

*This is an overstatement, of course, that applies to the most obsolete and least useful weapons. There must certainly be a spectrum of obsolescence along which old weapons models fall.

the form of providing technical experts and workers and also in the training of LDC nations either in their own country or in the donor country. In recent years, technical assistance not connected with specific projects has also been extended in many areas of expertise such as economic planning, medicine, agriculture, and management. Mostly, however, the technical assistance has been required to install new plants, get them started into production, and train local workers. Similarly, military specialists have been required to assemble and maintain equipment, train local military personnel, and serve as advisers. A given amount of military aid probably requires more technical assistance than the same amount of economic aid because the military is usually delivered more quickly and in larger packages. In the case of Soviet technical advisers, the LDC is required to pay the foreign exchange costs of transportation to and from the country and many local costs such as housing and medical care. These costs are often covered by grants under Western and Chinese technical aid. It has been estimated that in the aggregate, roughly 15 to 20 percent of drawings on Soviet project credits have gone to pay the costs of such technical assistance; in some of the more backward nations, however, the figure has reached 25 to 30 percent.[7]

In the early stages, the Soviets undoubtedly thought that political relations with the LDCs would be improved by having Soviet engineers in the LDCs and LDC students in the U.S.S.R. It is hard to sum up the net result of these experiences. At present, however, it is clear that expectations have not been fulfilled. Soviet technicians in Asia and Africa have often kept fastidiously to their enclaves, and the experiences of LDC students in the U.S.S.R. have been mixed; black students in particular have not gotten along well in recent years. Probably the most serious incident was the expulsion of many thousands of Soviet military technicians from Egypt in 1972. At best, exchanges of technicians and students have had little, if any, beneficial political effects.

The number of Soviet technical advisers in economic aid projects amounted to some 10,000-12,000 per year in the 1960s. Over the same period Eastern Europe has supplied around 5,000 or 6,000 technicians, and China has expanded its number to over 20,000, mostly in Africa.[8] Perhaps 15,000 LDC personnel have received technical training in Soviet institutes, and another 30,000 students, half from Africa, have attended Soviet universities and secondary schools on scholarship since 1955.[9] The number of new foreign students per year in the U.S.S.R. has actually declined since it hit a peak of 3,400 in 1962, a decline to which race problems have probably contributed. The total number of LDC students being trained in all the nations of the Communist bloc as of December 1972 was estimated at approximately 24,000.[10] Many foreign personnel have also received technical training on the job, either in factories being built in their own nations or in similar plants in the U.S.S.R. and Eastern Europe. A CMEA estimate put the total until 1970 at about 200,000, of whom 75 percent were trained by the U.S.S.R.[11] The socialist nations have been assisting in establishing more than twenty institutes of higher education in the developing nations which will have, eventually, an aggregate student body of more than 15,000.*

One further type of economic relationship between CMEA nations and the LDCs must be mentioned. We refer to the various forms of cooperation agreements among enterprises of the Eastern nations and between Eastern and Western as described in the preceding two chapters. Agreements of this kind have developed between members of CMEA and the developing nations since the early 1960s. In these agreements and ventures, the Eastern partner plays much the same role vis-à-vis the LDC that the Western partner does in East-West arrangements. The Eastern partner assists with selling, repairs, technical maintenance, and supply of spare parts, management, finance, and related matters for enterprises located on the LDC partner's territory.

---

*As this manuscript was about to go to press, a new source arrived with somewhat different figures from those in the above paragraph. Some of the data are presented below. In 1974, there were in the LDCs 24,440 economic and 6,880 military technicians from the U.S.S.R. Comparable figures for Chinese technicians were 22,935 and 1,035. Between 1955 and 1974, the following number of LDC military personnel were trained in Communist countries: U.S.S.R.–33,625; Eastern Europe–3,750; China–2,375. The comparable figures for numbers being trained in December 1974 were: 3,250, 100, and 700. The recent trend in the number of new trainees to all Communist nations was as follows: academic trainees: from 3,000 in 1967 to 4,645 in 1974; technical trainees: from 1,245 in 1967 to 4,380 in 1974; military trainees: from 1,205 in 1967 to 3,635 in 1974. Some of these data are clearly at odds with those presented in the text. Source: *Handbook of Economic Statistics, 1975* (Washington, D.C.: Central Intelligence Agency, August 1975), pp. 68-70.

The stock of these mixed companies is owned jointly, with the Eastern partner usually holding less than or up to 50 percent, but occasionally more. The Eastern partner is either the government itself or one of the foreign trade organizations. Apparently, the U.S.S.R. has been the only Eastern government which is not a stockholder per se and which does not share in the distribution of profits; however, its foreign trade organizations do. On the side of the LDCs, the partner is either the government, government-owned enterprises, or private enterprises. Compensation is most generally in the form of an annual guaranteed lump-sum payment. However, profit sharing, royalties, and other kinds of payments are also used. These payments are often made in the output of the venture or by other in-kind arrangements. According to CMEA sources, the ventures are viewed as temporary arrangements set up for limited periods of time, after which ownership is taken over by the developing country partner.[12]

Political and Military Background of Aid Flows[13]

The immediate postwar world was viewed in stark black-and-white terms by Stalin. It was a world divided into two hostile camps, Communist and capitalist-imperialist. No compromise between the two seemed possible. The Cominform (the old Communist International or Comintern) was resurrected, and fairly rigid control was exercised over foreign Communist parties. These parties isolated themselves from other indigenous left-wing movements and had as their goals Communist revolutions. Attempts at such revolutions were made in a number of LDCs, including India, Indonesia, Burma, Malaya, and the Philippines.[14] These extreme Soviet attitudes are somewhat surprising in view of the substantial "decolonization" and the sharp increase in the number of independent LDCs after World War II. However, it was argued that the apparent decolonization was not the end of imperialism and colonialism but simply the result of deals between Western capitalists and their governments and the wealthy local capitalists and landowners. The non-Communist leaders of the newly independent nations were viewed simply as the tools of these groups.[15]

This policy was not very successful and, among other events, Stalin's death in 1953 and the subsequent accession to power of the more ebullient, less dogmatic Khrushchev made a change in policies possible. Material conditions had also changed. The U.S.S.R. and the nations of Eastern Europe had recovered from the war and were growing rapidly; resources could be more easily spared for aid than had been true five years earlier. Finally, the Russians had the bomb and were well aware of the dangers of nuclear confrontation. Competition for the non-aligned Third World seemed much less fraught with danger than direct East-West confrontation, and it was in the direction of such competition that Soviet policies shifted. Khrushchev's aim was to ally himself with the LDCs and cut off the "imperialist" powers from their markets and sources of raw materials.[16] He and Marshal Bulganin took off on a series of much-publicized trips from capital to capital in the developing world, selling aid and moral support. The old tactic of Communist revolution was jettisoned for a policy of exploiting anti-imperialist and nationalist sentiments in the LDCs and trying for power by peaceful parliamentary means. Local Communist parties were directed to work with popular anti-imperialist and nationalist groups and leaders and were otherwise downgraded.

Political theory had to be modified, of course, to justify this change in policy. A new concept was invented to describe the independent LDC: the "national democratic state." In 1960, the conference of World Communist Parties stated:

In the present historical situation favorable international and internal conditions [are] being created in many countries for formation of an independent national democratic state, that is, a state that consistently defends its political and economic independence, struggles against imperialism and its military blocs, against military bases on its territory; a state that struggles against new forms of colonialism and the penetration of imperialist capital; a state that rejects dictatorial and despotic methods of government, a state in which the people are assured broad democratic rights and freedoms.[17]

Two or three years later, another theoretical construct, "revolutionary democracy," was added to the dogma to distinguish between non-Communist regimes which were just anti-imperialist (the national democracy) and those which were moving along a non-Capitalist path of development, gradually nationalizing industries, and with the potential for leading a revolution. Guinea, Ghana, and Mali were among the nations falling into this category, whereas India was a classic example of a national democracy.

The aid program was initiated by a small $3½ million loan to Afghanistan in January 1954, followed by another small loan later that year. In 1955 came the dramatic announcement that the U.S.S.R. would help finance the million-ton Bhilai steel mill in India to the tune of $136 million.[18] Soviet interests expanded from Southern Asia to the Middle East with the Soviet-Egyptian Arms Agreement in September 1955 and support of Egypt in the Suez Crisis in 1956. Most of the aid of the first five years concentrated on these few nations of Southern Asia and the Middle East, although other nations, including Indonesia, received smaller amounts of assistance.

Initial interest was in Southern Asia and the Middle East rather than in Latin America and sub-Saharan Africa. Latin America was undoubtedly shunned because of the dominance of U.S. power in the Western Hemisphere. Certainly, the potential for effective political influence in this area must have appeared relatively low to Soviet leaders. Sub-Saharan Africa also appeared far away, not so much in terms of distance or Western domination as in terms of its socioeconomic and political development. As a feudal-tribal continent not having achieved significant capitalist development, it was hardly a bright prospect in the foreseeable future from the standpoint of Marxist theory for either evolution or revolution to socialism. As a result, Africa was largely ignored by the Bolshevik leaders in the interwar and early postwar periods. After World War II, independence was first achieved in Asia and Southeast Asia by the larger and more strategic nations.

The picture changed abruptly in the late 1950s. Castro's overthrow of Batista in Cuba and his adoption of a Marxist ideology gave the Communist nations a base from which to operate in Latin America and a belief that success was possible. Interest in Africa developed in the 1950s as that continent exploded with independent nations led by men who could be depended on to fight imperialism and who were often viewed as "revolutionary democrats."[19] While support in the Western Hemisphere was confined for many years mainly to Cuba, at least a dozen African nations received assistance. Enthusiasm for both Latin America and Africa declined very quickly. In Latin America, the 1962 Cuban missile crisis and the 1965 American intervention in the

Dominican Republic made it clear that Western hemisphere penetration would have tough going. In addition, support of Castro was relatively very expensive. In Africa, the ousting of "revolutionary democrats" like Ben Bella (Algeria), Keita (Guinea), and Nkrumah (Ghana) put a damper on Soviet bloc enthusiasm.

In general, enthusiasm for aid programs had been dampened. In addition to the setbacks just mentioned, Sukarno was ousted from Indonesia, Sudanese Communists were massacred by other left-wing groups, and, somewhat later, Soviet military personnel were ousted from Egypt. Furthermore, the CMEA countries were all experiencing economic difficulties and slowdowns which induced a more cautious attitude toward extending credits. Finally, as one scholar puts it, there was "the morning after"[20]—the difficulties encountered in the actual implementation of aid agreements. These include such problems as equipment which operated efficiently under arctic or temperate conditions not working in the tropics; lack of local technicians or equipment to back up a project in case something happens to be missing or there is an accident; and inexperienced local workers misusing or breaking equipment, blaming the quality of the equipment and the donor's intentions for the results.

The CMEA nations nevertheless continued to extend credits at roughly the same rate while Khrushchev was in power. In particular, he jumped into the breach in his last year to support construction of the Aswan Dam in Egypt and continued negotiations that led to the support of the Bokharo steel mill in India. Many observers feel that Khrushchev's guarantee of support for the Aswan project, apparently made by him just before he was deposed in 1964 without prior consultation with other Soviet political and economic leaders, was a major proximate cause of his ouster. With his ouster, a significant force for optimism regarding aid programs was removed.

Brezhnev and Kosygin took a much more cautious and pragmatic view toward the aid programs. On the one hand, disillusioned by the lack of political payoff from aid programs, there has been a tendency to question again, as in the early 1950s, the significance of "independence" and to question also the promise which had been attributed to the development of national and revolutionary democracies. Once again, it was argued that there is only one road to socialism and that is via working-class leadership and revolution. On the other hand, having returned to this variety of ideological purity, Eastern nations had no commitment to Ben Bellas and Nkrumahs but were free to extend aid on the basis of pure power politics.[21] An example of the Soviet Union's changed emphasis was its completely neutral reaction to the overthrow of Mali's Modibo Keita in 1968, one of the soundest and most revolutionary leaders in Africa. The Soviet press did not even express regrets over his fall.[22] By this time black Africa was viewed as having very little strategic importance and the Eastern nations were no longer willing to devote resources to low priority political "adventures."*

The less enthusiastic position taken by the CMEA nations toward aid at the end of the 1960s was particularly embarrassing for two reasons. First, the Chinese launched their big aid drive at this time and were not reluctant to compare favorably themselves to the U.S.S.R. Second, in UNCTAD's eyes, the 1970s were to be the Second United Nations Development decade, with an aid goal of 1 percent of the GNP of the advanced industrial nations. With aid of less than .1 percent of GNP—and declining—the CMEA nations were on the spot. They refused to commit themselves to this or any other aid target, simply stating that they would extend aid where aid was warranted. On the other hand, they disclaimed responsibility for the poor economic situation in which the LDCs found themselves and thus disclaimed any moral commitment to extend aid. The moral commitment, presumably, was owed by the capitalist-imperialist powers which had exploited the LDCs over the past century.

The economic criteria for extending credits were changed in accordance with the changed political outlook. Before 1965, aid agreements were signed after only the most casual appraisals; many of the projects were for the construction of complete factories to be built largely by Eastern technicians using Eastern materials. After 1965, projects were much more carefully scrutinized for their possible benefits to both donor and recipient. Credits are no longer announced until feasibility studies are completed. Political stability and ability to absorb aid have become important criteria for loans. There is a tendency for the donor nations to concentrate more on the export of machinery and equip-

*It is worth noting, however, that despite the downgrading of ideology, the Allende government in Chile received almost $200 million from the U.S.S.R. and $115 million from Eastern Europe in 1971-1972.

ment and less on the construction with their own technicians of complete factories, in order to reduce their responsibility for the projects. Finally, an attempt has been made to reduce the "subsidy" implicit in many loans by raising somewhat the rate of interest and by requiring repayment in five to ten years instead of twelve to fifteen years. To justify this declining emphasis on aid, Soviet official sources have argued that the primary duty of the socialist nations to the workers of the world is to strengthen their own economies and to build socialism and communism at home, thereby preparing the "decisive condition for increasing aid to other detachments of the liberation struggle."[23]

The military aid program (Table 5.3, column 10), which is dictated by many of the same interests that guide the economic aid program, tends to be more erratic since much of the aid is purely and simply a response to a crisis situation. The same factors are responsible for the even greater concentration of military aid to a few countries. Thus, of the $8½ billion worth of military aid extended from 1955 to 1972, 80 percent was extended to five nations: Egypt, $2,685 million; India, $1,220 million; Indonesia, $1,100 million; Iraq, $1,000 million; and Syria, $715 million.[24] Military aid commitments were sizable in the late 1950s because of agreements with the Middle Eastern countries and Indonesia. The high level of commitments from mid-1962 to mid-1964 reflected the disputes between India and China, Indonesia and Malaysia, and the civil war in Yemen.[25] Another upsurge in spending occurred around the time of the Six Day War between Israel and the Arab nations in 1967. The sharp increase in 1970-1971 reflected, among other developments, the Soviet build-up of Egyptian air defenses and India's preparation for war with Pakistan. Soviet commitments in this period constituted about 30 percent[26] of their total military aid since 1955, and this makes it clear that the conservatism which has guided the economic assistance program did not constrain the military aid program to the same degree, because of the latter's greater and more political importance.

Some Data on Economic Aid

Some summary data on the Communist aid programs are presented in Tables 5.2 and 5.3. The data in Table 5.2 and in Columns 1 and 10 of

Table 5.3 are a useful background for the discussion in the preceding section.

TABLE 5.2
Communist Economic Loans and Grants to LDCs, 1954-1972
($ millions)

RECIPIENT COUNTRY	U.S.S.R.	EAST EUROPE	CHINA	TOTAL
	8,229	4,095	2,699	15,023
Africa	1,252	785	1,322	3,359
East Asia	154	306	281	741
Latin America	448	590	133	1,171
Near East and South Asia, total	6,375	2,414	918	9,707
Afghanistan	826	12	73	911
Egypt	1,198	671	106	1,975
India	1,593	382	—	1,975
Iran	562	435	—	997
Iraq	549	419	45	1,013
Pakistan	474	74	309	857

Additional data: The major loans and grants in 1973 and 1974 were (in millions of dollars) as follows. Soviet loans to: Argentina, 200; Pakistan, 216; India, 350; Iran, 188. Eastern European loans to: Argentina, 220; Algeria, 98; Egypt, 100; India, 105; Iran, 103; Syria, 185. Chinese loans to: Zaire, 100. From *Handbook of Economic Statistics, 1975* (Washington, D.C.: Central Intelligence Agency, August 1975), pp. 61-70.

SOURCE: Department of State, News Release, "Communist States and Developing Countries: Aid and Trade in 1972," August 1973, Table 1.

NOTE: Since some minor items were left out of this table (e.g., aid to Malta), the major subheadings do not add to the totals.

It is clear from Table 5.2 that the U.S.S.R. was the major aid donor of the Communist nations, contributing somewhat more than half of the $15 billion total. It is also clear that the bulk of Communist aid went to South Asia. This was particularly true of the U.S.S.R., which directed 77 percent of its total aid to this area. In fact, the major recipients of Soviet aid were two extremely important nations from a political and strategic standpoint, India and Egypt, along with four other nations close to the Soviet border, Afghanistan, Iran, Iraq, and Pakistan. Eastern Europe followed more or less in the Soviet pattern,

TABLE 5.3

Soviet Economic and Military Aid, 1954-1974

($ millions)

YEAR	1 COMMITMENTS	ANNUAL			CUMULATIVE					ANNUAL
		2 DELIVERIES	3 ESTIMATED REPAYMENTS	4 NET OUTFLOW, 2. − 3.	5 COMMITMENTS	6 DELIVERIES	7 ESTIMATED REPAYMENTS	8 NET OUTFLOW, 6. − 7.	9 % DELIVERED	10 ANNUAL MILITARY AID
1954	6	2	—	2	6	2	—	2	33.3	—
1955	146	8	—	8	152	10	—	10	6.6	110
1956	220	20	—	20	372	30	—	30	8.1	290
1957	233	40	—	40	605	70	—	70	11.6	240
1958	308	140	—	140	913	210	—	210	23.0	470
1959	821	87	10	77	1734	297	10	287	17.1	40
1960	611	86	25	61	2345	383	35	348	16.3	570
1961	562	174	30	144	2907	557	65	492	19.2	880
1962	24	228	40	188	2931	785	105	680	26.8	415
1963	200	276	60	216	3131	1061	165	896	33.9	390
1964A	742	372	85	287	3873	1433	250	1183	37.0	875
1964B					3794	1195	155	1040	31.5	
1965	416	315	80	235	4210	1510	235	1275	35.9	260
1966	1244	270	105	165	5454	1780	340	1440	32.6	450
1967	269	300	125	175	5723	2080	465	1615	36.3	515
1968	374	300	150	150	6097	2380	615	1765	39.0	465
1969	462	400	175	225	6559	2780	790	1990	42.4	330
1970	194	410	185	225	6753	3190	975	2215	47.2	985
1971	862	420	250	170	7615	3610	1225	2385	47.4	1365
1972	581	400	260	140	8196	4010	1485	2525	48.9	810
1973	622	400			8818	4410				1725
1974	563	635			9381	5045				1100

SOURCES: 1954-1964A from Janos Horvath, "Economic Aid Flow from the U.S.S.R.: A Recount of the First Fifteen Years," *Slavic Review* 29 (December 1970): 632; Horvath's figures are taken from U.S. government publications. 1964B-1972: column 1 is from Tansky, "Soviet Foreign Aid," p. 775; columns 2 and 3 are from Department of State, *News Release,* "Communist States and Developing Countries: Aid and Trade in 1972," August 1973, Table 5. Column 10: 1959-1960 from Department of State, "Communist States and Developing Countries: Aid and Trade in 1970," September 1971, p. 17; 1961-1972 from Department of State, "Communist States and Developing Countries: Aid and Trade in 1972," August 1973, Table 9: 1973-1974 from *Handbook of Economic Statistics, 1975* (Washington, D.C.: Central Intelligence Agency, August 1975), p. 65. There is a slight discrepancy between Tansky's figures and the later figures and the cumulative data are shifted to the later base in 1964.

with somewhat less concentration on Southern Asia and somewhat more on Latin America. Chinese aid, on the other hand, was much more concentrated, with about 50 percent going to Africa, which was relatively neglected by the U.S.S.R. and Eastern Europe. Also, as would be expected, China supplied a disproportionate share of the aid received by its neighbors in East Asia and by Pakistan, because of the latter's enmity with India. In fact, China was the major donor of aid over the 1970-72 period, after having extended virtually no aid over the previous three years. Between 1970 and 1972 China's new aid commitments totaled $1,681 million, compared with totals of $1,640 million and $1,301 million for the U.S.S.R. and Eastern Europe, respectively.[27] China's commitments in 1970-1972 amounted to about three-fifths of its total.*

The trends in Soviet commitments to aid are shown in Table 5.3. Looking at column 1, one sees slow beginnings in the mid-1950s, followed by a sharp increase in 1959 through 1961. This is followed by a virtual cessation of new commitments in 1962 and 1963. (A decline in military aid also occurs in these years.) Several factors have been mentioned as responsible for the sudden drop. First, as noted above, some disillusionment with the political payoff on aid had already set in. Second, the U.S.S.R. was having internal economic problems in this period: very bad weather had a disastrous impact on crops, leading to serious hard currency balance of payments problems as large-scale food imports from the West became necessary. Partly as a result of the poor crops but for organizational reasons as well, the rate of economic growth in these years was the lowest in the postwar period. Finally, some economists have argued (not very convincingly in my opinion) that there may have been a slowdown in new commitments because commitments were outpacing actual deliveries by such a large amount. Cumulative commitments are listed in column 5 and cumulative deliveries in column 6, with the percentage that column 6 is of column 5 listed in column 9. From column 9 we can see that, as of 1961, less than 20 percent of aid commitments had so far resulted in deliveries.

---

*The Tanzam railroad, an 1,100-mile project between Tanzania and Zambia which is being supported by China to the tune of $400 million, is the single largest Communist project ever undertaken.

Commitments rise again in the 1964-1966 period. Several factors may explain this. First, domestic economic conditions improved considerably. Second, as noted earlier, the opportunities presented by Western refusal to support the Aswan Dam and the Bokharo steel mill were too tempting for Khrushchev to turn down. Third, political relations with Pakistan, Iran, and Turkey had warmed up with aid agreements constituting part of the package. Marshall Goldman cites two additional factors. One aspect of the Sino-Soviet rift was a rivalry between the two nations for the political affections of many of the LDCs. This resulted in competitive aid-giving which, in the 1963-1965 period, led both nations to commit themselves to assist ten nations almost simultaneously. The other factor is what Goldman calls the "quicksand effect." This refers to the fact that unforeseen contingencies and requirements often develop out of an aid commitment. In order to maintain a project's effectiveness, a donor may have to provide supplementary assistance, a factor which Goldman believes increased Soviet aid commitments in this period.[28]

The cycle turns down again after the upsurge of 1966. The full extent of the downturn is appreciated if one views it in the perspective of steadily rising world prices and, over time, a much higher Soviet GNP. Clearly, the commitments in 1967 through 1970 were relatively small. This downturn would seem to reflect the Soviet dissillusionment with the aid program and the much more cautious approach to economic aid by Brezhnev and Kosygin. The cycle is reversed again, beginning in 1971. However, it is too soon to judge what factors have been responsible. The large increase in military aid commitments in 1970-1974 reflects, of course, Soviet buildup of Egyptian military capacities.

If commitments are marked by their cyclical character, deliveries show a much more stable and upward trend. This, of course, is to be expected. What is most interesting is the considerable lag of deliveries behind commitments. It is not until the sharp drop in commitments after 1967 that deliveries as a percentage of commitments begin to rise above the one-third mark (Table 5.3, column 9).* Deliveries are bound

*While not shown here, Eastern European deliveries lagged even further behind commitments. In 1968, deliveries reached 34.5% of commitments. See *Radio Liberty Dispatch*, "Trade and Aid to the Developing Countries," August 31, 1971, p. 17.

to lag behind commitments for some time, of course. There is considerable feeling among specialists, however, that the lag observed here is abnormal. Several factors are believed to be responsible. First, particularly in the Khrushchev era, credit agreements were often announced before any of the preparatory work on the projects had been completed. Since much of the aid took the form of shipment of complete factories which required a lot of preparatory work, the lag tended to be quite long. Second, many of the LDCs had what is called "poor absorptive capacity to receive aid." This means that they did not have properly trained personnel, funds to finance the local costs relating to the project, and so forth. Often, then, the disbursement of aid had to be slowed down because of the inability of the recipients to take care of their end of the project. It is illuminating that in the cases of countries with relatively high absorptive capacities, such as Egypt, India, and Iran, the lag between commitment and delivery tended to be shorter. Finally, further delays undoubtedly resulted from haggling over equipment specifications, costs of the successive stages of projects, and other problems of the kind that develop during the implementation of such agreements. It should be noted that such problems undoubtedly take longer to resolve under the excessively bureaucratic Soviet trade administration than in other countries.

The final dimension in the aid picture is repayment; these are estimated to have increased slowly but steadily since 1959 (Table 5.3, column 3). The actual current burden of an aid program is, of course, current deliveries (column 3) minus repayments (column 3), or what we have called "net outflow" (column 4). Soviet net outflows of $170 and $140 million in 1971 and 1972, respectively, are extremely small in comparison with the net flows from the sixteen Development Advisory Committee (DAC) nations* of $7.7 billion in 1971, of which $3.3 billion was contributed by the U.S. and $1.1 billion by France. The smallness of the burden of the net outflow for the U.S.S.R. is appreciated by relating the net outflow to GNP. At its peak in 1964, the net outflow was less than .1 percent of GNP in that year; in 1972, it had fallen to less than .05 percent. In contrast, the average ratio for all of the sixteen DAC nations in 1971 was .35 percent with ratios for the United States, France, and the United Kingdom of .32, .67, and .41,

*DAC consists of the OECD nations, Japan, and the United States.

respectively.[29] It is important to note that the Soviet ratio would be considerably higher if aid to Communist LDCs (Cuba, North Vietnam, etc.) were added to its aid burden. It would still be much below the ratios for the Western nations, however.

Some East-West Aid and Trade Comparisons[30]

AID

A number of East-West comparisons have already been noted; in this section, several others, relevant to an assessment of the desirability of Soviet bloc trade and aid, are presented.

As we have already indicated, Soviet bloc aid has comprised a mere fraction of the total aid that has been extended to the LDCs. This is the case not only because these nations constitute a numerical and economic minority among the advanced nations, but also because they simply have extended less aid, by almost any measure, than many of the advanced Western nations. Many scholars have pointed out that the Communist nations have given aid to many fewer nations than have the Western nations, that is, to less than half of the LDCs. This is not an independent fact, however, but a consequence of their smaller size and smaller aid programs. Given the dimensions of their aid programs, it has probably made sense for them to concentrate their funds in the most strategic areas, like India, Egypt, and peripheral nations, spreading the rest around in amounts just large enough to establish friendly relationships.

In the discussion so far, several distinctions between Eastern and Western aid have been glossed over. For example, no mention has been made of private capital flows from Western nations to the LDCs; discussion has been confined to official (government) flows. Actually, private capital flows represented one-third of total Western flows in 1960-1962 and close to half in 1969-1971.[31] The Communist nations view private investment as exploitation, of course, and much of it may involve exploitation; so might some official assistance, East or West. It all depends on how the terms are used. The fact is that some private investment, particularly that guaranteed by government organizations like the United States Export-Import Bank, is made on concessional terms and involves subsidy; at the same time, very little official assistance involves a 100 percent subsidy. All in all, Soviet bloc assistance, which is all governmental, contains very few (probably less than 5 percent of the total) pure grants, whereas perhaps close to half of Western government aid is on a pure grant basis. Where interest and repayment are required, Soviet bloc interest rates range between 2½ and 4 percent (most Chinese loans are interest free) and have to be repaid in five to fifteen years (Chinese loans, between twenty and thirty years); the Western span of rates is slightly higher but repayments can usually be made over longer periods. Western loans have often been generously refinanced when an LDC has been in balance of payments difficulties.

Another difference between Eastern and Western aid is the degree to which the aid is "tied." Untied aid is a situation in which the recipient receives a loan in convertible currency that can be spent anywhere. This is the best way to receive aid, since the recipient can shop around and get the most for his money. Tied aid is restricted to purchases in the donor nation which may often have to be made at higher prices than are available elsewhere. In fact, a Western nation that insists on tying its aid is likely to be one with balance of payments problems and, at going exchange rates, higher than world prices. Having hard-currency reserve problems, it may have no alternative to tying its aid; in effect, the exports, which result automatically, finance the aid. Because of commodity inconvertibility, the Communist nations must also tie their aid. In fact, because of commodity inconvertibility, not only is aid tied to purchases in the donor country, but it will usually be tied to the purchase of specific goods and services, so that these can be produced for the aid recipient. As it happens, a very large part of Soviet bloc aid has been in the form of "projects," such as the building of complete factories. Thus a large part of aid has been tied to the purchases of goods and technical services required to complete these projects. In the aggregate, almost 100 percent of Soviet bloc aid is tied, much of it to specific goods, whereas probably no more than half of Western official assistance is tied. From this standpoint (with all other things equal), Western aid is, dollar for dollar, more valuable. There is a caveat to this statement, however, which relates to the method of aid repayment. While it is true that the Soviet bloc ties much more of its aid than the

West, they also accept a much greater percentage of repayment in kind, that is, tied repayments. Generally speaking, repayment in commodities is less valuable to the donor and less costly to the aid recipient than is repayment in convertible currency. In effect, then, part of the relative loss experienced by the LDC in receiving tied aid from the Soviet bloc is made up for by the possibility of tied repayments. It is worth noting, however, that the degree of gain or loss from repaying in kind depends on the prices attached to the commodities used in repayment and the type of commodities employed. If an LDC exports a commodity which is in short supply in repayment for aid, and this commodity could be easily sold for hard currency, then the repayment can be viewed, in effect, as a repayment in hard currency.

A few other differences between Eastern and Western aid should be noted. First, technical aid is usually extended by the West on a grant basis, whereas the LDCs are required to pay for such aid from the East and these payments amount to 15-20 percent of total aid. Second, Western nations often extend financial aid designed to assist the LDCs meet local costs connected with particular projects. This is rarely, if ever, done by the East. Finally, as one would expect, almost all Eastern aid is to the public sector of the LDCs, whereas a considerable part of Western aid is to the private sector. It would be very difficult ideologically for the Eastern nations to contribute substantially to the development of private enterprise in an LDC.

TRADE

As noted at the beginning of this chapter, Communist bloc trade is only about 4 percent of total LDC trade, and LDC trade is roughly 7 and 15 percent of Eastern Europe and Soviet trade, respectively. The percentage of Eastern Europe-LDC trade has barely changed over the past fifteen years, although in absolute terms it has increased as fast as world trade; a modest increase has occurred, however, in Soviet-LDC trade, which rose from 7 to 15 percent of Soviet trade since 1956. As with aid, trade has been concentrated in a few nations, and some LDCs conduct a significant share of their trade with Communist nations. Those which are most dependent are:* Egypt (58, 31); Syria (36, 24);

*The figures in parentheses are the percentages that exports and imports, respectively, are of the total trade of the nation in 1971.

Sudan (32, 34); Tanzania (6, 27); India (21, 12); Iraq (1, 31); Turkey (12, 10); and Pakistan (18, 12).[32] Generally, however, the Soviet Union and Eastern Europe have not provided a great mass market for LDC products predicted, based on the 350 million population of these countries. Several factors are responsible. First, the Communist nations do trade less than comparable Western nations for reasons mentioned in Chapter 2. Second, they do concentrate their trade inordinately on other CMEA nations. Third, they do suffer from balance of payments pressures. Fourth, their per capita incomes are lower than those of the more advanced nations of Europe and North America. Finally, and this is related to the previous point, there is a tendency for the planners to bias imports in favor of necessities and against luxuries. This tends to reduce imports of tropical fruits, vegetables, and drinks, which constitute important exports of many LDCs. So, for example, it has been shown that in 1970 the U.S.S.R. imported (per capita) only half as many cacao beans, one-tenth as much coffee, one-twentieth as much citrus fruit, one-hundredth as many bananas, two-fifths as much jute, etc., as Italy, a nation of comparable GNP per capita.[33] Another study compares imports of a weighted average of coffee, tea, oranges, rice, sugar, and bananas for 1964 of the U.S.S.R. and Poland, on the one hand, with a large number of Western European nations on the other.[34] To adjust for differences in per capita GNP, the estimates are in terms of the number of dollars worth of these imports per $100 of per capita GNP. The figures for the U.S.S.R. and Poland are $.15 and $.18, respectively. The nine other nations in the sample rank from $.43 in the case of the United States to $1.63 for Ireland.* Even Yugoslavia imported $1.07 worth per $100 of per capita income. Still another study of the low level of Soviet bloc imports is that of Pryor, who calculates that in 1964 each of the CMEA nations ranked below each of eleven Western European nations in his sample as importers of tropical food products.[35] Updating this study would not change the results to a significant extent, although the position of the U.S.S.R. might be slightly improved. Perhaps the most comprehensive and suggestive set of calculations is provided by a *Radio Liberty Dispatch.*[36] The author

---

*The low figure for the United States is partly due to the fact that, at our very high level of per capita income, many of these products take on the character of necessities rather than luxuries, and increased amounts are not bought to any significant extent with increased income.

199

of this paper demonstrates the modesty of the socialist bloc imports from the LDCs by relating imports from the LDCs to GNP for several socialist and capitalist countries for the year 1967. His figures show that the United States's imports from the LDCs are 1.06 percent of GNP, or more than six times greater than the U.S.S.R.'s .16 percent. The smaller nations, with naturally larger trade/GNP ratios, register higher percentages. The figures for Poland, East Germany, Czechoslovakia, and Hungary are, respectively, .41, .42, .62, and .69 percents. In contrast, the figures for Canada, France, Germany, Japan, and the United Kingdom are 1.69, 2.76, 2.83, 3.78, and 4.13.

The Communist nations clearly have an aversion to importing "nonessentials." With the exception of certain important raw materials, most other products exported by the LDCs fall into the class of nonessentials. This is especially the case with the simple manufactured products that their developing industries are producing and upon which many of them will have to depend over the long run to balance their external accounts.

Relationship Between Economic Aid and Trade

There are some obvious relationships between aid and trade. First, when one nation extends a loan or grant to another, the recipient usually spends all or most of the loan on the donor's goods. This is especially true of Soviet bloc loans, which are virtually all tied specifically to the export of specific goods, services, or whole factories. Given commodity inconvertibility, it could hardly be otherwise. Second, in order to repay a loan, the borrower has to earn surplus foreign exchange. The socialist nations are, of course, always willing to accept convertible currency in repayment of their loans. Most of the LDCs, on the other hand, are always short of convertible currency reserves and prefer not to use what reserves they have for repayment, if this can be avoided, since the money usually has more value when it is spent in the West. For this reason, among others, the typical socialist loan can be repaid with exports of raw materials and food products, and a provision to this effect is usually included in the loan agreement; the particular products which are to be exported in payment are often specified. The prices at which the products are accepted in payment also have to be specified or some provision must be made for settling on a price at the time of repayment. This is an extremely important part of the agreement and has a significant impact on the distribution of the benefits of the aid. Low prices can rob the credit of much of its concessionary character, whereas relatively high prices redound to the benefit of the LDCs.

It is natural to raise a question regarding the extent to which trade between the centrally planned economies and the LDCs took place simply as a result of loans that had been extended. Analyses of the trade and aid flows over the first decade, 1955-1964, suggest that the relationship has not been very close, particularly for Eastern Europe. Thus, for example, Eastern European exports to the LDCs over this period totaled $6.1 billion, of which only 6.6 percent of $.4 billion was financed by aid disbursements. Soviet exports over this ten-year period totaled $4.3 billion, of which 34.9 percent were financed by aid disbursements amounting to $1.5 billion. Only 4.3 percent of China's $2.3 billion of exports could be attributed to aid.[37]

It might be argued that even though aid disbursements are a small part of exports, the very fact of having concluded an aid agreement may have fostered closer relationships leading to increased trade. Figures presented by the United Nations for the same period suggest that this is probably not the case to any significant degree. According to the data presented in Table 5.4, the annual rate of growth of trade between the U.S.S.R., Bulgaria, and China and their aid recipients was slightly higher than the rate of growth of their trade with all LDCs. On the other hand, the rate of growth of trade between all other Eastern nations and their aid recipients was actually slower than the rate of growth of trade with all LDCs. There are, of course, exceptions. Afghanistan's imports from the Soviet bloc, for example, were financed entirely through credit. On the other hand, many LDCs trading with the Communist countries have never received a ruble of credit.

The relationship between imports of the socialist nations from LDC aid recipients and the loan repayments by these nations also appears to be relatively tenuous although this may be due in part to the fact that repayments, so far, are not very substantial. A study by the United Nations shows that for five years, 1960-1964, repayments to the U.S.S.R. amounted to roughly 15 percent of imports from those same

TABLE 5.4
Relation Between Aid by Communist Nations to LDCs and Growth of Trade, 1955-1964
(annual rate of growth of trade, in percent)

COMMUNIST NATION	WITH AID RECIPIENTS	WITH ALL LDCS
U.S.S.R.	25.3	20.2
Rumania	10.4	12.9
China	17.1	11.3
Czechoslovakia	4.5	4.6
Poland	6.9	11.0
Eastern Germany	15.5	17.6
Hungary	8.1	8.4
Bulgaria	51.4	39.1
All Communist Nations	15.7	13.3

SOURCE: United Nations, "The Financing of Economic Development," in *World Economic Survey*, 1965, Part I, New York, 1965. p. 106.

nations.[38] The percentage for all the Communist nations, including the U.S.S.R., is less than 10 percent, suggesting that for the Communist nations other than the U.S.S.R., the percentage must have been in the neighborhood of 5 percent. There are exceptions to these generalizations, of course. A major case in point is Egypt, which substantially increased its exports of cotton to the U.S.S.R., and Czechoslovakia in the late 1950s, largely in repayment of military credits of a few years earlier.[39]

One is forced to conclude from the data available that, at least during the first decade, the relationship between aid and trade was not very strong. In fact, the data presented overstate the relationship, because it is certainly possible that some of the Communist nation exports to the LDCs, which were obviously financed by aid disbursements, might have taken place even without aid and some of the imports without repayment. This lack of relationship between aid and trade supports my earlier contention that aid is very much a "political" act and is not necessarily extended to nations with which the donor has a high trade complementarity and with which rapid development of trade may be expected on the basis of comparative advantage.

202

Chapter 6

Notes on Future
Problems and Prospects

Intrabloc

As an international trading bloc, the CMEA nations have fallen far short of their goals. Their many attempts to multilateralize their trade have failed, and after twenty-five years, trade is still rigidly bilateral. Related to this, their goal is currency convertibility. To this end, they have created a "transferable ruble." Yet their national currencies and the transferable ruble remain completely inconvertible. Nothing in the Comprehensive Program or any other program suggests that convertibility and multilateralism are around the corner. A major goal of the CMEA nations has been to integrate their economies. The degree of integration achieved, in terms of both commodity and factor flows, has been unimpressive. Bilateralism itself is a gross indicator of nonintegration. Plan coordination has not proceeded very far and, without the imposition of a supranational authority, is not likely to proceed much further—notwithstanding the impressive list of multinational projects in the Comprehensive Program. Finally, while trade creation was never an explicit goal of CMEA, it is a fact that CMEA comprises, in effect, a trade-diverting customs union.

It seems clear, at this point in history, that the "anarchy of the market" is better equipped than central planning to achieve multilateralism, convertibility, and integration. True, the Western international financial system has been beset by many crises, particularly in recent years, and others may be in the offing. Nevertheless, despite (and even during) these crises, the system has continued to function fairly effectively. Apparently it is easier to combine interests of and reconcile differences between autonomous national states through a relatively impersonal market system where the gains and losses impinge on the private business as well as public sectors than it is for national states to sit down together and determine directly how the gains and losses are to be allocated. An illustration of this phenomenon is the fact that in the EEC nations, integration has proceeded much more swiftly and easily through industrial cooperation in the private sector than in those industries that had been nationalized.*

There is, of course, a fairly clear path to the solution of many of CMEA's problems; that is the introduction of radical economic reforms which would substantially decentralize the operation of the socialist countries. Such reforms would, in theory at least, not only ameliorate their international economic problems but might also assist in the solution of domestic problems such as the declining growth rates. At least five sets of political problems impede the introduction of full-scale reforms. First, radical reforms would "inevitably transfer power from traditional Party power-holders into the hands of the economic professionals."[1] Those in power are not likely to take voluntary measures which would involve an attenuation or loss of that power. The fear of this certainly appears to have dominated the Soviet approach to reform. Second, and related, the abortive Czech reform of 1968 demonstrated very clearly what a close relationship there is between liberalization in the economic sphere and liberalization in the political and intellectual spheres. As a result, the Hungarians have done their best and have been fairly successful in suppressing the political and intellectual consequences of their economic reform. Nevertheless, the threat of such consequences is taken seriously, especially by the U.S.S.R. Third, the U.S.S.R. does want Eastern Europe to remain a "bloc," or sphere of influence. The existence of CMEA as a closely knit and interdependent trading group is one important mechanism in the maintenance of this "bloc." To this end, the U.S.S.R. has, as we have seen, been willing to forgo economic gains which it could have commanded by virtue of its superior economic and political-military power. The introduction of radical reforms would reduce intrabloc economic interdependence as

---

*The worst failure along these lines was inability to agree on a common color television system in the EEC, where TV is mostly government-owned.

tens of thousands of trading enterprises in each country made decisions not on the basis of national economic plans and international bilateral trading agreements but on the basis of purely commercial considerations.* Trade based on commercial considerations would, of course, involve a sharp shift in imports from the Eastern bloc to Western markets, since demands for Western products are so repressed. Eventually, of course, exports would also have to be shifted from East to West if the new import levels are to be maintained. Fourth, as long as the U.S.S.R. is the dominant power in CMEA and refused to introduce a radical reform, even if it does allow the Eastern European nations to introduce reforms these reforms will be difficult to implement internationally if the U.S.S.R. insists on maintaining CMEA as a tightly knit trading bloc. This is because intrabloc trade, especially that with the U.S.S.R., is such a large percentage of the trade of each CMEA member. Fifth, as we noted earlier in the case of Hungary, price stability and full employment are very high priority goals of the socialist nations. The need to implement these goals has impeded the Hungarian reform by reducing price flexibility and the rationality of Hungarian prices and preventing the kind of constant re-allocation of resources essential to efficiency in a dynamic economy. These problems will undoubtedly hamper attempts at more serious reforms in the other socialist nations. The counterpart of this problem under capitalism is the additional burden thrown on the international monetary mechanism by the fact that national policies in most Western nations do not allow balance of payments problems to be solved by domestic unemployment or deflation.

Aside from political factors, the U.S.S.R. has been less motivated by economic factors to reform international economic mechanisms than have the Eastern European nations. As we have noted, the U.S.S.R. is a large self-sufficient nation which trades (exports or imports) only about 2½-3 percent of its GNP, whereas trade/GNP ratios for Eastern European nations range from about 10 to 30 percent. For a small Eastern European country a balance of payments deficit is a much larger percentage of GNP than for the large U.S.S.R.; elimination of a deficit involves a much greater cut in domestic consumption; bilateralism

---

*Bilateral trading commitments lose much of their advantage if central economic planning is abandoned.

involves much greater losses; inability to trade to the optimum because of central planning involves much greater losses; and membership in CMEA has resulted in much greater losses from trade diversion. Clearly, the economic costs of not introducing radical reforms is high in Eastern Europe, much higher than in the U.S.S.R.

Looking into the future, two possible developments may lead to changes in this situation by increasing the economic costs to the U.S.S.R. of preserving the status quo. First, the developing shortages of raw materials, particularly in the energy field, have led to rapidly rising prices in the West. In fact, Soviet balance of payments problems were ameliorated temporarily in 1974 by increased receipts from sales to the West of natural gas and petroleum at these higher prices, as well as from the rise in the price of gold. At the same time, the "losses" to the U.S.S.R. from exports of these same products to CMEA nations at much lower prices, in exchange for products of much less value than those obtained from the West, have been rising. The Soviets could get much more in terms of foreign exchange and in valuable imports if they could redirect a good part of their raw material exports to the West. The costs of supplying Eastern Europe will rise over the next decade, because it does not appear that Soviet increases in energy output will keep up with increased requirements in both the U.S.S.R. and in Eastern Europe. Furthermore, the newer Soviet sources of oil and natural gas cost more.[2] Given these circumstances and the U.S.S.R.'s serious long-term hard-currency problems, one can envisage a growing reluctance on the part of the U.S.S.R. to continue to support Eastern Europe's raw material requirements, at least on the present scale. The Soviets will have to balance the economic costs of such support against the political advantages of economic interdependence, particularly an interdependence in crucial energy raw materials. If the decision is to reduce intrabloc trade, then nations like Hungary will have much more scope to benefit from their reforms in the international trade area, although these benefits will be offset in part by the loss of relatively cheap raw material supplies from the U.S.S.R. It seems likely that the other Eastern European nations would have more incentive to introduce radical economic reforms. As long as these economic reforms are prevented (as in Hungary) from spilling over into the political and intellectual life of the Eastern European nations, it is possible that they will not be reversed by the U.S.S.R. as the Czech reform was.

206

Second, the costs to the U.S.S.R. from its deficiencies in innovating and diffusing technology will probably continue to rise in the absence of a radical economic reform. Soviet leaders apparently hope that imports of technology from the West will reduce these costs to tolerable levels. This may well happen, but it is unlikely. The U.S.S.R. is much too large a country, with too many industries and products, to be able to affect its growth and efficiency significantly through imports of technology. This statement is made in the light of two major constraints which the U.S.S.R. would still have to face. Even if technology is imported, an unreformed Soviet economy would not quickly adapt or diffuse it, for reasons mentioned in Chapter 4. Thus, benefits to the nation that one might expect if, say, Japan imported a new process or product would not benefit the U.S.S.R. In the case of Japan, the innovation would probably be improved upon fairly quickly and would be adopted throughout the country and readied for export; in the U.S.S.R., more likely than not, introduction would be much slower and would probably never reach many sectors of industry, and there would be neither improvements nor exports. The second constraint lies in balance of payments considerations. There is a limit to how much technology the U.S.S.R. can afford to import from the West, even with fairly liberal credit. Considering that Soviet domestic investment annually exceeds $200 billion, it becomes clear that technology imports would have to be very sizable to be noticed. One estimate suggests that, optimistically, imports of technology are unlikely to raise the growth rate by more than, say, .3 percent per year.[3] My conclusion is that if the Soviet growth rate continues to decline, and no solution other than radical reform appears feasible to correct matters, then the Soviet leaders may opt for such a reform. Before this happens, however, many nonradical reforms will be tried, and the importation of Western technology will be pushed as far as possible.

East-West

Over the past twenty years there has been a trend toward improved East-West economic and political relationships. Improvement has recently accelerated with the more friendly attitude of the United States toward the Communist nations and, in particular, the U.S.-U.S.S.R. détente. Should détente remain a permanent fixture on the world scene, one might expect a steady improvement in East-West economic relations although serious economic problems may have to be overcome. To predict that the degree of détente which we are presently experiencing will be permanent, however, might be considered a rash judgment. Political turning points are usually unforeseen by most people. Furthermore, the present détente must still be viewed as relatively fragile, although it may become stronger as time goes on. There are many trouble spots in the world which could serve to catalyze a new Cold War—the Middle East and Sino-Soviet relations, for example. Furthermore, within the U.S. and the U.S.S.R. there are anti-détente forces and interest groups which could set back détente for many years. It is hard to predict, of course, what might happen if the U.S. chose a representative of such interests in a Presidential election, particularly when one considers that as outspoken an anti-Communist as Richard Nixon was an architect of the present détente. Nevertheless, one must face the fact that there are powerful anti-Communist groups in the United States. Similarly, knowledgeable Western observers have often noted that strong groups in the Soviet hierarchy oppose Secretary Brezhnev's policies or at least feel that the U.S.S.R. is not getting enough out of the "linkage" game that the two super powers are playing. In fact, it is the incommensurability of gains and losses in different dimensions which may make détente difficult to maintain. The U.S.-U.S.S.R. Trade Agreement was annulled because: there were groups in the U.S. which felt that the Soviet Union was getting too much and could and should be squeezed for further concessions; some groups in the U.S.S.R. obviously took an opposite view of the matter.

By how much East-West trade will increase over the next decade will also depend on the degree of political and economic integration achieved in CMEA. To the extent that there are problems in CMEA which cannot be overcome, there will be a tendency to look to the West. Much will depend upon whether the Soviet Union will continue to provide the other Eastern nations with relatively cheap food, oil, and other raw materials. The sharp rise in the hard currency prices of these commodities has raised the cost to the U.S.S.R. of such policies, policies designed to subsidize the political and economic cohesion of

CMEA. The Soviet Union's attitude toward economic reform will also play a significant role in the future of East-West trade.

If the internal and international economic performances of CMEA nations decline still further, so that the U.S.S.R. is finally driven to adopt radical economic reforms and to allow the other CMEA nations to do likewise, then there will be a sharp diversion from intrabloc to East-West trade. This would happen because under the reforms the Eastern nations would trade on more commercial principles and would stop discriminating in favor of each other to the extent that they do now. However, it now seems highly unlikely that radical economic reforms would be sanctioned by the U.S.S.R. in the near future.

An important economic constraint on greatly increased East-West trade is the persistent balance of payment deficit which the Eastern nations have with the West and for which there appears no easy solution (see Chapter 2). When East-West trade began to develop in earnest in the early 1960s, the deficits sustained were not a problem because there was no backlog of debt. Since that time, the ratios of debt service to value of hard-currency exports have risen steadily, and some have approached levels (.20 to .25) which are viewed in the West as the practical safe limit to the extension of credit in international trade. No doubt some additional credits will be forthcoming and the situation will be somewhat ameliorated by cooperative production and marketing arrangements in which payments are made in the form of output. Some investment of petrodollars may also be expected. Nevertheless, balance of payments considerations appear likely to act as long-run constraints on the expansion of East-West trade. They should also operate in the case of the Soviet Union, despite the recent windfall of some $3 billion a year as a result of higher prices of gold, oil, and other raw materials.

In fact, the advantages of that windfall were wiped out in 1975 by a decline in Soviet (and other Eastern European) exports due to the Western recessions as well as by the sharp rise in grain imports as a result of the poor harvest. The U.S.S.R. spends about .5 percent of its GNP on imports from the West and imports a total of only 2½-3 percent of its GNP. These amounts are certainly far below the profitable levels of trade. It is hard to believe that the U.S.S.R. could not profitably import another 1 or 2 percent of its GNP from the West, that is, $10 to $15 billion worth more of Western products. To do so, however, would require a great increase in hard currency exports, which seems unlikely at this point.

Finally, East-West trade, especially Soviet-American trade, may not expand to its profitable limits for strategic reasons. Neither nation appears to want to develop too high a level of interdependence with the other. The United States' greatest deficit at the moment is in energy resources, particularly oil and gas. Project Independence was implemented to achieve as much independence as possible not only from the Middle East but from the U.S.S.R. The Soviet Union, for its part, could undoubtedly benefit from reliance on regular imports of food from the U.S. instead of supplying both itself and most of the Eastern European nations with grain. Nevertheless, a decision has recently been made to expand agricultural production still further in the U.S.S.R. Obviously, the U.S.S.R. does want to be as independent as possible from a potential enemy for something so crucial as food. Neither nation is willing to obey the law of comparative advantage.

The Western LDCs

There are many imponderables in the future economic relations between the Eastern nations and the Western LDCs. I do not wish to speculate about such explosive and expensive relationships as those involved in Soviet military aid to the Middle Eastern nations. In the more normal trade and aid relations, a number of questions about the future may be raised, mostly having to do with the relatively less satisfactory performance of the socialist nations in meeting the needs and requirements of the LDCs.

The socialist nations have always tried to align themselves with the LDCs in the complaints of the latter nations against the advanced nations of the West. While their trade and aid with the LDCs has increased significantly since 1955, it is still on a very small scale when compared to that of the advanced Western nations. It is small not only because socialist nations are relatively small in GNP and not as affluent as the advanced Western nations, but because the Soviet bloc's efforts to accommodate the needs of the LDCs appear to be minor, even if one takes into account the "ability to pay" principle as it relates to their lower per capita incomes. This is demonstrated in the figures presented in Chapter 5 on the comparative aid and trade of socialist and capitalist nations, respectively, with the LDCs. The U.S.S.R. alone could provide an enormous market for raw material and food exports of the LDCs if it made the decision to do so. Yet Soviet policies have continued to be directed consistently toward import substitution and against any shift toward importing anything but necessities. Thus, the U.S.S.R. produces a higher percentage of synthetic rubber and imports a smaller percentage of natural rubber to meet its total requirements than do other industrial nations. Similarly, imports of tropical foods and light manufactured products from the LDCs are at a relatively low level. Policies of this sort—and with the socialist nations, import performance is a matter of state policy—are not calculated to help the LDCs with their balance of payments problems, including those which stem from the need to repay Soviet bloc loans. The Soviet bloc nations have shown no inclination to go along with the aid goals of the United Nations Second Development Decade (1971-1980). Branding the poverty of the LDCs a legacy of capitalism, they have attempted to avoid responsibility for having to take altruistic measures. In fact, not only have the total credits being extended declined relative to earlier peak years, but, as noted, the concessionary element in these loans has also declined as interest rates have been increased and repayment periods shortened.

The relatively poor recent performance of Soviet bloc trade and aid with the Western LDCs is probably attributable to three factors. First, domestic economic problems, as reflected in slower rates of economic growth, certainly would act to curb an altruistic impulse (aid), although it might serve to increase interest in trade in those directions in which additional profitable trade seemed possible. Second, with minor exceptions, the political payoffs to aid have been small, and in exceptional cases like India and the U.A.R., economic costs of political payoffs have been high. Where the political payoffs are high and certain, the U.S.S.R. is clearly willing to foot the bill—Cuba is the dramatic case in point (although the high costs of supporting Cuba are undoubtedly assumed with misgivings). The capitalist LDC world provides no such clear-cut quid pro quos (except perhaps for the military aid to the Middle East). Third, it does appear that the socialist nations are guided little by altruistic motives in their aid programs, particularly toward capitalist LDCs. Over time, expressions of this motive appear of less importance than ever.

Because aid and trade with the LDCs is so small, there is scope for improvement. Despite domestic economic problems, substantial increases could be financed at least by the U.S.S.R. without excessive strain. Therefore it would not be at all surprising to find large increases in trade with and aid to capitalist LDC nations which, for one reason or another, promise large political payoffs. The resources are there and will be used if the proper opportunities present themselves. However, these opportunities would probably have to be somewhat more attractive than has been the case in the past.

In a previous section, we discussed the possibility that there might be some disintegration of CMEA trade, either because of the introduction of radical reforms or because the U.S.S.R. decided that it wanted to sell its raw material surpluses to the West for hard currencies. Should either of these possibilities occur, a considerably larger amount of trade might develop between Eastern European nations and the capitalist LDCs. This would happen for two partly related reasons. First, disintegration of intrabloc trade would automatically involve more trade with capitalist nations, advanced and less developed. Second, if the U.S.S.R. shifted its exports of raw materials to the West, the Eastern European nations would be forced to fill in the deficits primarily with imports from the LDCs. Presumably, these imports would have to be financed with increases in exports to these nations—certainly easier for the Eastern European nations than increasing exports to the advanced Western nations. The result might be considerably closer economic relationships between Eastern Europe and some of the LDCs.

The Longer Run

A number of issues not discussed above may affect East-West and East-West-LDC relationships over the longer run.

A U.S.-U.S.S.R. Joint Committee on Cooperation in the Field of Environmental Protection was established in 1972, with many joint projects to be undertaken. The world is being linked closer together not only the telephone, telegraph, and radio but also by pollution and other forms of environmental despoliation.

The Eastern and Western nations bordering the Baltic Sea have been brought together by the fact that they are destroying that body of water. The potential destruction of the world's whale population, as well as of other animals, and joint use by nations of other interconnected resources (such as the earth's atmosphere) have also led to interaction at the political level to reconcile differences and reinforce mutual interests. Environmental interaction will undoubtedly develop in many other dimensions and with increasing rapidity. As environmental problems intensify, and they will do so at an accelerating pace, their economic implications will become more important and their political solutions more urgent. At the moment, some nations may have an incentive to despoil the environment at the expense of others (e.g., whaling). Over time, as pollution and other problems worsen, mutual interests in avoiding despoliation will be much stronger, and the problem confronting the political process will become the assignment of the costs of a solution.

A second economic problem which may threaten political stability over the long run is the growing inequality of income between the "haves" (Eastern and Western) and the "have-nots." It is a fact that the incomes of the advanced nations have been growing faster than those of the LDCs. The ultimate differentiation is the possibility of more and more mass starvation on one hand and increasing affluence on the other. Over the past twenty years, the relative importance of aid to the LDCs has declined. An attempt, largely unsuccessful, to reverse this trend was made in the United Nations Second Development Decade program. Over the very long run, in the absence of unforeseen developments, the problem of inequality and starvation appear to contain the roots of an explosion which would affect capitalist and Communist nations alike. Future East-West politics may be strongly affected by the course of development of this problem.

The economics of armaments and arms control are more fraught with political and military implications than any other, in the short as well as long run. It is almost beyond belief, particularly in the context of the discussion in the preceding paragraph, that current world military expenditures are well over a quarter of a trillion dollars—more than total world public expenditures on health, education, and foreign aid and of the same order of magnitude as the sum of the GNPs of the Western world's less developed nations. There are at least two aspects to the armaments problem in which economics and politics are related and in which developments may be expected in the future. First, the military establishments of the major nations, especially those of the U.S. and the U.S.S.R., constitute an enormous drain on the resources of each. As time goes on, as weapons systems become more and more expensive, as the futility of mutual armament buildups becomes more apparent (one hopes), then there may be more incentive to arrive at arms control agreements. The benefits to the world from turning the resources devoted to military purposes over to peaceful uses cannot be overestimated.

Second, the major arms producers (the U.S., U.S.S.R., U.K., and France) sell arms with which to fight their wars to other nations, especially the LDCs. Without such sales, there would probably be fewer hostilities and, of course, fewer casualties. Military trade and aid have two dimensions. On the one hand, they are often purely commercial, ways of earning foreign exchange or recouping military costs by selling surplus or obsolete equipment. On the other hand, they are part of partisan international politics and used to influence the outcomes of wars. In either event, arms trade must be viewed as a dangerous activity—possibly fatally dangerous if trade in nuclear arms ever develops—and an activity which, it is hoped, will eventually be subjected to international political control.

Finally, events connected with the Middle East War of October 1973 make it clear that economic warfare is approaching a potentially more dangerous phase than ever before. That a few Middle Eastern oil producers were able to threaten Western Europe and Japan with economic strangulation is a dramatic illustration of the danger. As the pressure on natural resources becomes greater, the ability of the supplier nations to blackmail the consumer nations may become even greater. There is a need for new rules of conduct, like those introduced under GATT and the IMF to outlaw tariff wars and beggar their neighbor policies, to control economic warfare. The major nations have never seen fit to push for such a set of rules because they have been least vulnerable to economic warfare. The Arab-Israeli war demonstrated that the oil producers of the Middle East have more power to practice economic warfare than either the United States or the

U.S.S.R.* Neither the United States nor (even less) the U.S.S.R. is very vulnerable to this kind of economic warfare, and it may be difficult to get an agreement on this matter. Nevertheless, over the long run, this problem will become more acute and will have to be dealt with on the political level.

*This power will be weakened as these small nations accumulate assets in the West as a result of their foreign exchange earnings, since these assets can be expropriated in return. Nevertheless, they would still hold the whip hand in a crisis.

Notes

Chapter 1

1. A. Alekseev and A. Borisenko, "A Price Basis of Its Own," *Problems of Economics*, April 1964, p. 47. Translated from Russian.

2. Quoted from Michael Kaser, *Comecon*, 2nd ed. (London: Oxford University Press, 1967), p. 253.

Chapter 2

1. Z. Fallenbuchl, "East European Integration: Comecon," in Joint Economic Committee, Congress of the United States, *Reorientation and Commercial Relations of the Economies of Eastern Europe* (Washington: U.S. Government Printing Office, 1974), p. 104.

2. For further discussion, see Andrea Boltho, *Foreign Trade Criteria in Socialist Economies* (Cambridge, England: Cambridge University Press, 1971).

3. Good sources on the foreign trade reforms are the United Nations *Economic Bulletin for Europe*, 20, no. 1 (1968): 43-50; *Economic Bulletin for Europe* 24, no. 1 (1973): 36-49; Matejka, Harriet. "Foreign Trade Systems." In *The New Economic Systems of Eastern Europe*, edited by H. H. Höhmann, M. Kaser, and K. C. Thalheim. Berkeley and Los Angeles: University of California Press, 1975.

Chapter 3

1. Stanley Wasowski, "Economic Integration in Eastern Europe" (Arlington, Va.: Institute for Defense Analysis, 1969), report, p. 24.

2. Peter Wiles, *Communist International Economics* (London: Blackwell, 1968), p. 382.

3. Imre Vajda, *The Role of Foreign Trade in a Socialist Economy* (Budapest: Corvina Press, 1965), p. 234.

4. Cf. Marshall I. Goldman, *The Spoils of Progress: Environmental Pollution in the Soviet Union* (Cambridge, Mass.: MIT Press, 1972).

5. Wasowski, "Economic Integration," p. 9.

6. Cf. Wiles, *Communist International Economics*, p. 456.

7. Ibid., p. 492.

8. Wiles feels that the second Yugoslavian case and China should be called commercial quarrels rather than economic warfare. Ibid., p. 507.

9. Ibid., p. 312.

10. Michael Kaser, *Comecon*, 2nd ed. (London: Oxford University Press, 1967), p. 12.

11. Ibid., p. 144, Table 2.

12. P. Ivanov, "Division of Labor and Coordination of Economic Plans," *Kommunist*, no. 18, 1964. Translated in *The American Review of Soviet and East European Foreign Trade*, May-June 1965, p. 27.

13. Bela Balassa, "Trade Creation and Trade Diversion in the European Common Market," *Economic Journal*, March 1967.

14. Frederic Pryor, *The Communist Foreign Trade System* (Cambridge, Mass.: MIT Press, 1963), p. 27.

15. These and other figures are primarily from: Janos Horvath, "Grant Elements in Intra-bloc Aid Programs," *The ASTE Bulletin*, Fall 1971; Marshall Goldman, *Soviet Foreign Aid* (New York: Praeger, 1966).

16. Wiles, *Communist International Economics*, p. 448.

17. Joint stock companies were also established in Manchuria and Communist China. Cf. Goldman, *Soviet Foreign Aid*, chap. 1.

18. Horvath, "Grant Elements," p. 9.

19. Robert Freedman, *Economic Warfare in the Communist Bloc* (New York: Praeger, 1970), p. 19, citing Djilas.

20 Ibid., chap. 2.

21. Z. Brzezinski, *The Soviet Bloc: Unity and Conflict*, 2nd ed. (Cambridge, Mass.: Harvard University Press, 1967), pp. 172-174.

22. The U.S.S.R. advanced $1.3 billion in credits and cancelled debts of $1.8 billion from the Eastern European nations in 1956-1957. Brzezinski, *The Soviet Bloc*, pp. 285-286.

23. Herta W. Heiss, "The Council of Mutual Economic Assistance—Developments Since the Mid-1960s," in Joint Economic Committee, Congress of the United States, *Economic Developments in Countries of Eastern Europe* (Washington: Government Printing Office, 1970), p. 533.

24. Kaser, *Comecon*, p. 114.

25. Franklyn D. Holzman, *Foreign Trade Under Central Planning* (Cambridge, Mass.: Harvard University Press, 1974), chaps. 11 and 12.

26. Translated quotations from the article appear in Brzezinski, *The Soviet Bloc*, pp. 451-452.

27. The following discussion of economic warfare against Albania and China is based on Freedman, *Economic Warfare*.

28. *The Soviet Bloc*, p. 397.

29. Freedman, *Economic Warfare*, p. 113.

30. Quoted in Ibid., p. 125.

31. The Charter is reproduced as Appendix IV in Kaser, *Comecon*; the Basic Principles appear in somewhat abridged form as Appendix VI of that book.

32. "Council of Mutual Economic Assistance," p. 535.

33. *Comecon*, p. 165.

34. *Foreign Trade*, no. 2 (1972), p. 7.

35. Quoted in Z. Fallenbuchl, "East European Integration: Comecon," in Joint Economic Committee, Congress of the United States (Washington: Government Printing Office, 1974), p. 90.

36. A G.D.R. spokesman, quoted in J. M. Montias, *Economic Development in Communist Rumania* (Cambridge, Mass.: MIT Press, 1967), p. 202.

37. Cited in Ibid., p. 194.

38. Cited in Ibid., pp. 210-211.

39. Ibid., p. 223.

40. According to Kaser, *Comecon*, p. 107, Gomulka was the real originator of these proposals.

41. Ibid., pp. 106-107.

42. Ibid.

43. Cited in Ibid., p. 108.

44. Wiles, *Communist International Economics*, p. 325, citing J. F. Brown's article in (Soviet) *Survey*, October 1963.

45. Basic Principles of CMEA (1962), cited in Kaser, *Comecon*, p. 252.

46. The history of these price changes is not absolutely clear. For the history and its ambiguities, see Kaser, *Comecon*, pp. 179-185; Montias, *Economic Development*, pp. 188; 191-192; and Edward Hewett, *Foreign Trade in CMEA* (Cambridge: Cambridge University Press, 1974), chaps. 1 and 2.

47. Kaser, *Comecon*, p. 185.

48. C. H. McMillan, "Factor Proportions and the Structure of Soviet Foreign Trade," *ACES Bulletin*, Spring 1973, pp. 57-82; Hewett, "Prices and Resource Allocation in Intra-CMEA Trade," unpublished.

49. *Handbook of Economic Statistics, 1975* (Washington, D.C.: Central Intelligence Agency, August 1975), p. 70.

50. Horvath, "Grant Elements" is the best single source I know of on these matters.

51. These figures draw on chap. 5 and on Raymond Mikesell, *The Economics of Foreign Aid* (Chicago: Aldine, 1968), p. 241.

52. This section is based on Heiss, "The Council of Mutual Economic Assistance," pp. 539-541; Kaser, *Comecon*, pp. 214-216; Fallenbuchl, "East European Integration," p. 128.

53. Heiss, "The Council of Mutual Economic Assistance," p. 538.

54. Ibid.

55. Ibid., p. 539.

56. Fallenbuchl, "East European Integration," pp. 131-132.

57. United Nations, *Economic Bulletin for Europe* 23, no. 2 (1971), p. 26.

58. Quoted in Stanley Wasowski, ed., *East-West Trade and the Technology Gap* (New York: Praeger, 1970), p. 13.

59. Ibid., p. 18.

60. Henry Schaeffer, *Comecon and the Politics of Integration* (New York: Praeger, 1972), p. 15.

61. An English translation of the Comprehensive Program was published in *Soviet and Eastern European Foreign Trade*, Fall-Winter 1971-1972, White Plains, N.Y. All citations here are from this source. The CMEA Secretariat in Moscow has also published an English language version. The full title is "Comprehensive Programme for the Further Extension and Improvement of Cooperation and Development of Socialist Economic Integration by the CMEA Member Nations."

62. Ibid., pp. 215-217.

63. Ibid., pp. 253-292.

64. Fallenbuchl, "Comecon Integration," *Problems of Communism*, March-April 1973, p. 39.

65. Ibid., p. 37.

66. *Soviet and Eastern European Foreign Trade*, p. 191.

67. Ibid., p. 222.

68. Ibid., p. 210.

69. Ibid., p. 211.

70. Ibid., pp. 232-240.

71. Schaeffer, *Comecon and the Politics of Integration*, p. 112.

72. Cf. Abram Bergson, "Economic Development Under Two Systems," *World Politics*, July 1971.

Chapter 4

1. Josef Wilczynski, *The Economics and Politics of East-West Trade* (London: Macmillan, 1969), p. 106. The agreement between the U.S. and U.S.S.R. was signed in 1972 and terminated by the U.S.S.R. in February 1975.

2. Gunnar Adler-Karlsson, *Western Economic Warfare*, 1947-67 (Stockholm: Almqvist & Wiksell, 1968), p. 156.

3. Quoted from Kennan's *Memoirs: 1925-1950*, p. 343, in Karin Kock, *International Trade Policy and the GATT, 1947-67* (Stockholm: Almqvist & Wiksell, 1969), p. 188.

4. Adler-Karlsson, *Western Economic Warfare*, p. 177.

5. Nicolas Spulber, "Effects of the Embargo on Soviet Trade," *Harvard Business Review*, November-December 1952.

6. Adam Ulam, *The Rivals* (New York: Viking, 1971), p. 227.

7. Cited from official sources in Harold Berman and John Garson, "Possible Effects of the Proposed East-West Trade Relations Act Upon U.S. Import, Export and Credit Controls," *Vanderbilt Law Review*, March 1967, p. 300.

8. M. Ernst, "Postwar Economic Growth in Eastern Europe," in Joint Economic Committee, Congress of the United States, *New Directions in the Soviet Economy*, Part IV (Washington: Government Printing Office, 1966), p. 880.

9. Robert Campbell, *The Soviet-Type Economies* (Boston: Houghton Mifflin, 1974), p. 120.

10. Ibid., p. 120.

11. Thad Alton, "Economic Structure and Growth in Countries of Eastern Europe," in Joint Economic Committee, Congress, *Economic Development in Eastern Europe* (Washington: Government Printing Office, 1970), pp. 42, 63.

12. Abram Bergson, "Toward a New Soviet Growth Model," *Problems of Communism*, March-April 1973, pp. 1-9.

13. Government estimate cited by Herbert Levine, "An American View of Economic Relations with the U.S.S.R.," unpublished, 1974, p. 5.

14. Robert M. Solow, "Technical Change and the Aggregate Production Function," *Review of Economics and Statistics*, August 1957.

15. Michael Kaser and C. F. G. Ransom, "Relations With Eastern Europe," in C. R. Denton, *Economic Integration in Europe* (London: Weidenfeld and Nicolson, 1968), p. 100.

16. Samuel Pisar, *Coexistence and Commerce* (New York: McGraw-Hill, 1970), p. 113; Z. Brzezinski, *Alternative to Partition* (New York: McGraw-Hill, 1962), p. 68.

17. Pisar, *Coexistence and Commerce*, pp. 111-114.

18. Ibid., p. 105.

19. Brzezinski, *Alternative to Partition*, p. 62.

20. Pisar, *Coexistence and Commerce*, p. 106.

21. Wilczynski, *Economics and Politics of East-West Trade*, pp. 106-109.

22. Derived from Alan Brown and Paul Marer, "New Options for the United States in East-West Trade," *Studies in Comparative Communism*, April 1971.

23. Robert Kretschmar and Robin Foor, *The Potential for Joint Ventures in Eastern Europe* (New York: Praeger, 1972), p. x. Other useful sources are Pisar, *Coexistence and Commerce*, chap. 18; and Marshall Goldman, "The East Reaches the Markets," *Foreign Affairs*, July 1969.

24. Kretschmar and Foor, *Potential for Joint Ventures*, chap. 1.

25. A list of these commodities is found in Michael Kaser, "Comecon's Commerce," *Problems of Communism*, July-August 1973.

26. J. F. Brown, F. Ermarth, and R. Salloch, "Eastern Europe and the Common Market," *Communist Affairs*, March-April 1968.

27. Henry Kissinger, Congressional briefing, mimeographed, June 15, 1972, p. 3.

28. John Hardt and George D. Holliday, *U.S.-Soviet Commercial Relations: The Interplay of Economics, Technology, Transfer, and Diplomacy* (Washington, D.C.: Committee on Foreign Affairs, United States House of Representatives, 1973).

29. Ibid.

30. Michael Boretsky, "Comparative Progress in Technology, Productivity, and Economic Efficiency: U.S.S.R. vs. U.S.A.," Joint Economic Committee, Congress of the United States, *New Directions in the Soviet Economy*, Part II-A (Washington, D.C.: Government Printing Office, 1966), p. 149.

31. Cited in Joint Economic Committee, Congress of the United States, *Soviet Economic Prospects for the Seventies* (Washington, D.C.: 1974), p. 643.

32. Report to the President by the Special Committee on U.S. Trade Relations with East European Countries and the Soviet Union, Department of State, pp. 14-15.

33. These events are chronicled in Joint Economic Committee, *Soviet Economic Prospects*, pp. 643-659.

34. Cited in Ibid., p. 645.

35. Personal conversation with Peter Peterson, spring 1972.

36. Cited in Herbert Feis, *The Diplomacy of the Dollar* (New York: W. W. Norton, 1966), p. 22.

37. *New York Times*, April 7, 1975, p. 3.

38. *New York Times*, January 31, 1976, p. 5.

39. Ibid., p. 5.

40. Moscow Narodny Bank, *Press Bulletin*, September 26, 1973, pp. 5-6; International Monetary Fund, *Survey*, May 20, 1974, p. 151.

41. Henry Schaeffer, *The Eastern Reassessment of the EEC* (Munich: Radio Free Europe Research, May 1972), p. 18.

Chapter 5

1. V. Vassilev, *Policy in the Soviet Bloc on Aid to Developing Countries* (Paris: OECD, 1969), p. 77.

2. Carole A. Sawyer, *Communist Trade With Developing Countries: 1955-1965* (New York: Praeger, 1970), p. 59.

3. Cited in Ibid., p. 61.

4. Cited in Ibid., pp. 3-4.

5. Cited in Ibid., pp. 63-65.

6. Leo Tansky, "Soviet Foreign Aid to the Less Developed Countries," in Joint Economic Committee, Congress of the United States, *New Directions in the Soviet Economy*, Part IV (Washington: Government Prining Office, 1966), pp. 947-974.

7. Tansky, "Soviet Military Aid, Technical Assistance, and Academic Training," in Raymond Duncan, *Soviet Policy in Developing Countries* (Waltham, Mass.: Ginn, 1970), pp. 47-48; Tansky, "Soviet Foreign Aid: Scope, Direction, and Trends," in Joint Economic Committee, Congress of the United States, *Soviet Economic Prospects for the Seventies* (Washington: Government Printing Office, 1973), pp. 770-772.

8. Department of State, news release, "Communist States and Developing Countries: Aid and Trade in 1972," August, 1973, Table 6. Many of the Chinese "technicians" are in fact relatively unskilled workers.

9. Tansky, "Soviet Military Aid," pp. 770-772.

10. Department of State, "Communist States and Developing Countries," Table 8.

11. United Nations, *Innovations in the Practice of Trade and Economic Cooperation Between the Socialist Countries of Eastern Europe and the Developing Countries* (New York: United Nations, 1970), p. 25.

12. See Ibid., pp. 26-28.

13. For further discussion, see Duncan, *Soviet Policy in Developing Countries*; see, in particular, notes by Duncan and the following articles: Ishwer C. Ojha, "The Kremlin and Third World Leadership: Closing the Circle," pp. 9-28; Marshall Goldman, "Soviet Foreign Aid Since the Death of Stalin: Progress and Problems," pp. 29-41; Philip Mosely, "The Kremlin and the Third World," pp. 287-297; Robert Legvold, "The Soviet Union's Changing View of Sub-Saharan Africa," pp. 62-82; Tansky, "Soviet Military Aid," pp. 42-61.

14. Duncan, *Soviet Policy in Developing Countries*, p. xvi.

15. Ibid., p. 6; Ojha, "The Kremlin and Third World Leadership," pp. 9-13.

16. Mosely, "The Kremlin and the Third World," p. 288.

17. Cited in Duncan, *Soviet Policies in Developing Countries*, p. 6.

18. Marshall Goldman, *Soviet Foreign Aid* (New York: Praeger, 1967), pp. 29-30.

19. Legvold, "The Soviet Union's Changing View," p. 62.

20. Goldman, *Soviet Foreign Aid*, p. 31.

21. Ojha, "The Kremlin and Third World Leadership," pp. 26-28.

22. Legvold, "The Soviet Union's Changing View," pp. 73-75.

23. This sentence contains paraphrases of and quotation from a *Pravda* editorial, October 27, 1965, cited in Ibid., p. 74.

24. Tansky, "Soviet Foreign Aid," p. 772.

25. Tansky, "Soviet Military Aid," pp. 43-44.

26. Tansky, "Soviet Foreign Aid," p. 772.

27. Department of State, "Communist States and Developing Countries," Tables 2, 3, 4.

28. Goldman, *Soviet Foreign Aid*, pp. 36-38.

29. Western figures from Department of State, news release, "Official Development Assistance and the Developing World," August 1973, Tables 5 and 6.

30. A useful if somewhat polemical summary is provided in "Trade and Aid to Developing Countries: Contrasts in World Performance," *Radio Liberty Dispatch*, August 31, 1971.

31. Department of State, "Official Development Assistance," Table 2.

32. Ibid., Table 13. This table did not contain figures for Afghanistan, whose percentages were around 40 percent in 1969.

33. "Soviet Markets Disappoint Developing Countries," *Radio Liberty Dispatch*, March 12, 1973, p. 6.

34. Franklyn D. Holzman, *Foreign Trade Under Central Planning* (Cambridge, Mass.: Harvard University Press, 1971), p. 168.

35. Frederick L. Pryor, "Trade Barriers of Capitalist and Communist Nations Against Foodstuffs Exported by Tropical Underdeveloped Nations," *Review of*

Economics and Statistics, November 1966, pp. 406-411. There are some methodological errors in Pryor's work, but their correction would probably leave his results unchanged. Cf. Holzman, *Foreign Trade*, chap. 7.

36. "Trade and Aid to Developing Countries," p. 29.

37. Sawyer, *Communist Trade With Developing Countries*, p. 49.

38. "The Financing of Economic Development," in *World Economic Survey, 1965–Part 1* (New York: United Nations, 1966), p. 101.

39. Tansky, "Soviet Military Aid," p. 44.

Chapter 6

1. John Hardt, "East European Economic Development: Two Decades of Interrelationships and Interactions with the Soviet Union," in Joint Economic Committee, Congress of the United States, *Economic Developments in Countries of Eastern Europe* (Washington: Government Printing Office, 1970), p. 37. This provides an excellent survey of the issues.

2. An excellent discussion of some of these issues is Robert Campbell, "Some Issues in Soviet Energy Policy for the Seventies," Joint Economic Committee, Congress of the United States, *Soviet Economic Prospects for the Seventies* (Washington: Government Printing Office, 1974), pp. 44-45.

3. Franklyn D. Holzman and Robert Legvold, "The Economics and Politics of East-West Relations," *International Organization*, Winter 1975. Republished in C. Fred Bergsten and Laurence B. Krause, eds., *World Politics and International Economics* (Washington: The Brookings Institution, 1975).

Sources and References

Chapter 1

Buky, Barnabas. "Hungary's NEM on a Treadmill." *Problems of Communism*, September-October, 1972.

Bergson, Abram. *Economics of Soviet Planning*. New Haven: Yale University Press, 1964.

Bornstein, Morris, ed. *Plan and Market*. New Haven: Yale University Press, 1973.

Campbell, Robert. *The Soviet-Type Economies*. Boston: Houghton Mifflin, 1974.

Fainsod, Merle. *How Russia is Ruled*. Revised edition. Cambridge, Mass.: Harvard University Press, 1967.

Gamarnikow, Michael, "Balance Sheet on Economic Reforms." In Joint Economic Committee, Congress of the United States, *Reorientation and Commercial Relations of the Economies of Eastern Europe*. Washington, D.C.: Government Printing Office, 1974.

Granick, David. "The Hungarian Economic Reform." *World Politics*, 1973.

Gregory, Paul, and Stuart, Robert. *Soviet Economic Structure and Performance*. New York: Harper & Row, 1974.

Grossman, Gregory. "Economic Reforms: A Balance Sheet." *Problems of Communism*, November-December, 1966.

Höhmann, H. H., Kaser, M., and Thalheim, K. C., eds. *The New Economic Systems of Eastern Europe*. Berkeley and Los Angeles: University of California Press, 1975.

Chapter 2

Boltho, Andrea. *Foreign Trade Criteria in Socialist Economies*. Cambridge: Cambridge University Press, 1971.

Brown, A., and Neuberger, E. *International Trade and Central Planning*. Berkeley: University of California Press, 1968.

Fallenbuchl, Z. "East European Integration: Comecon." In Joint Economic Committee, Congress of the United States, *Reorientation and Commercial Relations of the Economies of Eastern Europe*. Washington, D.C.: Government Printing Office, 1974.

Holzman, Franklyn D. *Foreign Trade Under Central Planning*. Cambridge, Mass.: Harvard University Press, 1974.

Kaser, Michael. *Comecon*. 2nd ed., London: Oxford University Press, 1967.

Matejka, Harriet. "Foreign Trade Systems." In *The New Economic Systems of Eastern Europe*, edited by H. H. Höhmann, M. Kaser, and K. C. Thalheim. Berkeley and Los Angeles: University of California Press, 1975.

United Nations. 1968 and 1973. *Economic Bulletin for Europe*, vol. 20, no. 1, pp. 43-50; vol. 24, no. 1, pp. 36-49.

Wilczynski, Josef. *The Economics and Politics of East-West Trade*. London: Macmillan, 1969.

Wiles, P. H. D. *Communist International Economics*. Oxford: Basil Blackwell, 1968.

Chapter 3

Brown, Alan, and Neuberger, Egon. *International Trade and Central Planning*. Berkeley: University of California Press, 1968.

Brzezinski, Z. *The Soviet Bloc: Unity and Conflict*. 2nd ed. Cambridge, Mass.: Harvard University Press, 1967.

"Comprehensive Programme for the Further Extension and Improvement of Cooperation and Development of Socialist Economic Integration by the CMEA Member Nations." *Soviet and East European Foreign Trade*, Fall-Winter, 1971-72.

Fallenbuchl, Z. "Comecon Integration." *Problems of Communism*, March-April 1973.

Fallenbuchl, Z. "East European Integration: Comecon." In Joint Economic Committee, Congress of the United States, *Reorientation and Commercial Relations of the Economies of Eastern Europe*. Washington, D.C.: Government Printing Office, 1974.

Freedman, Robert. *Economic Warfare in the Communist Bloc*. New York: Praeger, 1970.

Goldman, Marshall. *Soviet Foreign Aid*. New York: Praeger, 1966.

Heiss, Herta W. "The Council of Mutual Economic Assistance—Developments Since the Mid-1960's." In Joint Economic Committee, Congress of the United States, *Economic Developments in Countries of Eastern Europe*. Washington, D.C.: Government Printing Office, 1970.

Hewett, Edward. *Foreign Trade Prices in CMEA*. Cambridge: Cambridge University Press, 1974.

Holzman, Franklyn D. *Foreign Trade Under Central Planning*. Cambridge, Mass.: Harvard University Press, 1974.

Horvath, Janos. "Grant Elements in Intra-bloc Aid Programs." *The ASTE Bulletin*, Fall 1971.

Joint Economic Committee, Congress of the United States, *Reorientation and Commercial Relations of the Economies of Eastern Europe*, Washington, D.C.: Government Printing Office, 1974.

Kaser, Michael. *Comecon*. 2nd ed. London: Oxford University Press, 1967.

Mendershausen, Horst. "Terms of Trade Between the Soviet Union and Smaller Communist Countries." *Review of Economics and Statistics*, May 1959.

——————"The Terms of Soviet-Satellite Trade." *Review of Economics and Statistics*, May 1960.

Montias, J. M. *Economic Development in Communist Rumania*. Cambridge, Mass.: MIT Press, 1967.

Pryor, Frederic. *The Communist Foreign Trade System*. Cambridge, Mass.: MIT Press, 1963.

Schaeffer, Henry. *Comecon and the Politics of Integration*. New York: Praeger, 1972.

Tansky, Leo. "Soviet Foreign Aid: Scope, Direction and Trends." In Joint Economics Committee, Congress of the United States, *Soviet Economic Prospects for the Seventies*, Washington, D.C.: Government Printing Office, 1973.

Ulam, Adam. *Expansion and Coexistence: Soviet Foreign Policy*. New York: Praeger, 1974.

Wasowski, Stanley, ed. *East-West Trade and the Technology Gap*. New York: Praeger, 1970.

Wasowski, Stanley, "Economic Integration in Eastern Europe." Arlington, Va.: Institute for Defense Analysis, December 1969. Report.

Wiles, Peter. *Communist International Economics*. London: Basil Blackwell, 1968.

Chapter 4

Adler-Karlsson, Gunnar. *Western Economic Warfare, 1947-67*. Stockholm: Almqvist and Wiksell, 1968.

Alton, Thad. "Economic Structure and Growth in Eastern Europe." In Joint Economic Committee, Congress of the United States, *Economic Development in Eastern Europe*, Washington, D.C.: Government Printing Office, 1970.

Bergson, Abram. "Toward a New Soviet Growth Model." *Problems of Communism*, March-April 1973.

Boretsky, Michael. "Comparative Progress in Technology, Productivity, and Economic Efficiency: USSR vs. USA." In Joint Economic Committee, Congress of the United States, *New Directions in the Soviet Economy, Part II-A*, Washington, D.C.: Government Printing Office, 1966.

Brown, A., and Marer, P. "New Options for the United States in East-West Trade." *Studies in Comparative Communism*, April 1971.

Brown, J. F., Ermarth, F., and Salloch, R. "Eastern Europe and the Common Market." *Communist Affairs*, March-April 1968.

Brzezinski, Z. *Alternative to Partition*. New York: McGraw-Hill, 1962.

Campbell, Robert. *The Soviet-Type Economies.* Boston: Houghton Mifflin, 1974.

Ernst, M. "Postwar Economic Growth in Eastern Europe." In Joint Economic Committee, Congress of the United States, *New Directions in the Soviet Economy, Part IV.* Washington, D.C.: Government Printing Office, 1966.

Goldman, Marshall. "The East Reaches for Markets." *Foreign Affairs*, July 1969.

Hardt, John, and Holliday, George D. *U.S.-Soviet Commercial Relations: The Interplay of Economics, Technology, Transfer, and Diplomacy.* Committee on Foreign Affairs, United States House of Representatives, Washington, D.C., 1973.

Holzman, Franklyn, and Legvold, Robert. "The Economics and Politics of East-West Relations." *International Organization*, Winter 1975.

Joint Economic Committee, Congress of the United States. *Reorientation and Commercial Relations of the Economies of Eastern Europe.* Washington, D.C.: Government Printing Office, 1974.

_____ *Soviet Economic Prospects for the Seventies.* Washington, D.C.: Government Printing Office, 1973.

Kaser, Michael. "Comecon's Commerce." *Problems of Communism*, July-August 1973.

Kaser, M., and Ransom, C. F. G. "Relations With Eastern Europe." In C. R. Denton, *Economic Integration in Europe.* London: Weidenfeld and Nicolson, 1968.

Kock, Karin. *International Trade Policy and the GATT, 1947-67.* Stockholm: Almqvist & Wiksell, 1969.

Kretschmar, Robert, and Foor, Robin. *The Potential for Joint Ventures in Eastern Europe.* New York: Praeger, 1972.

Mackintosh, J. M. *The Strategy and Tactics of Soviet Foreign Policy.* London: Oxford University Press, 1962.

Pisar, Samuel. *Coexistence and Commerce.* New York: McGraw-Hill, 1970.

Schaeffer, Henry. *Eastern Reassessment of the EEC.* Munich: Radio Free Europe Research, May 1972.

Spulber, Nicolas. "Effects of the Embargo on Soviet Trade." *Harvard Business Review*, November-December 1952.

Ulam, Adam. *Expansion and Coexistence: Soviet Foreign Policy.* New York: Praeger, 1974.

_____ *The Rivals*, New York: Viking, 1971.

Wilczynski, J. *The Economics and Politics of East-West Trade.* London: Macmillan, 1969.

Wolf, Thomas. *U.S. East-West Trade Policy.* Lexington, Mass.: D. C. Heath, 1973.

Chapter 5

Duncan, Raymond, ed. *Soviet Policy in Developing Countries.* Waltham Mass.: Ginn, 1970.

Goldman, Marshall. *Soviet Foreign Aid.* New York: Praeger, 1967.

Holzman, Franklyn D. *Foreign Trade Under Central Planning.* Cambridge, Mass.: Harvard University Press, 1974. Chapters 7, 16, 17.

Horvath, Janos. "Economic Aid Flow From the USSR: A Recount of the First Fifteen Years." *Slavic Review,* December 1970.

Kanet, Roger E., ed. *The Soviet Union and the Developing Nations.* Baltimore: Johns Hopkins University Press, 1974.

Pryor, Frederic L. "Trade Barriers of Capitalist and Communist Nations Against Foodstuffs Exported by Tropical Underdeveloped Nations." *Review of Economics and Statistics,* November 1966.

Sawyer, Carole A. *Communist Trade With Developing Countries: 1955-1965.* New York: Praeger, 1970.

Tansky, Leo. "Soviet Foreign Aid: Scope, Direction, and Trends." In Joint Economic Committee, Congress of the United States, *Soviet Economic Prospects For the Seventies,* Washington, D.C.: Government Printing Office, 1973.

—————."Soviet Foreign Aid to the Less Developed Countries." In Joint Economic Committee, Congress of the United States, *New Directions in the Soviet Economy, Part IV,* Washington, D.C.: Government Printing Office, 1966.

—————."Soviet Military Aid, Technical Assistance, and Academic Training." In Raymond Duncan, *Soviet Policy in Developing Countries.* Waltham, Mass.: Ginn, 1970.

United Nations. "The Financing of Economic Development." In *World Economic Survey, 1965-Part 1,* Chapter IV. New York, 1966.

United Nations. *Innovations in the Practice of Trade and Economic Cooperation Between the Socialist Countries of Eastern Europe and the Developing Countries.* New York, 1970.

Vassilev, V. *Policy in the Soviet Bloc on Aid to Developing Countires.* Paris: Organization for Economic Co-operation and Development, 1969.

Chapter 6

Bergsten, C. Fred, and Krause, Lawrence B., eds. *World Politics and International Economics.* Washington, D.C.: The Brookings Institution, 1975.

Burks, R. V. "Political Hazards of Economic Reform." In Joint Economic Committee, Congress of the United States, *Reorientation and Commercial Relations of the Economies of Eastern Europe.* Washington, D.C.: Government Printing Office, 1974.

—————."The Political Implications of Economic Reform." In *Plan and Market,* edited by M. Bornstein. New Haven: Yale University Press, 1973.

Campbell, Robert. "Some Issues in Soviet Energy Policy for the Seventies." In Joint Economic Committee, Congress of the United States, *Soviet Economic Prospects for the Seventies.* Washington, D.C.: Government Printing Office, 1973.

Hardt, John. "East European Economic Development: Two Decades of Interrelationships and Interactions with the Soviet Union." In Joint Economic Committee, Congress of the United States, *Economic Developments in Countries of Eastern Europe*, Washington, D.C.: Government Printing Office, 1970.

Holzman, Franklyn D. *Foreign Trade Under Central Planning.* Cambridge, Mass.: Harvard University Press, 1974. Pp. 220-229.

————. "Future East-West Economic Issues." In *The Future of the International Economic Order: An Agenda for Research*, edited by Fred Bergsten. Lexington, Mass.: D. C. Heath, 1973.

Holzman, F. D., and Legvold, Robert. "The Economics and Politics of East-West Relations." *International Organization*, Winter 1975. (Also in Bergsten & Krause, 1975.)

Joint Economic Committee, Congress of the United States, *Reorientation and Commercial Relations of the Economies of Eastern Europe.* Washington, D.C.: Government Printing Office, 1974.

————.Congress of the United States, *Soviet Economic Prospects for the Seventies*, Washington, D.C.: Government Printing Office, 1973.

Index

Brezhnev Doctrine, 113-115
Brzezinski, Z., 89
Bulganin, Nikolai A., 140, 186
Bulgaria, 75, 82, 95, 101, 107, 151;
economic reforms in, 18; U.S.S.R.'s
discrimination in trade with, 84-86

Canada, 200
Capital flows: among CMEA nations,
103-106, 121, 122; IIB and, 120-
122; from Western nations to LDCs,
private, 196-197; *see also* Aid; aid
to LDCs; loans or credits
Central economic planning, 5-7; Foreign Trade Institutions and Behavior, 21-50; East-West trade and,
135; economic reforms and, 111,
see also Reforms, economic; new
technology and, 146-147; as over-
full employment planning, 7-10;
productivity levels and, 145-146;
quality of products and, 144
Centralization, political, 4
Chile, 189*n*
China, 68, 98, 105, 110, 135, 136,
160; aid to LDCs by, 175, 181,
183, 193, 201; Albania and, 88,
89; LDCs' trade with, 177; U.S.S.R.
and, economic relations between 87,
89-92; *see also* Sino-Soviet dispute
China Coordinating Committee
(CHINCOM), 136, 139
CMEA, *see* Council of Mutual Economic Assistance
COCOM (Coordinating Committee),
136, 137, 139, 149
Cold War, 66-67, 126; East-West trade
and, 132-139; economic warfare
and, 125
Commodity inconvertibility, 43, 108,
179
Common Market, *see* European Economic Community (EEC)
Communist party, political centralization and, 4

Comprehensive Program, 116-121, 203
Consultative Group, 136
Controls: administrative, 13-14; direct, central planning with, 5-7;
trade, in East-West trade, 135-140,
149-151
Convertibility of currency, 119, 172;
see also Inconvertibility, currency;
inconvertibility, commodity
Cooperation agreements, *see* Joint
ventures
Coordination of plans, CMEA and, 92-
95, 97, 98, 116-119
Council of Mutual Economic Assistance
(CMEA or Comecon), xiii, 51, 59,
86; Basic Principles of, 13, 92, 97;
bilateralism and, 108, 109; capital
flows among nations of, 103-106;
Charter of (1960), 92-93, 97; Comprehensive Program of, 116-121,
203; coordination of plans and, 92-
95, 97, 98; customs union analysis
of, 70-74; economic growth slowdown among nations of (1960s),
110-111, 123, 144-146, 148; EEC
and, 142-143, 155-156, 170-171;
equalization of development and
per capita income and, 96-97, 121;
establishment of, 68-69; future
problems and prospects for 203-
207; IBEC and, 108, 109; IIB and,
120-121; IMF and, 171-173; inconvertibility and, 108-109; integration
of, 62, 63, 81-83, 86-87, 110-113,
121-122, 203, *see also* Comprehensive Program; Supranationality;
interested-party principle of, 93;
post-Khrushchev developments in,
110-122; labor flows among countries of, 106-107; LDC cooperation
agreements with, 184-185; LDCs in,
95-96; LDCs' trade with countries
of, 176-180, 198-202, 210-212;
multilateralization and, 94, 95, 108,
109, 120; pricing system of, 99-
103; scientific-technical coopera-

tion and, 107-108; specialization and, 94-98; supranational power vs. national sovereignty and, debate over, 92-99, 110, 112-114; upgrading of (early 1960s), 86-87, 92; *see also* East-West economic relations; Intrabloc economic relations

Credits, *see* Loans or credits

Cuba, 105, 187-188, 211

Currencies: collective, 119; inconvertibility of, *see* Inconvertibility, currency; *see also* Exchange rates

Customs, *see* Tariffs

Customs union model (customs union analysis), 56-59, 70-74

Czechoslovakia, 63, 66, 75, 82, 102, 105, 110, 133, 134, 149, 158*n*, 200, 202; CMEA integration and, 112; economic reforms in, 19, 47, 48, 111, 113, 204; 1968 invasion of, Brezhnev Doctrine and, 113-116

Détente, U.S.-U.S.S.R., 55, 127, 131, 151, 159-173; economic and strategic considerations in, 161-165; linkage politics and, 159-161; prospects for, 208

Devaluation (depreciation), reasons for, 31-33

Developing countries, *see* Less developed countries

Dumping, 38-39

East Germany (German Democratic Republic; G.D.R.), 66, 76, 82, 102, 106, 107, 110, 200; CMEA integration and, 112-113; economic reforms in, 19, 47, 48; 1953 unrest in, 79; reparations paid to U.S.S.R. by, 75-76

East-West economic relations: CMEA integration and, 112; Cold War and (1945 to mid-1950s), 132-139; conduct of, 129-132; Comprehensive Program and, 117; data on magnitude of, 127-129; détente and, *see* Détente, U.S.-U.S.S.R.; discrimination by West against U.S.S.R. in, 84-86; economic warfare and, 124-126, 137; future problems and prospects for, 207-210; intensification of economic interest in (early 1960s), 143-148; intrabloc trade and, 124, 127, 143-144, 209; joint ventures and, 152-155; political and economic developments in early and mid-1960s and, 148-159; prices in intrabloc trade and in, compared, 83-86; technology-related problems and, 146-148, 207

Eastern Europe: Chinese trade with, 91; *see also* East-West economic relations; Intrabloc economic relations; *and specific countries*

Economic goals and policies of Communist states, 12-15

Economic growth, 13, 15; decline in rates of, among CMEA nations, 110-111, 123, 144-146, 148; *see also* Equalization of development levels

Economic integration, 107; Comprehensive Program and, 116-121; definition of, 59; CMEA and, 62, 63, 81-83, 86-87, 110-113, 121-122, 203; EEC and, 142

Economic integration models, 56-63

Economic power: aid to LDCs and, 175-176; economic warfare and, 64-66; intrabloc economic and political relations and, 51-56; *see also* Economic warfare

Economic reforms, *see* Reforms, economic

Economic warfare, 55, 63-66, 214-215; against Albania, 87-89; against China,

Latin America, 187, 193
Lend-Lease debt, Soviet, 165-167
Less developed countries (LDCs),
174-202; aid to, *see* Aid to less
developed countries; in CMEA, 95-
96; CMEA countries' trade with,
176-180, 198-202, 210-212; Eastern bloc vs. Western trade with,
198-200; future problems and prospects for economic relations with,
210-212; inequality of income between advanced nations and, 213;
loans to, *see* Loans or credits to
LDCs; share in world trade of,
25; U.S. trade with, 199, 200;
U.S.S.R. trade with, 174, 178,
198-202
Liberman reform proposals, 111, 141
Linkage politics, 54-55, 127, 159-161,
170, 208
Loans or credits: to Communist countries, 125; to Communist countries,
during Cold War, 134-135; in East-
West trade, 149-150; by IIB, 120-
122; intrabloc, 61; to LDCs, *see*
Loans or credits to LDCs; to
U.S.S.R. by U.S., 167, 169; by
U.S.S.R. to China, 90, 91; by
U.S.S.R. to Eastern nations, 81,
103, 105-106, *see* Aid; capital flows
Loans or credits to LDCs, 45-46; by
Communist countries, 180-181,
188-191, 200-202; repayment of,
195, 197, 200-202, *see also* Aid;
aid to LDCs

McMillan, C. H., 102, 103
McMillan, Harold, 140
Malaysia, 178
Malenkov, Georgi, 138, 139
Managerial incentives, 10-12, 16, 27
Manchuria, 75
Marin, Louis, 167
Market socialism, 113

Market structure, 5-7
Marshall, Gen. George, 133
Marshall Plan, 68, 133-134
Material balances, 6-7, 11
Mendershausen, Horst, 83
Mikoyan, Anastas I., 141
Military aid, by Soviet bloc to LDCs,
174, 182-183, 190, 192, 194, 211
Miller, J. Irwin, 163
Molotov, Vyacheslav, 133
Mongolia, 93
Monopolistic (monopsonistic) power,
54; of U.S.S.R., in intrabloc trade,
84, 86
Monopoly, foreign-trade, 21-26
Montias, J. M., 96
Most-favored-nation (MFN) treatment:
Cold War and denial of, 136-137;
GATT and, 156-159; tariffs and, 36-
38; U.S.-U.S.S.R. trade agreement
of 1972 and, 167-170; Jewish emi-
gration issue and, 169
Multilateralism: CMEA and, 94, 95, 108,
109, 120; Comprehensive Program
and, 119; in East-West trade, 143-
144, 149, 172; IIB and, 120, *see
also* inconvertibility
Multinational enterprises, 153, 154
Mutual Defense Assistance Act (Battle
Act), 136, 139

National democracy, concept of, 186,
187
National sovereignty: Brezhnev Doctrine
and, 114; CMEA and issue of, 92-99;
see also Supranationality
Nationalization of means of production,
4-5
NATO, 140, 142, 155
New Economic Policy, 152
New York Times, 170
Nixon, Richard M., 165
North Korea, 135
North Vietnam, 105-106
Notional exchange rates, 34, 35

Scott, Harold, 163
Sino-Soviet dispute, 87, 89-90, 110
Smoot-Hawley Tariff Act of 1930, 136
Socialism, market, 113
Solow, Robert M., 146
Sovereignty, national, *see* National
   sovereignty
Soviet Union, *see* Union of Soviet
   Socialist Republics
Special Drawing Rights (SDRs), 172
Specialization, CMEA and, 94-98
Stalin, Joseph, 66, 77, 78, 80, 97,
   138, 185
Stans, Maurice, 165
State-trading between governments,
   130-131
Steel industry, in Rumania, 98-99
Stevenson Amendment, 169
"Stop prices," 1950, 100
Subsidies to enterprises, 9-10, 32
Supranationality: Brezhnev Doctrine
   and, 113, 114; CMEA and issue of
   national sovereignty versus, 92-99,
   110, 112-114; EEC and, 142
Syria, 190

Tariffs: dumping and countervailing,
   39; in East-West trade, 136-137;
   most-favored-nation problems and,
   36-38; two- and three-column, 37-
   38; *see also* GATT; Most-favored-
   nation (MFN) treatment
Taxes: excise, 9; Hungarian price reforms and, 49; import-turnover, in
   Hungary, 49, 50; sales, 9-10
Technical assistance to LDCs, 182-184
Technical-scientific cooperation, 107-
   108
Technology: East-West trade and, 146-
   148; 207; U.S.-U.S.S.R. economic
   relations and, 162-163
Third World, *see* Less developed countries
Tito, Marshal (Josip Broz), 77-80, 88

Tourist exchange rate, 29, 30, 32
Trade Agreement Extension Act of 1951,
   136
Trade agreements: bilateral, *see* Bilateral
   trade agreements; East-West, 24, 131-
   132, 150
Trade aversion, 24-26
Trade balance, exchange rates and, 30-31
Trade controls, in East-West trade, 135-
   140, 149-151
Trade creation, 57, 58, 74n
Trade diversion, 57-58
Trading with the Enemy Act, 135
Turkey, 194
"Turnkey" plants, 148, 153

Ulbricht, Walter, 112
Underdeveloped countries, *see* Less
   developed countries
Unemployment, 12-13
Union of Soviet Socialist Republics
   (U.S.S.R.): aid and loans to LDCs
   from, 175, 181-184, 186-196, 201-
   202; aid to Albania from, 88, 89; aid
   to China from, 90, 91; aid to Communist countries from, 103-106;
   Albania as economic-warfare target
   of, 87-89; autarkic tendencies of, 24-
   25; balance-of-payments problems of,
   41-42; China and, economic relations
   between, CMEA integration and, 86-
   87, 112, 114; CMEA pricing system
   and, 100, 102-103; Comprehensive
   Program and, 117-119; détente between U.S. and, *see* Détente, U.S.-
   U.S.S.R.; discriminatory prices imposed on Eastern nations by, 83-86,
   102; East-West trade and, 125-127,
   129, 130, 132, 135, 137-141, 143,
   148-151, 156, 159-173, 208-210;
   economic reforms in, 16-18, 46-47,
   111, 112, 141, 204-205, 209; economic warfare (economic pressures)
   by, 64-66, 87-92, 125; GATT and,